CAMBRIDGE LATIN AMERICAN STUDIES

64

RESISTANCE AND
INTEGRATION

*For my mother, Chris Maddison,
and father, Morgan James,
with love and gratitude*

*In memory of Bryn Morgan,
Welsh miner, 1908–79*

*and Daniel Hopen,
disappeared in Argentina,
August 1976*

RESISTANCE AND INTEGRATION

PERONISM AND THE ARGENTINE WORKING CLASS, 1946–1976

DANIEL JAMES

Assistant Professor, Department of History, Yale University

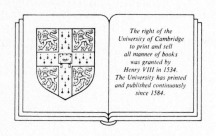

The right of the
University of Cambridge
to print and sell
all manner of books
was granted by
Henry VIII in 1534.
The University has printed
and published continuously
since 1584.

CAMBRIDGE UNIVERSITY PRESS

Cambridge

New York   New Rochelle   Melbourne   Sydney

Published by the Press Syndicate of the University of Cambridge
The Pitt Building, Trumpington Street, Cambridge CB2 1RP
32 East 57th Street, New York, NY 10022, USA
10 Stamford Road, Oakleigh, Melbourne 3166, Australia

First published 1988

Printed in Great Britain by Redwood Burn Limited, Trowbridge, Wiltshire

British Library cataloguing in publication data
James, Daniel
Resistance and integration: Peronism and
the Argentine working class, 1946–1976.
– (Cambridge Latin American studies 64)
1. Argentina – Politics and government
– 1943–1955   2. Argentina – Politics
and government – 1955–1983
I. Title
982'.06   F2849

Library of Congress cataloguing in publication data
James, Daniel.
Resistance and integration.
(Cambridge Latin American studies; 64)
Bibliography: p.
Includes index.
1. Labor and laboring classes – Argentina – Political
activity – History – 20th century.   2. Trade-unions –
Argentina – Political activity – History – 20th century.
3. Peronism – History.   4. Government, Resistance to –
Argentina – History – 20th century.   5. Argentina –
Politics and government – 1943–1955.   6. Argentina –
Politics and government – 1955–1983.   I. Title.
II. Series.
HD6603.5.J36   1988   322'.2'0982   87–25681

ISBN 0 521 34635 5

Contents

Acknowledgements

The research on which this book is based was financed through grants from the following bodies: Social Science Research Council (Great Britain), Foreign Area Fellowship Program (New York), and the University of Cambridge junior fellows travel fund. I would like to express my appreciation to these bodies for their support.

The intellectual and personal debts that go into any work of this type are bound to be enormous. Professor John Lynch and Richard Moseley-Williams first planted the seeds of my interest in Argentine history and were sympathetic and stimulating teachers. I have studied Argentina and its labour movement for over fifteen years and in the course of that time I have argued and discussed the history and the present of the Argentine working class with many people. Many of the views and opinions expressed here are borrowings, hybrids, adaptations which have emerged from those discussions. Intellectual originality is, it seems to me, an extremely rare commodity and for my part I willingly thank the following friends and colleagues for their part in this book. I can only hope that such an association does not displease them and that they recognise, in at least a partial way, the essence of shared ideas and discussions.

I must first and foremost thank my friend Alberto Belloni, who willingly spent many hours and days discussing labour history and sharing his own experiences with a naive foreigner. Much of any understanding I have of the passion, the ambiguity and the tragedy of the Argentine working-class history I owe to him. In the many years that followed our first meeting he has, in the most trying of personal circumstances, always been willing to continue to share his thoughts, his anger, his compassion and his overwhelming intellectual curiosity. Another Argentine friend, Alberto Ferrari, placed his deep knowledge of Argentine politics and society at my disposal. I have also benefited from many discussions with Juan Carlos Torre, who consistently provoked me and made me question commonplaces about Argentine workers and their unions. These and other Argentine friends always managed to suppress their instinctive scepticism about that intrinsically condescending and improbable species – the academic Latin Americanist. For their good manners and good humour I thank them.

Judith Evans was a good friend and good adviser, who has always shared her passion for things Argentine. My colleague and friend Emilia Viotti da Costa has been a consistent source of encouragement and good editorial advice. More than that, though, she has shared her unflagging intellectual curiosity with me and provoked me to justify and rethink many, many assumptions. Graduate students at Yale have also provided me with a stimulating intellectual environment; in particular Albert Vourvoulias, Romi Gandolfo and Jeff Gould all contributed to this work. Walter Little offered sound and generous advice. The usual caveats, of course, apply in that none of the above are responsible for the final product presented here.

Last, but in no sense least, my thanks to Lynn Di Pietro for her patience and above all for simply being there.

Introduction

Over the last forty years the Peronist union movement has been a crucial actor in the drama of modern Argentine history. It has been the principal institutional channel for, and beneficiary of, the Argentine working class's allegiance to Perón as a person and Peronism as a movement. A vital pillar of the Peronist regime from 1946 to 1955, the unions have remained the main mobilisers of the Peronist masses and the union leadership has acted as the chief broker of this power in its negotiations with other sectors of the Argentine polity, above all the armed forces. Indeed, a dominant theme of contemporary Argentine history has been the role of the union movement as the chief interlocutor between the armed forces and civil society; the fate of modern Argentina has frequently seemed to hinge on the outcome of an uneasy but ever present dialogue between generals and union bosses. The power accruing to the union movement from this situation has been enormous; frequently repressed, the unions have nevertheless presented themselves to even the most hostile military governments as an irreducible social and political force.

This book seeks, at a most basic level, to trace the development of Peronism within the unions in the 1955–73 period. What was the relationship between union leaders and members? How valid is the popular conception of union power which emphasises corruption, violence and power politicking? What were the real sources of union, and more particularly union leadership, power? By asking and trying to answer these obvious but important questions we can hope to go beyond the surface plausibility of popular images.

The book also addresses the wider issue of the relationship between Peronism and the Argentine working class and the meaning of that relationship for workers in general and the trade unions in particular. Frequently, this issue has been approached from the perspective of more general notions concerning populism. The result of this has been an emphasis on the aberrant quality of working-class participation within Peronism. Such participation has been treated as something of an historical conundrum requiring explanation, most usually in terms of notions such as manipulation, passivity, cooptation, and not uncommonly, irrationality. This work does not offer an all-embracing theory of populism. Indeed, from the historian's point of view I would suggest that part of the problem with many existing analyses has been the level of abstraction at which they have operated. Macro-explanatory frameworks have not been able to cope with the concrete questions and exceptions they themselves have often suggested. The specificity of concrete social movements and historical experience have escaped through the broad mesh of such frameworks.

First and foremost, I have attempted to explore the historical experience of Argentine workers in the decades following the overthrow of Juan Perón in 1955. Within this general framework, two terrains of analysis have interested me in particular: the Peronist union hierarchy and its relationship with its rank and file, and the issue of Peronist ideology and its impact on the working class. Considerable emphasis has been placed in this work on grounding our analysis of these issues in an understanding of the concrete experience of the Peronist rank and file. I feel that this emphasis is important for two reasons. First, because a grass-roots perspective is essential if we are to analyse the themes of major concern to this book. A better understanding of the actions and perceptions of rank-and-file Peronist unionists is essential to this enterprise.

In addition, however, this aspect is crucial because it has largely been overlooked by writers on this subject. One has a curiously ambiguous feeling reading much of the material written on modern Argentine history. The working class is present in such analysis; political reality and the nature of the dominant Argentine political and intellectual discourse clearly compel such a presence. Yet, this presence has a certain unreality about it. The working class usually appears as a cypher, almost an ideal construct at the service of different ideological paradigms. The essence of these abstractions derives from broader notions concerning the relationship of workers and Peronism. From Gino Germani and modernisation sociology we find the passive, manipulated urban masses which result from an incomplete modernisation process. Marxism and Latin American communism and socialism present us with inexperienced proletarians incapable of realising their true class interests, dominated by bourgeois ideology and controlled and manipulated by demagogic politicians and a ruthless union bureaucracy. Finally, the Peronist left and many radical youth sectors of the late 1960s and early 1970s offered a vision of exemplary proletarians forging a peculiarly Argentine movement towards socialism and national liberation. Behind these paradigms lurk a series of global antinomies which have dominated the general debate over populism and the working class: traditional/modern, cooptation/autonomy, false consciousness/class consciousness, and of particular importance for Peronism in the post-1955 era, resistance and integration. What these abstractions fail to give us is generally any sense of the concrete historical experience of working people and their complex, ambiguous, frequently contradictory responses.

I would suggest that this lack results, partly at least, from the long-standing failure of much academic theory to come to terms adequately with the complexity of working-class experience. It is also partly due, however, to the extraordinary polemical relevance of past historical models and experience in contemporary Argentina. Past historical experience is evidently a crucial bedrock of contemporary ideological and political debate in most societies. In Argentina, however, the past has been lived as the present in a peculiarly intense way. It has been precisely a perception of this fact which has underlain much of the aura of pessimism and fatalism which has informed public and intellectual attitudes toward the Argentine 'enigma'. Argentines have seemed condemned to endure a present dominated by symbols drawn from past conflicts and experiences. National figures, social and political movements from the past have frequently become mythologies which serve as symbols whose function is to rationalise, justify and give emotional coherence to present political needs.

In the case of the working class such mythologising has implied a simplifying and an idealising of the painful complexities of working-class experience. Much of the internal debate within Peronism over the last thirty years has indeed revolved around the conflicting idealisations and stereotypes of working-class history and experience. Similarly, an understanding of the development of the Peronist left and guerrilla groups in the late 1960s and 1970s must be based on an understanding of their mythologies of the working class and its role in Peronism in general and particularly during the decade following Perón's ouster in 1955. Such mythologies are both bad for historical understanding and pernicious for political practice by groups who have claimed to symbolise and represent this working class. Uncovering some of the reality behind these myths concerning the working-class presence in Peronism is one of the major preoccupations of this work.

The sources used for this study have been primarily threefold. First, I have made use of archival resources that existed in Argentina. These included national newspapers, magazines from the period, trade union newspapers and journals, yearbooks and materials available in government agencies, principally the Ministry of Labour. Second, I was fortunate enough to have access to a large number of unofficial Peronist newspapers, rank-and-file newspapers, pamphlets, and barrio broadsheets. These were almost exclusively part of private personal holdings not available to the general public. Third, I have relied heavily on interviews, conversations, and discussions with participants active within the unions in this period.

The general approach adopted in terms of the organisation of this work has been a narrative analytical one. The chapters follow a chronological order. It should be emphasised that within such an approach selection has been made. This work is not a history of Argentina in the decades following the overthrow of Perón. Many issues have been referred to obliquely, or only as they had bearing on the labour movement. Thus, for example, the relations between civilian authorities and the military, or the intrigues within the armed forces, are referred to very briefly and only as they affect the overall context within which the Peronist unions had to operate.

The first chapter, 'Peronism and the working class, 1943-55', provides an interpretation of the relationship between Peronism and the working class in the period of the formation of the Peronist movement and the Peronist governments. It seeks, in particular, to examine the roots of the working class's identification with Peronism so that we may better understand the reaction of the working class to the situation created by the overthrow of Perón. Part Two, 'The Peronist Resistance,' deals with the resistance of the working class and other sectors of the Peronist movement to the military regimes which governed Argentina from 1955 to 1958. Part Three, 'Frondizi and integration: temptation and disenchantment', analyses the period of Arturo Frondizi's government, 1958–62. In Part Four, 'The Vandor era', I have studied the development of the Peronist union movement's power under the dominant influence of Augusto Vandor, the metal workers' leader, in the period from the overthrow of Frondizi to the miliary coup of June 1966. Finally, Part Five, 'Workers and the *Revolución Argentina*', offers an analysis of the period of military government from 1966 to 1973.

PART ONE

The background

1

Peronism and the working class, 1943–55

– Speak freely. What is the problem? You speak Tedesco. The colonel will understand you better. – Well... – You are Tedesco? Son of Italians, no? – Yes, colonel. – I thought so. What's up Tedesco? – Very simple, colonel; a lot of work and very little cash. – That's clear. Where? – We work on the night shift in ... They pay us 3 pesos and 30 centavos each night. – That's a disgrace! We'll fix that immediately. I will call the owners of the factory so that they sign a contract with you people. How much do you want to earn? – We would settle for 3 pesos and 33 cents but the just wage would be 3.50 a night. – Everything will turn out alright. It's impossible that they still exploit workers in this way. – Thank you colonel. – Tedesco, you stay. The rest can go and rest easy.

Mariano Tedesco, founder of the *Asociación Obrera Textil*

Well look, let me say it once and for all. I didn't invent Perón. I'll tell you this once so that I can be done with this impulse of good will that I am following in my desire to free you a little of so much bull shit. The truth: I didn't invent Perón or Evita, the miraculous one. They were born as a reaction to your bad governments. I didn't invent Perón, or Evita, or their doctrines. They were summoned as defence by a people who you and yours submerged in a long path of misery. They were born of you, by you and for you.

Enrique Santos Discépolo

Organised labour and the Peronist state

Under the guidance of successive conservative governments the Argentine economy had responded to the world recession of the 1930s by producing internally an increasing number of manufactured goods it had previously imported.[1] While generally maintaining adequate income levels for the rural sector, and guaranteeing the traditional elite's privileged economic ties with the United Kingdom, the Argentine state stimulated this import substitution by a judicious policy of tariff protection, exchange controls and the provision of industrial credit.[2] Industrial production more than doubled between 1930/5 and 1945/9; imports which in 1925/30 accounted for almost one quarter of the Argentine GNP had been reduced to some 6% in the 1940/4 quinquennium. From importing some 35% of its machinery and industrial equipment in the first period, Argentina imported only 9.9% in the second.[3] In addition the Second World War saw a considerable amount of export-led industrial growth as Argentine manufactured goods penetrated foreign markets.[4] By the mid 1940s Argentina was an increasingly industrialised economy; while the traditional rural sector remained the major source of foreign exchange earnings, the dynamic centre of capital accumulation now lay in industry and manufacture.

Changes in the social structure reflected these economic developments. The number of industrial establishments increased from 38,456 in 1935 to 86,440 in 1946. At the same time the number of industrial workers proper increased from 435,816 to 1,056,673 in 1946.[5] The internal composition of this industrial labour force had also changed. New members were now drawn from the interior provinces of Argentina rather than from overseas immigration, which had effectively ceased after 1930. They were attracted to the expanding urban centres of the littoral zone, in particular to the Greater Buenos Aires area outside the limits of the Federal Capital. By 1947 some 1,368,000 migrants from the interior had arrived in Buenos Aires attracted by the rapid industrial expansion.[6] In the overwhelmingly industrial suburb of Avellaneda, across the Riachuelo river from the Capital, out of a total population in 1947 of some 518,312 over 173,000 had been born outside the city or province of Buenos Aires.[7]

While the industrial economy expanded rapidly the working class did not benefit from this expansion. Real wages declined in general as salaries lagged behind inflation. Faced with concerted employer and state repression, workers could do little to successfully improve wages and work conditions. Labour and social legislation remained sparse and sporadically enforced. Outside the workplace the situation was little better as working-class families confronted, unaided by the state, the social problems of rapid urbanisation. A survey of 1937 found, for example, that 60% of working-class families in the Capital lived in one room.[8]

The labour movement which existed at the time of the military coup of 1943 was divided and weak. There existed in Argentina four labour centrals: the anarchist Federación Obrera Regional Argentina (FORA), now simply a rump of anarchist militants; the syndicalist Unión Sindical Argentina (USA), also considerably reduced in influence; finally there was the Confederación General de Trabajo (CGT), which was divided into two organisations, a CGT No. 1 and another CGT No. 2.[9] The influence of this organisationally fragmented labour movement on the working class was limited. Perhaps some 20% of the urban labour force was organised in 1943, the majority of them being in the tertiary sector. The great majority of the industrial proletariat was outside effective union organisation. The most dynamic group to attempt to organise in non-traditional areas were the communists who had some success in organising in construction, food processing and wood working. However, the vital areas of industrial expansion in the 1930s and 1940s – textiles and metal working – were still virtually *terra incognita* for labour organisation in 1943. Of 447,212 union members in 1941 the transport sector and services accounted for well over 50% of membership, while industry had 144,922 affiliates.[10]

Perón, from his position as Secretary of Labour and late Vice President of the military government installed in 1943, set about addressing some of the basic concerns of the emerging industrial labour force.[11] At the same time he set about undermining the influence of rival, radical competitors in the working class. His social and labour policy created sympathy for him among both organised and unorganised workers. In addition, crucial sectors of the union leadership came to see their future organisational prospects as bound up in Perón's political survival, as traditional political forces from both left and right attacked his figure and policies in the course of 1945. The growing working-class support for Perón which this engendered first crystallised in the 17 October 1945 demonstration which secured his release from confinement and launched him on the path to victory in the presidential elections of February 1946.[12]

While there had been many specific improvements in work conditions and social legislation in the 1943–6 period the decade of Peronist government from 1946 to 1955 was to have the most profound effect on the working class's position in Argentine society. First, the period saw a great increase in the organisational strength and social weight of the working class. A state sympathetic to the extension of union organisation and a working class eager to translate its political victory into concrete organisational gains combined to effect a rapid increase in the extension of trade unionism. In 1948 the rate of unionisation had risen to 30.5% of the wage-earning population, and in 1954 it had reached 42.5%. In the majority of manufacturing industries the rate was between 50% and 70%.[13] Between 1946 and 1951 total union membership

increased from 520,000 members to 2,334,000. Industrial activities
such as textiles and metal working, where unionisation had been weak
or non-existent prior to 1946, by the end of the decade had unions with
membership numbering in the 100,000s. In addition a large number of
state employees were also unionised for the first time. Accompanying
this massive extension of unionisation there was, for the first time, the
development of a global system of collective bargaining. The contracts
signed throughout Argentine industry in the 1946–8 period regulated
wage scales and job descriptions and also included a whole array of
social provisions concerning sick leave, maternity leave, and vaca-
tions.[14]

   The organisational structure imposed on this union expansion was
important in moulding the future development of the union movement.
Unionisation was to be based on the unit of economic activity, rather
than that of the individual trade or enterprise. In addition, in each area
of economic activity only one union was granted legal recognition to
bargain with employers in that industry. Employers were obliged by
law to bargain with the recognised union, and conditions and wages
established in such bargaining were applicable to all workers in that
industry regardless of whether they were unionised or not. Beyond
that, a specific centralised union structure was laid down, encompass-
ing local branches and moving up through national federations to a
single confederation, the Confederación General de Trabajo (CGT).
Finally, the role of the state in overseeing and articulating this structure
was clearly established. The Ministry of Labour granted a union legal
recognition of its bargaining rights with employers. Decree 23,852 of
October 1945, known as the Law of Professional Associations, which
established this system, also established the right of the state to oversee
considerable areas of union activity. Thus, the legal structure assured
unions many advantages: bargaining rights, protection of union officials from victimisation, a centralised and unified union structure,
automatic deductions of union dues and the use of these dues to under-
write extensive social welfare activities. It also, however, made the state
the ultimate guarantor and overseer of this process and the benefits deriving from it.

   While the massive expansion of union organisation assured the working class recognition as a social force in the sphere of production, the
Peronist period also saw the integration of this social force within an
emerging political coalition overseen by the state. From labour's point
of view the precise nature of their political incorporation within the
regime was not immediately apparent. The general contours of this pol-

itical integration only emerged in the course of Perón's first presidency and they were to be confirmed and developed during the second. The first period, from 1946 to 1951, saw the gradual subordination of the union movement to the state and the elimination of the old-guard leaders who had been instrumental in mobilising the support of organised labour for Perón in 1945, and who had formed the Partido Laborista to act as labour's political expression. Their notions of political and organisational autonomy, and the conditional nature of their support for Perón, did not combine well with his political ambitions. Nor, it must be said, did their insistence on the principle of labour autonomy match the dominant perceptions of the rapidly expanding union membership.[15] Moreover, the weight of state intervention and the popular political support for Perón among their members inevitably limited the options open to the old-guard union leadership. Increasingly the unions were incorporated into a monolithic Peronist movement and were called upon to act as the state's agents vis-à-vis the working class, organising political support and serving as conduits of government policy among the workers.

As the outline of the justicialist state emerged in the second presidency, with its corporatist pretensions of organising and directing large spheres of social, political and economic life, the role officially allotted to the union movement in incorporating the working class into this state became clear. The attractions of such a relationship were great for both leaders and rank and file. An extensive social welfare network was in place operated through the Ministry of Labour and Social Welfare, the Fundación Eva Perón, and the unions themselves. Labour leaders were now to be found sitting in the congress; they were routinely consulted by the government on a range of national issues; they entered the Argentine diplomatic corp as labour attachés.[16] In addition, concrete economic gains for the working class were clear and immediate. As Argentine industry expanded, impelled by state incentives and a favourable international economic situation, workers benefited. Real wages for industrial workers increased by 53% between 1946 and 1949. Although real wages would decline with the economic crisis of the regime's last years, the shift of national income towards workers was to be unaffected. Between 1946 and 1949 the share of wages in the national income increased from 40.1% to 49%.[17]

While there were demonstrations of working-class opposition to aspects of Peronist economic policy, there was little generalised questioning of the terms of the political integration of labour within the Peronist state. Indeed, a crucial legacy of the Perón era for labour was the integration of the working class into a national political community and a corresponding recognition of its civic and political status within that community. Beyond that, the experience of this decade bequeathed to the working-class presence within that community a remarkable degree of political cohesion. The Peronist era largely erased former political loyalties among workers and entrenched new ones. Socialists, communists, and radicals who had competed for working-class allegiance prior to Perón had been largely marginalised in terms of influence by 1955. This marginalisation was partly due to state repression of non-Peronist politicians and labour leaders. Principally, however, it reflected the efficacy of Perón's social policy, the advantages of state patronage and the inadequacies of non-Peronist competitors for working-class allegiance. For socialists and radicals Peronism was to remain a moral and civic outrage; a demonstration of the backwardness and lack of civic virtue of Argentine workers. This position had determined their opposition to the military government of 1943–6, their support of the Unión Democrática, and their consistent hostility to Perón throughout the following decade.

The Communist Party attempted to adopt a more flexible position than its erstwhile allies. Soon after the election victory the party changed its characterisation of Peronism as a form of fascism, dissolved its union apparatus and ordered its militants to enter the CGT and its unions in order to work with the misguided Peronist masses and win them over.[18] Yet it, too, was never able to recover from the political error of supporting the anti-Peronist coalition, the Unión Democrática, in the 1946 elections; nor was it able to offer a credible alternative to the clear gains to be derived from integration within the Peronist state. While at the local level some of its militants were able to maintain credibility and lead some important strikes, politically the party could never challenge the hegemony of Peronism among organised labour. The importance of this legacy of political cohesion can be clearly appreciated if we also bear in mind the relative racial and ethnic homogeneity of the Argentine working class, and the concentration of this working class within a few urban centres, above all Greater Buenos Aires. Together these factors helped give the Argentine working class and its labour movement a weight within the wider national community which was unparalleled in Latin America.

Workers and the political appeal of Peronism

The relationship between workers and their organisations and the

Peronist movement and state is, therefore, clearly vital for understanding the 1943–55 period. Indeed, the intimacy of the relationship has generally been taken as defining the uniqueness of Peronism within the spectrum of Latin American populist experiences. How are we to interpret the basis of this relationship, and beyond that, the significance of the Peronist experience for Peronist workers? Answers to this question have increasingly rejected earlier explanations which saw working-class support for Peronism in terms of a division between an old and new working class. Sociologists like Gino Germani, leftist competitors for working-class allegiance, and indeed Peronists themselves, explained worker involvement in Peronism in terms of inexperienced migrant workers who, unable to assert an independent social and political identity in their new urban environment and untouched by the institutions and ideology of the traditional working class, were *disponible* (available) to be used by dissident elite sectors. It was these immature proletarians who flocked to Perón's banner in the 1943–6 period.[19]

In the revisionist studies working-class support for Perón has been regarded as representing a logical involvement of labour in a state-directed reformist project which promised labour concrete material gains.[20] With this more recent scholarship the image of the working-class relationship to Peronism has shifted from that of a passive manipulated mass to that of class-conscious actors seeking a realistic path for the satisfaction of their material needs. Political allegiance has, thus, been regarded, implicitly at least, within this approach as reducible to a basic social and economic rationalism. This instrumentalism would seem to be borne out by common sense. Almost anyone enquiring of a Peronist worker why he supported Perón has been met by the significant gesture of tapping the back pocket where the money is kept, symbolising a basic class pragmatism of monetary needs and their satisfaction. Clearly, Peronism from the workers' point of view was in a fundamental sense a response to economic grievances and class exploitation.

Yet, it was also something more. It was also a political movement which represented a crucial shift in working-class political allegiance and behaviour, and which presented its adherents with a distinct political vision. In order to understand the significance of this new allegiance we need to examine carefully the specific features of this political vision and the discourse in which it was expressed, rather than simply regard Peronism as an inevitable manifestation of social and economic dissatisfaction. Gareth Stedman Jones, commenting on the reluctance of social historians to take sufficient account of the political, has recently observed that 'a political movement is not simply a manifestation of distress and pain, its existence is distinguished by a shared conviction articulating a political solution to distress and a political diagnosis of its causes'.[21] Thus if Peronism did represent a concrete solution to felt material needs, we still need to understand why the solution took the specific political form of Peronism and not another. Other political movements did speak to the same needs and offer solutions to them. Even programmatically there were many formal similarities between Peronism and other political forces. What we need to understand is Peronism's success, its distinctiveness, why its political appeal was more credible for workers – which areas it touched that others did not. To do this we need to take Perón's political and ideological appeal seriously and examine the nature of Peronism's rhetoric and compare it with that of its rivals for working-class allegiance.

Workers as citizens in Peronist political rhetoric

Peronism's fundamental political appeal lay in its ability to redefine the notion of citizenship within a broader, ultimately social, context. The issue of citizenship *per se*, and the question of access to full political rights, was a potent part of Peronist discourse, forming part of a language of protest at political exclusion that had great popular resonance. Part of the power of such elements in Peronist political language, came from a recognition that it formed part of a traditional language of democratic politics which demanded equal access to political rights. This tradition had found its principal prior embodiment in the Unión Cívica Radical and its leader Hipólito Yrigoyen. The Radical Party prior to 1930 had mobilised the urban and rural middle classes and a not inconsiderable section of the urban poor with a rhetoric permeated with symbols of struggle against the oligarchy, and with a traditional language of citizenship, political rights and obligations.[22] Peronism was certainly eclectic enough to lay claim to, and absorb elements of, this Yrigoyenist heritage.[23]

In part, too, the force of such a concern for the rights of political citizenship lay in the scandal of the *década infame*, the infamous decade which followed the military overthrow of Yrigoyen in 1930.[24] The *década infame*, which stretched in fact from 1930 until the military coup of 1943, witnessed the reimposition and maintenance of the conservative elite's political power through a system of institutionalised fraud and corruption. It was the epoch of 'Ya votaste, rajá pronto para tu casa' (You've already voted, get along quickly to your home!), enforced by the hired thugs of the conservative committees.[25] In Avellaneda Don Alberto Barceló controlled Argentina's emerging industrial centre with the aid of a police force, a political machine, the underworld and votes from the dead, much as he had done since the First World War.[26] In the province of Buenos Aires Governor Manuel Fresco coordinated a similar machine of clientelism and corruption. The only island of relative political rectitude was in the Federal Capital where fraud was rarely practised. Political corruption set a tone of social degeneration of the traditional elite, epitomised in the seemingly endless series of scandals involving public figures and foreign economic groups which was to furnish the emerging groups of nationalists with many of their targets.[27]

Beyond that, such institutional corruption bred a broader public cynicism. In the words of one author 'this was a corruption which gave lessons'.[28] The political and moral malaise embodied in this situation clearly engendered a crisis of confidence and legitimacy in established political institutions. Peronism could, therefore, draw political capital by denouncing the hypocrisy of a formal democratic system which had little of democracy's real content. Moreover, the weight of Peronist claims to this heritage was reinforced by the fact that even those parties formally opposed to the fraud of the 1930s were perceived to have compromised themselves with the conservative regime. This was particularly the case with the Radical Party which after a period of principled abstention between 1931 and 1936 had, under the leadership of Manuel T. de Alvear, reentered the political fray to act as a loyal opposition in a political system it knew it would never be allowed to dominate. The crisis of legitimacy extended, therefore, far beyond the conservative elite itself and was a constantly reiterated theme of Peronist propaganda in 1945 and 1946. As the organ of the Partido Laborista expressed it during the run up to the 1946 elections: 'The old traditional parties, for many years passed, have ceased to be voices of the people in order to act instead in small circles of clear unpopular character, deaf and blind to the worries of that mass whose aid they only think to call upon when elections come around.'[29]

Nevertheless, Peronism's political appeal to workers cannot be explained simply in terms of its capacity to articulate claims to political participation and a full recognition of the rights of citizenship. Formally the rights associated with such claims – universal suffrage, the right of association, equality before the law – had long existed in Argentina. The Saenz Peña Law of 1912, the law of universal suffrage, continued in operation in Argentina throughout the *década infame*. Similarly there existed in Argentina a long-established tradition of representative social and political institutions. Peronism's articulation of democratic demands was, therefore, a claim for a *re*establishment of previously recognised rights and claims. Moreover, Perón had no monopoly of this language of political exclusion. Indeed it was a language which his opponents in the Unión Democrática used against him, accusing him of representing a closed, undemocratic system, and it was a discourse which would continue to form the basis of political opposition to Perón throughout his regime and after his fall from power. Finally, it was, in the sense that it addressed the general issue of citizenship, not an appeal directed specifically at workers but, by definition, at all voters whose rights had been abused.

Perón's political success with workers lay, rather, in his capacity to recast the whole issue of citizenship within a new social context.[30] Peronist discourse denied the validity of liberalism's separation of the state and politics from civil society. Citizenship was not to be defined any longer simply in terms of individual rights and relations within political society but was now redefined in terms of the economic and social realm of civil society. Within the terms of this rhetoric to struggle for rights in the sphere of politics inevitably implied social change. Indeed, by constantly emphasising the social dimension of citizenship Perón explicitly challenged the legitimacy of a notion of democracy which limited itself to participation in formal political rights and he extended it to include participation in the social and economic life of the nation. In part this was reflected in a claim for a democracy which included social rights and reforms, and in an attitude which treated with scepticism political claims couched in the rhetoric of formal liberalism. This was most starkly apparent in the election campaign of 1946. The political appeal of the Unión Democrática was almost entirely expressed in a language of liberal democratic slogans. In the political manifestos and speeches there was virtually no mention made of the social issue. Instead, one finds a political discourse entirely framed in terms of a rhetoric of 'liberty', 'democracy', 'the constitution', 'free elections', 'freedom of speech'.[31]

Perón, in contrast, constantly reminded his audiences that behind the phraseology of liberalism lay a basic social division and that a true democracy could only be built by doing justice to this social issue. In a speech in July 1945 in which he responded to growing opposition demands for elections he said: 'If some ask for liberty we too demand it ... but not the liberty of fraud ... nor the liberty to sell the country out, nor to exploit the working people.'[32] Luis Gay, the secretary general of the Partido Laborista, echoed this perception in a speech at the formal proclamation of Perón's presidential ticket in February 1946:

Political democracy is a lie on its own. It is only a reality when it is accompanied by an economic reconstruction of the economy which makes democracy possible on the terrain of practical happenings. They are lying who don't agree with this concept and only speak of the constitution and of that liberty which they defrauded and denied right up to the coup of 3 June 1943.[33]

It seems clear that this kind of rhetoric struck a deep chord with working people emerging from the *década infame*. Manuel Pichel, a delegate of the CGT, stated in the first official demonstration organised by the CGT to back Perón against the mounting opposition attack in July 1945: 'It is not enough to speak of democracy. We don't want a democracy defended by the reactionary capitalists, a democracy which would mean a return to the oligarchy is not something we would support.'[34] Mariano Tedesco, a textile workers' leader, recalled some years later that 'people in 1945 had already had a belly-full. For years they had seen the satisfaction of their hunger delayed with songs to liberty.'[35] In a similar vein, the scepticism with which the formal symbols of liberalism were met is forcibly evoked in an anecdote Julio Mafud recalls from the year 1945. Mafud remembers a group of workers responding to a questioner who asked if they were worried about freedom of speech if Perón were to be elected in the upcoming election. They had replied, 'Freedom of speech is to do with you people. We have never had it.'[36]

More fundamentally still, Perón's recasting of the issue of citizenship implied a distinct, new vision of the working class's role in society. Traditionally the liberal political system in Argentina, as elsewhere, had recognised the political existence of workers as individual, atomised citizens with formal equality of rights in the political arena, at the same time as it had denied, or hindered, its constitution as a social class at the political level. Certainly, faithful to the liberal separation of state and civil society, it had denied the legitimacy of transferring the social identity built around conflict at the social level to the political arena. Rather, any unity, social cohesion and sense of distinct interests attained in civil society were to be dissolved and atomised in the political marketplace where individual citizens sought, through the mediation of political parties, to influence the state and thus reconcile and balance the competing interests which existed in civil society.

Radicalism, for all its rhetoric of 'the people' and 'the oligarchy', never challenged the presuppositions of this liberal political system. Indeed, its clientelistic political machine, built around local bosses, was ideally placed to act as the broker of the individual citizens' claims in the political marketplace.[37] Peronism, on the other hand, premised its political appeal to workers on a recognition of the working class as a distinct social force which demanded recognition and representation as such in the political life of the nation. This representation would no longer be achieved simply through the exercise of the formal rights of citizenship and the primary mediation of political parties. Instead, the working class as an autonomous social force would have direct, indeed privileged access, to the state through its trade unions.

The uniqueness of this vision of working-class social and political integration in the Argentina of the 1940s becomes apparent if we examine the distinctive way Perón addressed the working class in his speeches both during the election campaign of 1945–6 and after.[38] In contrast to the more traditional *caudillo* or political boss Perón's political discourse did not address workers as atomised individuals whose only hope of achieving social coherence and political meaning for their lives lay in establishing ties with a leader who could intercede for them with an all-powerful state. Instead Perón addressed them as a social force whose own organisation and strength were vital if he were to be successful at the level of the state in asserting their rights. He was only their spokesman and could only be as successful as they were united and organised. Continually Perón emphasised the frailty of individuals and the arbitrariness of human fate, and hence the necessity for them to depend on nothing but their own will to achieve their rights. Those rights and interests would have to be negotiated with other social groups. Within this rhetoric, therefore, the state was not simply an all-powerful dispenser of desired resources which distributed these – through its chosen instrument, the leader – to passive individuals. Rather, it was a space where *classes* – not isolated individuals – could act politically and socially with one another to establish corporate rights and claims. Within this discourse the ultimate arbiter of this process might be the state, and ultimately the figure of Perón identified with the state, but he did not on his own constitute these groups as social forces; they had a certain independent, and irreducible, social, and hence political, presence.[39]

Clearly there were strong elements of a personalist, almost mystical *caudillismo* attached to the position of both Perón and Evita Perón within Peronist rhetoric. Partly this resulted from the different political needs of Perón and Peronism at different times. From a secure position of state power the need to emphasise working-class organisational autonomy and social cohesion was evidently less than in the period of political contest preceding the achievement of that power. Indeed such an emphasis would soon conflict with the new demands of the state. Even during the pre-1946 period the personalist elements of Perón's political appeal were present, as witness the consistent, overwhelming chant of 'Perón! Perón!' which dominated the mobilisation of 17 October 1945. Nevertheless, even at the height of the adulation of Evita and the growing state-sponsored cult of Perón's personal power during the second presidency, this personalist element was not present entirely at the expense of a continued affirmation of the social and organisational strength of the working class.

This affirmation of the workers as a social presence and their incorporation directly into the affairs of state evidently implied a new conception of the legitimate spheres of interest and activity of the working class and its institutions. This was most evident in Perón's assertion of the workers' rights to be concerned with, and to help determine, the economic development of the nation. It was within the context of this new vision of the working class's role in society that the issues of industrialisation and economic nationalism, key elements in Peronism's political appeal, were to be situated. Peronist rhetoric was open enough to absorb existing strands of nationalist thought. Some of these went back, once again, to the Yrigoyenist heritage, particularly his conflict with foreign petroleum companies in his last years in office. Other elements were absorbed from the groups of nationalist intellectuals which emerged in the 1930s and whose ideas were influential among the military. Thus, for example, terms such as *cipayo* and *vendepatria* became incorporated into the political language of Peronism to refer to those forces which wished to maintain Argentina within the economic orbit of the United States or the United Kingdom as a provider of agricultural and pastoral products.[40] Such a language became symbolic of a commitment to industrialisation overseen and guided by a commitment to *Argentina potencia* in contrast to the *Argentina granja* of Peronism's opponents.

The success of Perón's identification of himself with the creation of an industrial Argentina and the political appeal of such symbolism did not reside primarily in programmatic terms. Given the evident concern of an emerging industrial workforce with the issue of industrialisation, and Peronism's strenuous self-identification with this symbol, and later monopoly of the language of economic development, it would be tempting to explain such a success in terms of a unique attachment on

the part of Perón to such a programme. Yet, in terms of political programmes and formal commitments, the association of Peronism with
industrialisation and of its opponents with a rural, pastoral Argentina
was scarcely accurate. Emphases varied greatly and the commitment
was rarely consistent, but very few of the major political parties in
Argentina denied by the 1940s the need for some sort of state-
sponsored industrialisation. The most articulate sector of the conservative elite had affirmed their recognition of the irreversibility of
industrialisation with the *Plan Pinedo* of 1940. The Radical Party
had also increasingly adopted a pro-industrialisation stance and the
Yrigoyenist wing of the party adopted in April 1945, with the Declaration of Avellaneda, an economic blueprint every bit as industrialist
as that of Perón. The left, too, in the form of the communists and
socialists had consistently used an anti-imperialist rhetoric throughout
the 1930s.[41]

The real issue at stake in the 1940s was not, therefore, so much industrialisation *versus* agrarian development, or state intervention *versus*
laissez-faire. Rather it was the issue of the different potential meanings
of industrialism, the social and political parameters within which it
should take place which were at stake. It was Perón's ability to define
these parameters in a new way which appealed to the working class, and
his ability to address this issue in a particularly credible way for
workers that enabled him to appropriate the issue and symbol of industrial development and make it a political weapon with which to distinguish himself from his opponents.

The success of this appropriation was partly a matter of perception.
Certainly, the association of Perón's political opponents in 1945 and
1946 with the bastions of traditional rural society, the *Sociedad Rural*
and the Jockey Club, weakened the credibility of their commitment to
industrialism. In a similar way, their close association with the US am-
bassador did not strengthen belief in their devotion to national
sovereignty and economic independence. In terms of image making the
identification of Peronism with industrial and social progress, with
modernity, was an established fact by the end of the presidential election campaign of 1946. It was not, however, solely a matter of images
and public relations. More fundamentally the working class recognised
in Perón's espousal of industrial development a vital role for itself as an
actor in the greatly expanded public sphere which Peronism offered to
it as a field for its activity. Indeed Perón consistently premised the very
notion of national development on the full participation of the working
class in public life and social justice. Industrialisation within his

discourse was no longer conceivable, as it had been prior to 1943, at the expense of the extreme exploitation of the working class. In a speech delivered during the election campaign Perón had affirmed: 'In conclusion: Argentina cannot continue to stagnate in a somnolent rhythm of activity to which so many who had come and lived at her expense had condemned her. Argentina must recover the firm pulse of a healthy and clean living youth, Argentina needs the young blood of the working class.'[42] Within Peronist rhetoric social justice and national sovereignty were credibly interrelated themes rather than simply enunciated abstract slogans.

A believable vision: credibility and concreteness in Perón's political discourse

The issue of credibility is crucial for understanding both Perón's successful identification of himself with certain important symbols such as industrialism and, more generally, the political impact of his discourse on workers. Gareth Stedman Jones, in the essay to which we have already referred, notes that to be successful 'a particular political vocabulary must convey a practicable hope of a general alternative and a believable means of realising it such that potential recruits can think in its terms'.[43] The vocabulary of Peronism was both visionary and believable. The credibility was in part rooted in the immediate, concrete nature of its rhetoric. This involved a tying down of abstract political slogans to their most concrete material aspects. As we have already seen, in the crucial years 1945 and 1946 this was clearly contrasted with a language of great abstraction used by Perón's political opponents. While Perón's rhetoric was capable of lofty sermonising, particularly once he had attained the presidency, and depending on the audience he was addressing, his speeches to working-class audiences in this formative period have, for their time, a unique tone.

They are, for example, framed in a language clearly distinct from that of classic radicalism, with its woolly generalities concerning national renovation and civic virtue. The language of 'the oligarchy' and 'the people' was still present but now usually more precisely defined. Their utilisation as general categories to denote good and evil, those who were with Perón from those against, was still there but now there was also a frequent concretising, sometimes as rich and poor, often as capitalist and worker. While there was a rhetoric of an indivisible community – symbolised in 'the people' and 'the nation' – the working class was given an implicitly superior role within this whole, often as the repository of national values. 'The people' frequently were transformed into 'the working people' (*el pueblo trabajador*): the people, the nation and the workers became interchangeable.

A similar denial of the abstract can be found in Peronism's appeal to economic and political nationalism. In terms of the formal construction from the state of Peronist ideology, categories such as 'the nation' and 'Argentina' were accorded an abstract, mystical significance.[44] When, however, Perón specifically addressed the working class, particularly in the formative period, but also after, one finds little appeal to the irrational, mystical elements of nationalist ideology. There was little concern with the intrinsic virtues of *Argentinidad* nor with the historical precedents of *criollo* culture as expressed in a historical nostalgia for some long-departed national essence. Such concerns were mainly the province of middle-class intellectuals in the various nationalist groups which attempted, with little success, to use Peronism as a vehicle for their aspirations. Working-class nationalism was addressed primarily in terms of concrete economic issues.

Moreover, Peronism's political credibility for workers was due not only to the concreteness of its rhetoric, but also to its immediacy. Perón's political vision of a society based on social justice and on the social and political integration of workers into that society was not premised, as it was for example, in leftist political discourse, on the prior achievement of long-term, abstract structural transformations, nor on the gradual acquisition at some future date of an adequate consciousness on the part of the working class. It took working-class consciousness, habits, life styles and values as it found them and affirmed their sufficiency and value. It glorified the everyday and the ordinary as a sufficient basis for the rapid attainment of a juster society, provided that certain easily achievable and self-evident goals were met. Primarily this meant support for Perón as head of state and the maintenance of a strong union movement. In this sense Peronism's political appeal was radically plebeian; it eschewed the need for a peculiarly enlightened political elite and reflected and inculcated a profound anti-intellectualism.

The glorification of popular life styles and habits implied a political style and idiom well in tune with popular sensibilities. Whether it was in symbolically striking the pose of the *descamisado* (shirtless one) in a political rally, or in the nature of the imagery used in his speeches, Perón had an ability to communicate to working-class audiences which his rivals lacked. The poet Luis Franco commented cryptically on Perón's 'spiritual affinity with tango lyrics'.[45] His ability to use this affinity to establish a bond with his audience was clearly shown in his speech to those assembled in the Plaza de Mayo on 17 October 1945. Towards the end of that speech Perón evoked the image of his mother, 'mi vieja': 'I said to you a little while ago that I would embrace you as I would my mother because you have had the same griefs and the same thoughts that my poor old lady must have felt in these days.'[46] The reference is apparently gratuitous, the empty phraseology of someone who could think of nothing better to say until we recognise that the sentiments echo exactly a dominant refrain of tango – the poor grief-laden mother whose pain symbolises the pain of her children, of all the poor. Perón's identification of his own mother with the poor establishes a sentimental identity between himself and his audience; with this tone of nostalgia he was touching an important sensibility in Argentine popular culture of the period.[47] Significantly, too, the speech ended on another 'tangoesque' note. Perón reminded his audience as they were about to leave the Plaza, 'remember that among you there are many women workers who have to be protected here and in life by you same workers'.[48] The theme of the threat to the women of the working class, and the need to protect their women, was also a constant theme of both tango and other forms of popular culture.

Perón's use of such an idiom within which to frame his political appeal often seems to us now, and indeed it seemed to many of his critics at the time, to reek of the paternalistic condescension of the traditional *caudillo* figure. His constant use of couplets from Martín Fierro, or his conscious use of terms taken from *lunfardo* argot grates on modern sensibilities. However, we should be careful to appreciate the impact of his ability to speak in an idiom which reflected popular sensibilities of the time. In accounts by observers and journalists of the crucial formative years of Peronism we frequently find the adjectives *chabacano* and *burdo* used to describe both Perón himself and his supporters. Both words have the sense of crude, cheap, coarse and they also implied a lack of sophistication, an awkwardness, almost a country bumpkin quality. While they were generally meant as epithets they were not descriptions Peronists would necessarily have denied.

Indeed this capacity to recognise, reflect and foster a popular political style and idiom based on this plebeian realism contrasted strongly with the political appeal of traditional working-class political parties. The tone adopted by the latter when confronted by the working-class effervescence of the mid 1940s was didactic, moralising and apparently addressed to a morally and intellectually inferior audience. This was particularly the case of the Socialist Party. Its analysis of the events of 17 October is illustrative of its attitude and tone:

The part of the people which lives its resentment, and perhaps only for its resentment, spilt over into the streets, threatened, yelled, trampled upon and assaulted newspapers and persons in its demon-like fury, those persons who were the very champions of its elevation and dignification.[49]

Behind this tone of fear, frustration and moralising lay a discourse which addressed an abstract, almost mythical working class. Peronism on the other hand was prepared, particularly in its formative period, to recognise, and even glorify, workers who did 'threaten, yell, and trample with a demon-like fury'. Comparing Perón's political approach to that of his rivals one is reminded of Ernst Bloch's comment concerning Nazism's preemption of socialist and communist appeal among German workers that 'the Nazis speak falsely but to people, the communists truthfully, but of things'.[50]

Perón's ability to appreciate the tone of working-class sensibilities and assumptions was reflected in other areas. There was, for example, in Peronist rhetoric a tacit recognition of the immutability of social inequality, a common sense, shrug of the shoulders acceptance of the reality of social and economic inequities, a recognition of what Pierre Bourdieu has called 'a sense of limits'.[51] The remedies proposed to mitigate these inequities were plausible and immediate. Perón, in a speech in Rosario in August 1944, had emphasised the apparently self-evident reasonableness of his appeal, the mundaneness behind the abstract rhetoric of social equality: 'We want exploitation of man by man to cease in our country and when this problem disappears we will equalise a little the social classes so that there will not be in this country men who are too poor nor those who are too rich.'[52]

This realism implied a political vision of a limited nature but it did not eliminate utopian resonances; it simply made such resonances – a yearning for social equality, for an end to exploitation – more credible for a working class imbued by its experience of the *década infame* with a certain cynicism regarding political promises and abstract slogans. Indeed the credibility of Perón's political vision, the practicability of the hope it offered, was affirmed on a daily basis by its actions from the state. The solutions it offered the working class did not depend on some future apocalypse for confirmation but were rather directly verifiable in terms of everyday political activity and experience. Already by 1945 the slogan had appeared among workers which was to symbolise this credibility: 'Perón cumple!' (Perón delivers).

The heretical social impact of Peronism

Peronism meant a greatly increased social and political presence for the working class within Argentine society. The impact of this can be measured in institutional terms by reference to such factors as the intimate relationship between government and labour during the Perón era, the massive extension of unionisation, the number of union-sponsored members of congress. These are factors that are clearly demonstrable empirically and often measurable statistically. There are, however, other factors which need to be taken into account in assessing Peronism's social meaning for the working class – factors which are far less tangible, far more difficult to quantify. We are dealing here with factors such as pride, self-respect and dignity.

The meaning of the 'década infame': working-class responses

In order to assess the importance of such factors we must return to the *década infame*, for it was clearly a benchmark against which workers measured their experience of Peronism. Popular culture of the Peronist era was dominated by a temporal dichotomy which contrasted the Peronist present with the recent past. As Ernesto Goldar has noted in his analysis of Peronist popular fiction this dichotomy was accompanied by a corresponding contrast of values associated with the *hoy* of 1950 and the *ayer* of the 1930s.[53] Some of these evaluative contrasts referred to the concrete social changes associated with better social welfare, improved wages and good union organisation. Yet, others spoke to a wider, more personal social realm outside improvements in the world of the production line, the wage packet or the union. These suggest strongly that the *década infame* was experienced by many workers as a time of profound collective and individual frustration and humiliation.

While we lack a comprehensive account of the elements which made up the social universe of the working class in the pre-Perón period, the evidence of anecdote, personal testimony, popular cultural forms and working-class biography nevertheless can provide us with suggestive fragments of a whole picture. The harsh conditions and discipline attested to by most observers of the period evidently had an impact in the wider working-class community. Cipriano Reyes notes, for example, in his memoirs of his organising experiences in the meatpacking plants of Berisso in the 1930s and 1940s that 'the company was the master of the lives and dwellings of its workers ... when a workman didn't pay his debts the tradesman went to see the personel chief of the *frigorífico* and the offender was fired or suspended. The vigilance was incredible; everything was controlled'.[54]

This sort of control was probably most fierce in working-class communities dominated by a single large concern, such as the meatpacking plants. Nevertheless, the wider social implications arising from such a situation of employer dominance were not confined to the extreme case of the company town. Angel Perelman remembers leaving school at ten in order to enter a metal-working workshop in the Federal Capital where he worked 'without any fixed hours ... the time we finished was fixed by the boss ... the sum total of happiness for a working-class family consisted in keeping your job'. The 1930s were, he remembers, 'the era of the desperate, the ingenious and the petty theft'.[55] Another writer, commenting on the wider implications of the labour situation in the same era observed that: 'Fear of unemployment in this period led to humiliation. You had to be quiet, not talk. The lack of elemental defensive actions led to a moral decline, to cynicism. Within the factory the worker was alone, deprived of all social consciousness.'[56] Although such sweeping generalisations about moral decline and cynicism being characteristic of working-class attitudes in the 1930s need to be treated with caution, there is other evidence which tends to point in a similar direction.

Some of the most suggestive of this evidence is to be gleaned from popular cultural forms and in particular the tango. The social universe depicted in the tangos of the 1930s was universally bleak. The traditional themes of tango are still present – the betrayal of love, the nostalgia for a simpler past centred on an idyllic recreation of the *barrio* or *arrabal*, the affirmation of the virtues of valour and courage – but to this has now been added, in some of the most popular and significant tangos, a wider social context. In the tangos of Enrique Santos Discépolo, in particular, the impossibility of a meaningful relationship between a man and a woman has come to symbolise the impossibility of any social relationship which is not based on greed, egotism and a total lack of moral scruples in a world based on injustice and deceit. A crucial figure in many of Discépolo's tangos is the *gilito embanderado* – the naive little man, humiliated by poverty and society, who still has illusions that he can survive in the world while being morally honest and decent or, more ingenuously still, that he can effect some change in an unjust world.[57] The object of the tango then becomes to disabuse him of his illusions by confronting him with a reality where 'Not even God saves those who are lost.'[58] The tone is one of bitterness and resignation. The popular wisdom about social life embodied in the narrative recommends an adoption of the dominant values of egotism and immorality. At its most extreme this implied an understanding – if not approval – of the attraction for the poor of the logic of the *mala vida* – prostitution, pimping and crime.[59] The alternative was a resigned acceptance or 'an obstinate silence' for those who could not conform to this dominant social ethos.[60]

Now evidently care must be taken in drawing conclusions about working-class attitudes from tango and other popular cultural forms of the period. Tango, for example, was increasingly a commercialised art form whose connection with the working-class *barrio* was very tenuous by the 1930s. What reached the general public was largely determined by record companies and commercial success and failure depended on the reception in the wider consumer market and the theatres and music halls of downtown Buenos Aires. It seems likely, too, that the bohemian element which had always been a crucial part of tango was given greater prominence as tango lyricists came more and more from the urban lower middle class. Certainly, the desperate lament of Discépolo's great tango, 'Cambalache', written in 1935, that 'Everything is equal, nothing is better; it's the same to be a jack ass as a great professor' rings with the educated middle class's disenchantment with society's failure to recognise true merit. The lyrics of the *década infame* lack, too, some of the optimism and social engagement found in some of the tangos of an earlier era. Yet the immense popularity of these tangos among the working class of Buenos Aires seems to attest to the fact that whatever the manipulations of the culture industry, whatever the caveats we place on the reading of working-class consciousness directly from the lyrics of tango, they did respond to certain attitudes and experiences recreated in tango which they recognised as authentic to themselves and their experience.

However, even if we recognise the suggestiveness of such evidence we must also recognise that cynicism, apathy or resignation were not the only responses available to workers. Luis Danussi who would become, after 1955, a leader of the print workers's union found when he first arrived in Buenos Aires in 1938 a city which was 'tumultuous and possessed a frantic union activity, offering a broad field for action; national congresses, zonal, municipal congresses of workers and unions' according to his biographers.[61] The militant working-class culture characteristic of an earlier epoch was still present. This culture was centred around the existence of 'unions, atheneums, libraries, the distribution of pamphlets, papers, reviews, leaflets and books; demonstrations, committees for the release of political prisoners, theatre groups, cooperatives, communities and attempts at a solidarity life style. Also campaigns were carried out against alcoholism, tobacco, picnics were organised, lectures discussed and the spirit of mutual aid inculcated.'[62] Elements of this sort of traditional militant culture shared by socialists, communists, anarchists and syndicalists alike still flourished. They found an expression in the numerous committees formed in the 1930s to aid the Spanish Republicans, and they were still a living presence in unions such as the print workers which Luis Danussi entered.

Danussi himself had an anarchist background before arriving in Buenos Aires, but workers from outside this culture could be attracted by it and use it as a channel to express their resentment at exploitation and as part of their search for political solutions. Angel Perelman notes, for example, that:

I learned about capitalist exploitation and class struggle first in that factory rather than in the books ... at the age of fourteen, and with already four years as a worker I couldn't help but be interested in politics. How could I not have been interested? There were many demonstrations by the unemployed. Some left-wing parties protested against the reigning misery. Union meetings ... brought together the most militant and determined workers. I began to attend all sorts of meetings and acts.[63]

Other evidence, too, suggests an increase in union activity and attendance at union meetings in the late 1930s and early 1940s as unemployment decreased, industry expanded and the union movement recovered somewhat from the decline of the years following the coup of 1930. Union membership responded to an improved national and international climate, increasing by some 10% between 1941 and 1945.[64]

Yet this positive organisational and collective response to the conditions of the pre-1943 period does not seem to have been the predominant one. Evidently there was a wide spectrum of working-class experience and response. The working-class militants themselves recognised, however, that the militant culture of the union or ideological grouping touched only a minority of the working class. Danussi's biographers stress that 'to open up the road for union organisation was enormously difficult, in many respects because of police and employer repression, but what represented an almost insuperable obstacle to overcome was the indifference and disbelief of the workers themselves, reluctant to organise in defence of their own interests'.[65]

Something of the feeling of impotence and resignation which we may suggest characterised the response of many workers to the experience of the pre-1943 period can be found in the personal testimony of the non-militant. The following two excerpts from such testimony are offered in an attempt to convey the essence of this feeling. The first comes from a worker who had worked in the ports along the Paraná River, particularly in the port of Rosario:

Question: What were the thirties like for you?

Don Ramiro: Well life was very hard back then … working people weren't worth anything and we got no respect from those who controlled everything. You had to know your place and keep in line. I used to vote for the Radicals in the twenties but after 1930 things got really bad. The conservative bosses ran the whole show. On election day I would go down to the town hall to vote but I couldn't get in … You see I was known as someone they couldn't trust so they would stop me voting. By law they couldn't, but that was a joke, what was the law back then? There would be a group of them, heavies, paid by the local conservative committee … everyone knew them … and they would block the doorway when you wanted to go in. You could see their guns bulging under their jackets.

Question: You mean they would use force to stop you voting? They would threaten you?

Don Ramiro: No. They never did that openly … not to me at least, they didn't have to … you knew you would have to pay for it somehow if you went against them. It was a sort of game for them.

Question: So what did you do?

Don Ramiro: What could you do? Nothing. You'd go home. Complain maybe to your friends about those bastards. If you made a fuss they would get you one way or another and it wouldn't do any good anyway. You were nothing to them. But later with Perón that all changed. I voted for him.

Question: How did it change?

Don Ramiro: Well, with Perón we were all machos.[66]

The second excerpt comes from a younger worker from Buenos Aires who entered the workforce in the late 1930s:

Lautaro: One thing I remember about the thirties was the way you were treated. You felt you didn't have rights to anything, everything seemed to be a favour they did for you through the church or some charity or if you went and begged the local political boss he'd help you get medicine or get into a hospital. Another thing I remember about the thirties is that I always felt strange when I went to the city, downtown Buenos Aires – like you didn't belong there, which was stupid but you felt that they were looking down on you, that you weren't dressed right. The police there treated you like animals too.

Question: Were unions or politics important to you at that time?

Lautaro: Well, I voted for the socialists usually. My brother was more interested in them, though I always thought that they were at least honest. But I never thought that it would do any good. The same really with unions. We didn't have a union in the shops where I worked – it must have been in the early forties, before Perón. We had plenty to complain about but I don't recall that we thought seriously about the union. That was just the way things were, you just had to put up with it ... with everything, their damn arrogance, the way they treated you. Some of the activists my brother hung out with wanted to change that but they were exceptions I think. Not many workers thought of being heroes then.[67]

Private experience and public discourse

It is against the background of this working-class experience of the pre-1943 period that the profounder social impact of Peronism must be considered. With the crisis of the traditional order inaugurated by the military coup of 1943 far more was challenged than the political and institutional authority of the conservative elite. By 1945 political crisis had provoked, and was itself compounded by, a questioning of a whole set of social assumptions concerning social relationships, forms of deference and largely tacit understandings about 'the natural order of things', 'the sense of limits', of what could and could not be legitimately questioned and spoken. In this sense Peronism's power ultimately lay in its capacity to give public utterance to what had until then been internalised, lived as private experience. As Pierre Bourdieu has written:

Private experiences undergo nothing less than *change of state* when they recognise themselves in the *public objectivity* of an already constituted discourse, the objective sign of recognition of their right to be spoken and to be spoken publicly. 'Words wreck havoc,' says Sartre, 'when they find a name for what had up till then been lived namelessly.'[68]

It is surely in this context that the fragments presented in the preceding section acquire their significance. In particular we can appreciate the image of silence which runs through them: 'You have to be silent, not talk'; 'an obstinate silence'; or Don Ramiro's response when asked what he did about the power of the political bosses, 'Nothing. You'd go home. Complain maybe to friends.' Peronist discourse's ability to articulate these unformulated experiences was the basis of its truly heretical power. Now there were other heretical discourses – in the sense of offering alternatives to establishment orthodoxy – present in the form of socialist, communist and radical rhetoric. However, as we have seen, these were unable to acquire unchallenged authority as valid expressions of working-class experience. Peronism had the enormous advantage over these other political forces of being an 'already constituted discourse' articulated from a position of state power, and this vastly increased the legitimacy it bequeathed on the experiences it expressed.

The heretical social power Peronism expressed was reflected in its use of language. Terms expressive of notions of social justice, fairness, decency – whose expression had been silenced (or ridiculed as in tango) – were now to become central to the new language of power. More than this, though, we find that terms which had previously been symbolic of working-class humiliation and explicit lack of status in a deeply status-conscious society now acquired diametrically opposite connotations and values. The most famous example is clearly the implications attached to the word *descamisado* (shirtless one). The word had been used originally as an epithet by anti-Peronists prior to the election of 1946 to refer to Perón's working-class supporters.[69] The explicit connotation of social, and hence political and moral, inferiority was based on a criteria of social worth which took one of the most evident signs of working-class status – work clothes – and treated that as a self-evident badge of inferiority. Peronism took the term and inverted its symbolic significance, turning it into an affirmation of working-class value. This inversion was magnified by the attachment of the *descamisados* in official rhetoric to the figure of Eva Perón, their designated protectress.[70]

Perhaps more significantly still we find terms current in the pre-1943 period to refer even more scornfully to the working class now being transformed, inverted, in a similar fashion. *Negro* in general usage referred to inhabitants from the interior of the country and often had clear ethnic, pejorative, connotations. The traditional elite had disrespectfully referred to Yrigoyen's supporters as *los negreros radicales*.[71] With the mass influx of internal migrants to the industry of Buenos Aires in the 1930s the word was commonly used as synonymous with manual workers and *negrada* was used as a generic equivalent of proletariat. The connotations were unmistakable: *una negra* meant in *porteño* slang a woman of 'low condition', *negrear* meant to pick up such women for sexual purposes. As José Gobello notes in his *Diccionario Lunfardo*, all but one of the variants of *negro* carry the strong sense of inferiority and disrespect.[72] The use of *negrada* as a synoym for the proletariat of the 1930s thus had a strong social symbolism which was at the root of its use by anti-Peronist forces. *La negrada de Perón, las cabecitas negras*, were frequent terms of derision used by Perón's political opponents from the mid 1940s on. Their incorporation into the language of Peronism conferred on them a new status. The fact that *la negrada* found expression and affirmation in this public discourse meant that a range of experiences normally associated with the term – and which by being so designated had been ruled illegitimate, unworthy of concern and hence condemned to be suffered silently, internalised or expressed obliquely in certain anguished forms of popular culture – could now be spoken and enter into the realm of public discussion, social concern and hence political action.

Something of this heretical social meaning was apparent in the vast upsurge of working-class mobilisation which stretched from 17 October 1945 until the election victory of February 1946. This mobilisation demonstrated workers' capacity to mobilise and defend their perceived interests. In addition, however, it also expressed a more diffuse social challenge to accepted forms of social hierarchy and symbols of authority. This was particularly noticeable during the demonstration of 17 October. While most attention has been directed to the ultimate political object of the demonstration – the personal figure of Perón and his release from confinement – the mobilisation itself, and the forms it took, themselves suggest an ampler social significance. Most sensitive observers of the event have agreed on the dominant tone of irreverence and ironic good humour among the demonstrators on that day. Felix Luna has summarised the atmosphere as one resembling 'a great fiesta, of carnival groups, of candomblé'.[73] The communist press spoke disparagingly of clans with *aspecto de murga*, which took part in the demonstration.[74] The use of the word *murga* is interesting since in popular usage it referred to groups who at carnival and other festivals dressed up and went around singing, dancing and playing instruments. While such behaviour was acceptable within the strict limits of carnival, and restricted to working-class *barrios*, its breaking out of these confines in a demonstration with a clear political content represented a symbolic subversion of accepted codes of behaviour and deference for the working class.

An important part of this subversion related to the area in which such behaviour was taking place – to implicit notions of spatial hierarchy. As the irreverent crowds moved out of the working-class suburbs of the outer limit of the Federal Captial or crossed the Puente Alsina from Avellaneda and beyond, and converged on the central area and the Plaza de Mayo in front of the presidential palace, they violated such notions. The behaviour of the workers as they moved through the wealthier suburbs compounded the blasphemy implicit in such a violation. The ditties they sang became increasingly insulting and ridiculing of the wealthy, the *gente decente* (decent folk), of *porteño* society. One of the many refrains directed at the puzzled onlookers of the Barrio Norte as they watched the emergence of the 'invisible Argentina'[75] under their balconies went: 'Get off the corner you mad oligarch, your mother doesn't love you and nor does Perón.'[76]

The fact that the culmination of the demonstration was the Plaza de Mayo was itself significant. Up until 1945 the Plaza in front of the presidential palace had been very much the territory of the *gente decente* and workers who ventured there without jacket or tie were not infrequently moved on or even arrested. A much published photograph taken on 17 October shows workers with shirt sleeves rolled up, sitting and bathing their feet in the fountains of the plaza. The symbolism implicit here can be readily appreciated if contrasted with the feeling of unease expressed by Lautaro whenever he visited the central area of the Federal Capital in the years prior to Perón.

Much of this irreverence, blasphemy, dancing and reappropriation of public space characteristic of 17 October and the election campaign which followed would seem to constitute a form of 'counter-theatre', of ridicule and abuse against the symbolic authority and pretensions of the Argentine elite.[77] The result was, certainly, a puncturing of elite self-assurance. It also represented a recovery of working-class pride and self-esteem, encapsulated in Don Ramiro's pithy summary of the change wrought by Perón: 'Well, with Perón we were all machos.' Perhaps above all it marked an affirmation of the working class's existence and a defiant end to silence and privatisation of grievance. This mixture of symbolic meanings is astutely captured in Felix Luna's recollection of his own memories of 17 October as he and his student friends, all anti-Peronist radicals, watched the columns of workers march through the city:

Well, there they were. As if they wanted to show all their power, so that nobody could doubt that they really existed. There they were all over the city, shouting in groups which seemed to be the same group multiplied by hundreds. We looked at them from the side walk, with a feeling akin to compassion. From where did they come? So they really existed? So many of them? So different from us? Had they really come on foot from those suburbs whose names made up a vague unknown geography, a *terra incognita* through which we had never wandered ... During all those days we had made the rounds of the places where they spoke of preoccupations like ours. We had moved through a known map, familiar: the faculty, Recoleta for the burial of Salmon Feijoo, the Plaza San Martin, the Casa Radical. Everything up till then was coherent and logical; everything seemed to support our own beliefs. But that day when the voices began to ring out and the columns of anonymous earth-coloured faces began to pass by we felt something tremble which until that day had seemed unmoveable.[78]

The limits of heresy: the ambivalence of Peronism's social legacy

It would be misleading, however, to leave the characterisation of

Peronism's social impact on the working class at this level. Peronism in power did not regard the working-class ebullience and spontaneity of the period from October 1945 to February 1946 in the same favourable light as it had done when it had been a contender for power. Indeed, much of the Peronist state's efforts between 1946 and its demise in 1955 can be viewed as an attempt to institutionalise and control the heretical challenge it had unleashed in the earlier period and to absorb this challenge within a new state-sponsored orthodoxy. Viewed in this light Peronism was, in a certain sense, a passive, demobilising social experience for workers. It stressed increasingly in its official rhetoric the controlled, limited mobilisation of workers under the aegis of the state. Perón himself frequently referred to his concern with the dangers of 'unorganised masses', and in the ideal Peronist scenario unions acted very much as instruments of the state in both mobilising and controlling workers. This cooptative side of the Peronist experience was reflected in the fundamental slogan addressed from the state to workers in the Perón era exhorting them to go peacefully 'From home to work, and from work to home.'

Formal Peronist ideology reflected this concern. It preached the need to harmonise the interests of capital and labour within the framework of a benevolent state, in the interest of the nation and its economic development. Perón, in his May Day speech of 1944, had said, 'We seek to surpass the class struggle, replacing it by a just agreement between workers and employers, based on a justice that springs from the state.'[79] Peronist ideology distinguished between exploitative, inhuman capital and progressive, socially responsible capital committed to the development of the national economy. Workers had nothing to fear from the latter: 'International capital is an instrument of exploitation, but national capital is an instrument of welfare; the first represents misery, the second prosperity.'[80] Peronist ideology stressed, too, as a logical extension of this premise that the interests of the nation and its economic developments were to be identified with the workers and their unions. Workers were seen as sharing with national, non-exploitative capital a common interest in defence of national development against the depradations of international capital and its internal allies, the oligarchy, who wanted to prevent Argentina's independent development.

In the context of our discussion concerning Peronism's social implications for workers, and its success in channelling and absorbing what we have called its heretical social potential, several factors need to be borne in mind. The Peronist state clearly did have considerable success in controlling the working class, socially and politically, and while class conflict was in no sense abolished, and the idyll of social harmony portrayed by official propaganda was not realised, relations between capital and labour did improve. The feared plebeian vengeance of the *porteño* sans culotte, apparently presaged in the social and political turmoil of 1945/6, did not materialise. Several reasons for this success can be suggested. The working class's ability to satisfy its material aspirations within the parameters set by the state is one; the personal prestige of Perón another. The ability of the state and its related cultural, political and ideological apparatus to promote and inculcate notions of class harmony and common interest must also be weighed. We must be careful, however, not to analyse this solely in terms of manipulation and social control. The efficacy of official ideology depended crucially on its ability to tie in with working-class perceptions and experience. Peronist rhetoric, like any other, drew its authority ultimately from its capacity to tell its audience what they wanted to hear.

As an example of what we mean we may take the treatment of the Day of the Workers, 1 May, in official Peronist rhetoric. A document published in 1952 by a state agency, entitled *Emancipation of the Workers*, was typical of official efforts in this direction. At its centrepiece is a collection of photographs, with a written commentary under each. The first photos show workers gathering to celebrate Labour Day with red flags and black-and-red anarchist banners raised high. Mounted police are visible in the photos. The commentary tells the story: 'Labour day as it was formerly celebrated in the country; taking part in the celebrations signified real courage.' 'The police, strongly armed and ready for anything, hindered workers from proclaiming their just aspirations.' The third photo bears witness to a 'sad account of the tragic happenings of Labour Day of thirty years ago'. The photos show those wounded or killed by the police. The next three photos are in explicit contrast and carry the moral of the story. They show a huge May Day demonstration in the Plaza de Mayo, full of union banners but now no red flags. 'In the new Argentina created by General Perón, 1 May is joyfully celebrated by a united people.' 'Labour Day is always a popular event of the greatest importance in Argentina.' The photo shows crowds of workers on their way to Government House to listen to a speech by Perón.[81]

This piece is evidently illustrative of Peronism's capacity to absorb and appropriate, and neutralise, the symbols of older rival class traditions. More importantly for our discussion is the way in which this appropriation involved altered meanings. The point can scarcely be missed: the symbolic contrast in the text is unavoidable. Far from being an affirmation of an identity forged in class conflict, a symbol of struggle and the holding fast for the sake of principle as it had been for an earlier generation of militants, May Day in the pre-Perón era now symbolised sadness, pain and impotence etched on the bandaged faces as they stare out of the text. On the other hand, May Day under Perón means happy faces walking toward the presidential palace, an atmosphere of tranquillity and harmony, an absence of panic, no police and no injuries. Now, clearly, this is government propaganda but the point is that its efficacy depended partly at least on its ability to tap a receptiveness to its message among workers.

Such a receptiveness existed among Argentine workers. Its roots, we may suggest, lie, once more, in the working-class experience of the pre-1943 era. The lessons of that experience were an important theme of popular culture in the Peronist years. Goldar summarises the treatment of the issue in popular fiction in the following way: 'The Day of the Workers during the *década infame* will be of struggle, repression, internationalist slogans, impotent rebellion; "your hunger, the hatred of those people, your misery, the waiting, the dirty and torn clothes, the worn out coat, the hoarse voices, struggling only so that life would be nothing more than tiredness and old dreams".'[82] In contrast to this picture of conflict and pain associated with May Day before Perón, the image associated with the post-1946 era will be one of tranquillity, where 1 May will be a fiesta of labour and the bloody meetings will become fading memories of the past.

Similar attitudes to the symbols of the class struggles of the past can be found in personal testimony. A long-time activist prominent in the founding of the Partido Laborista, explaining why he became involved in politics in 1945, said: 'I decided to collaborate in politics so that the working people, my class, could obtain the right to live better without the danger of having to confront tragedies like *Semana Trágica*, the massacre of Patagonia, 1921, Gualeguaychu, Berisso, Avellaneda, Mendoza and many other cases too numerous to mention.'[83]

We should be careful not to interpret such testimony solely in terms of working-class incorporation. Such fragments clearly do represent a yearning for social advancement without the pain of class conflict, for stability and routine in comparison with the arbitrariness and impotence associated with the earlier period. Though such a yearning could, as we shall see, coexist with a recognition of the reality of a lack of harmony. Moreover, the bedrock on which such attitudes rested—what gave them, and the official rhetoric which reflected them, credibility – was the notion of dignity and regained self respect. Time and again this seems to surface as the irreducible, minimal social meaning of the Peronist experience for workers. Enrique Dickmann, at more than eighty years of age, with more than fifty years as a militant and leader of the Socialist Party, attempted, finally, reluctantly to come to terms with what Peronism had meant for the working class:

I have spoken to many workers in the Federal Capital and in the interior, and each one says, 'Now I am something, I am someone.' And I asked a worker his opinion and in his ingenuous simplicity he said this to me: 'So that you can understand the change produced by this government I will tell you that when in the old Department of Labour we had to discuss some question with the boss, the boss would be seated and I, the worker, would be standing; now I, the worker, am seated and the boss is the one who is standing.'[84]

In summarising our analysis of the nature of the Peronist experience for Argentine workers in the 1943–55 period we must start by stating the obvious: Peronism marked a critical conjuncture in the emergence and formation of the modern Argentine working class. Its existence and sense of identity as a coherent *national* force, both socially and politically, can be traced to the Perón era. The legacy acquired during this period was not to be easily shed after Perón's fall from power. This legacy was not, however, a straightforward one. Its impact on workers was both socially and politically complex. We have suggested, for example, that its appeal for workers cannot be reduced simply to a basic class instrumentalism. An adequate attention to Peronism's specifically political appeal would, we have suggested, uncover a particular political discourse which, while emphasising the righting of social and economic inequities, linked these to a vision of citizenship and the working class's role in society. This vision was expressed in a distinct rhetoric and political style of particular appeal to Argentine workers.

There are several implications to be drawn from this analysis. First, Perón's support among workers was not solely based on their class experience within the factories. It was also a political allegiance generated by a particular form of political mobilisation and discourse. Clearly the two bases for mobilisation should not be counterposed – certainly not in the form of the classic dichotomy between 'old' and 'new', 'traditional' and 'modern' working class. A political rhetoric needs to speak to perceived class needs if it is to have success in politically mobilising workers, but this does not exhaust the range of its appeal. As Sylvia Sigal and Juan Carlos Torre have commented, in Latin America the public plaza rather than the factory has frequently been the main point of constitution of the working class as a political force.[85]

This raises a related issue. The working class did not come to Peronism already fully formed and simply adopt Peronism and its rhetoric as the most conveniently available vehicle to satisfy its material needs. In an important sense the working class was constituted by Perón; its self-identification as a social and political force within national society was, in part at least, constructed by Peronist political discourse which offered workers viable solutions for their problems and a credible vision of Argentine society and their role within it. This was evidently a complex process, involving for some workers a *re*-constitution of their sense of identity and political loyalty as they abandoned established allegiances and identities. The construction of the working class did not necessarily imply the manipulation and passivity associated with Germani's powerful image of *masas disponibles* against which so much of the literature on Peronism has been directed.[86] A two-way process of interaction was clearly involved and if the working class was partly constituted by Peronism then Peronism was itself also in part a creation of the working class.

Socially, too, the heritage bequeathed to the working class by the Peronist experience was a profoundly ambivalent one. Certainly, for example, Peronist rhetoric preached and official policy increasingly sought to realise an identification with, and incorporation of, the working class into the state. This implied, as we have suggested, working-class passivity. The official Peronist vision of the working class's role tended to be that of a profoundly soporific idyll in which workers would move contentedly from a harmonious work environment to the union vacation resort and from there to the state dependencies which would resolve their personal and social problems. Beyond the state Perón himself would be the ultimate guarantor of this vision.

Similarly, the union movement emerged from this period with a deeply imbedded reformism. This rested on a conviction of the need to achieve conciliation with employers and to satisfy its members' needs by establishing an intimate relationship with the state. This relationship implied a commitment on the part of the union leadership to the notion of controlling and limiting working-class activity within the limits established by the state and to acting as a political conduit into the working class. In this sense Peronism could be considered to have played a prophylactic role in preempting the emergence of autonomous activity and organisation.

Yet the Peronist era also bequeathed an immensely increased sense of class solidity and potential national importance to the working class. Moreover, the array of social welfare legislation and labour law did represent a massive achievement in terms of working-class rights and recognition; an achievement which reflected labour mobilisation and class consciousness and not simply passive acceptance of the state's largesse. The development of a centralised, mass union movement – no matter how much under the aegis of the state it might be – inevitably confirmed the existence of workers as a *social* force within capitalism. This meant that at the level of the union movement, for all the success of an increasingly bureaucratised leadership in acting as the mouthpiece of the state, conflicting class interests *did* break through and working-class interests *were* articulated by this union movement. There was always a limit to how far the integration of the unions within the Peronist state could be relied upon to ensure the acceptance of policies which were not perceived to be in the workers' interests. In general, the union leadership was remarkably faithful in fulfilling its role for the state, but in return the state, and fundamentally this meant Perón himself, had to provide at least the minimum basis of a *quid pro quo*. The relationship was not that of a diktat but, rather, that of a bargain which had to be negotiated.

Similarly, the weight of a formal philosophy of conciliation and class harmony, an ideology which emphasised values crucial to the reproduction of capitalist social relations, was considerable. However, the effectiveness of such an ideology was limited in everyday practice by the development of a culture which affirmed ideas of workers' rights within society at large and within the workplace in particular.

Peronism aspired to be a viable hegemonic alternative for Argentine capitalism, as a promoter of economic development based on the social and political integration of the working class. In this respect comparisons of Peronism with the New Deal policies of Roosevelt, and the development of welfare state capitalism in Western Europe after 1945 clearly have merit, in that they all to varying degrees marked the confirmation of the working class's 'economic civil rights', while at the same time confirming, and indeed strengthening, the continued existence of capitalist production relations. At the same time, however, Peronism in an important sense defined itself, and was defined by its working-class constituency, as a movement of political and social *opposition*, as a denial of the dominant elite's power, symbols and values. It remained, in a fundamental way, a potentially heretical voice, giving expression to the hopes of the oppressed both within the factory and beyond, as a claim for social dignity and equality.

The tensions arising from this ambiguous legacy were considerable. Ultimately we may suggest that the most fundamental of these centred on the conflict between Peronism's meaning as a social movement and its functional needs as a specific form of state power. In this sense to speak of Peronism as a monolithic movement obscures more than it clarifies. For those who were aspirants to positions of power in the administrative bureaucracy and the political machine Peronism was embodied in a set of formal policies and institutions. For employers who supported Perón it represented a risky gamble of an expanded internal market, state-sponsored economic incentives and a guarantee against radical control of labour, in return for which they had to accept a working class with a greatly increased institutional power and sense of its own weight. For sectors of the middle class Peronism represented, perhaps, greater opportunities for jobs within an expanded state sector. For the mass of Perón's working-class support formal social policies and economic benefits were important but not finally definitive of Peronism's import. Peronism was, perhaps, most enduringly for them a vision of a more decent society in which they recognised for themselves a vital role, a vision couched in a language with which they could identify. It represented, too, a political culture of opposition, of rejection of all that had gone before – politically, socially, and economically; a sense of blasphemy against the norms and self-esteem of the traditional elite.

Now, for those who controlled the political and social apparatus of Peronism this oppositional culture was a burden, since it meant that Peronism was unable to establish itself as a viable hegemonic option for Argentine capitalism. They recognised the social and political mobilising potential inherent in the working class's adherence to Peronism, and they used this as a bargaining counter with rival contenders for political power – a sort of *après moi le déluge* tactic. Finally, however, they had to recognise that this was akin to riding the tiger. Certainly the dominant economic and social forces in Argentine society, who had initially been forced to tolerate Peronism, recognised by the early 1950s the danger inherent in such ambivalence. From the point of view of Peronism as a social movement, however, this oppositional element represented an enormous advantage since it gave to Peronism a dynamic substratum that would survive long after peculiarly favourable economic and social conditions had faded, and which even the increasing sclerosis of ten years of sycophancy and corruption could not undermine. It would be this substratum which would form the basis of rank-and-file resistance to the post-1955 regimes and lay the basis for the reassertion of Peronism as the dominant force within the Argentine workers' movement.

PART TWO

The Peronist Resistance, 1955–8

2

The survival of Peronism: resistance in the factories

The unofficial committee presented itself to Captain Tropea, the interventor, and he told us that these men would definitely not return to
work in the *frigorífico*. This was at 8.50 a.m. At 9 the plant stopped
spontaneously, 100%. And the strike lasted six days. And in the end they
had to bring those *compañeros* from Villa Devoto in official government
cars and reinstate them in their jobs.

Sebastian Borro

They didn't know how to reply ... they were the sons of a paternalistic
government and their father had left them ... they were like orphans.

Alberto Belloni

'Ni vencedores, ni vencidos': the Lonardi interregnum

The collapse of compromise: Lonardi and the Peronist union leadership

The first government of the *Revolución Libertadora*, that of General
Eduardo Lonardi, represented an interregnum in the relationship between the Peronist union movement and the non-Peronist state authorities. After adopting an initial hostile stance which had led the
secretary general of the CGT, Hugo di Pietro, to proclaim that 'every
worker will fight with arms and those means he has to hand',[1] the CGT
in practice made no attempt to mobilise workers in support of Perón's
regime. The day following his bellicose statement, Di Pietro was calling
on the workers to remain calm and denouncing 'some groups who are
trying to create disturbances'.[2] The CGT's attitude was in line with
Perón's own fatalistic reaction to the coup and, with the virtual abdica-
tion of the political wing of the movement, the CGT certainly showed
no inclination to stand alone and adopt an aggressive stance toward the
rebels. With the swearing in of Lonardi as the provisional president on
23 September, and the conciliatory tone of his inaugural speech with its
theme of 'Ni vencedores, ni vencidos' (neither victors, nor vanquished), the stage was set for a seven-week attempt at working out a

rapprochement between the Peronist union movement and the first non-Peronist government.

On the 24 September the CGT responded to Lonardi's speech by emphasising 'the need to maintain the most absolute calm ... each worker must be at his post on the road that leads to harmony'.[3] The following day a delegation was received by Lonardi who assured them of his government's respect for the measures of social justice attained and for the integrity of the CGT and its member organisations. The general atmosphere of restrained benevolence was reinforced by the appointment of Luis B. Cerrutti Costa as Minister of Labour; Cerrutti Costa had until that time been the chief legal adviser of the Unión Obrera Metalúrgica. One of his first acts was to instruct the Dirección Nacional de Seguridad to reopen the union locals which had been closed down or occupied by anti-Peronists. This issue was, indeed, the major obstacle to the fragile *modus vivendi* being constructed.

By the end of September the unions of print workers, railroad workers, bank workers, petroleum, meatpacking and garment workers had all been abandoned by Peronists in face of attacks from armed groups of anti-Peronists. These armed groups, known as civil commandos, consisted mainly of Socialist and Radical party activists. They had played a prominent part in the rebellion against Perón and saw themselves as a civilian militia which would be a guarantee against any Peronist resurgence. As such they tended to receive support from sections of the armed forces in their attacks on union locals and headquarters. It was in order to preempt the growing pressure on Lonardi and Cerrutti Costa by these sectors of the armed forces who gave support to the civil commandos that the CGT issued a communique on 3 October calling on the government to end the armed occupations that were occurring in some unions, and, at the same time, reaffirming its desire to have democratic elections as soon as possible. As a further step toward defusing the situation the executive council of the CGT resigned and appointed in its place a provisional triumvirate made up of Andrés Framini, the leader of the textile workers, Luis Natalini of the power workers and Dante Viel of the public employees' union.

In a signed agreement made public on 6 October the CGT and the government committed themselves to holding elections in all unions within 120 days and to the appointment of interventors by the CGT in those unions which found themselves in an irregular situation – chiefly those occupied by anti-Peronists. These interventors would oversee the election process.[4] At this stage the prospects for the future of government/union understanding seemed promising. A number of union centrals had been returned to Peronist hands. In the case of the railroad workers the Peronist leadership had personally interviewed Lonardi after the occupation of their central building and the installation of an anti-Peronist leadership, and he had ordered the reinstatement of the former leadership.[5] In addition the response of the unions of the 6 October agreement on elections was immediate and by the following day numerous unions had announced the date for their elections. In the following week the number continued to rise, often the call to elections being accompanied by other measures aimed at drawing the sting from the anti-Peronist attack. At the very least this often involved the resignation of the existing leaders. In some unions the gestures went further; the leadership of the bakery workers' union, for example, resolved that all documents and books should be placed at the disposal of whoever wished to see them.[6] In the pasta makers' union a committee was established to oversee the election; the committee was to be made up of different political tendencies and was to carry out a detailed investigation of the actions of the previous leadership.[7]

The anti-Peronist unionists remained less than convinced by these gestures. Indeed, they were becoming increasingly vociferous in expressing their anxieties over this process and determined to press the government for its reversal. Their concern was easy to understand. In a fundamental sense they were opposed to the Lonardi government's entire policy toward the Peronist unions. This opposition was based on their fundamental attitude toward, and analysis of, Peronism which will be analysed in another section of this chapter. In the more immediate term, in October 1955 they were opposed to the inauguration of an electoral process in the unions which would almost certainly lead to the confirmation of Peronist domination of the individual unions and, thus, the CGT. They were alarmed by the fact that despite the rash of resignations of Peronist leaders and the initiation of the election process, the elections were going to remain under overall Peronist control. These fears were compounded by the government's action in agreeing to the installation of CGT interventors in unions where there was overt conflict between Peronist and non-Peronist. The unions most affected by this policy were precisely those in which the anti-Peronist forces were strongest.

Throughout October socialists, radicals and syndicalists became increasingly strident in their complaints at the Ministry of Labour's failure to bring the *Revolución Libertadora* sufficiently to bear on union affairs.[8] Moreover, the growing spirit of conciliation seemed to be enhanced by the CGT's urging of workers to treat 17 October – the crucial day in the Peronist calendar – as a normal workday.

In fact, however, the government, and Cerrutti Costa in particular, were well aware of the anti-Peronist unionists' misgivings, and the consequent pressure exerted by those sectors of the government strongly influenced by them, to abandon their conciliatory policy.[9] Responding to this pressure, on 20 October the Ministry warned many Peronist unions that had on their own initiative started the election procedure that they must first have their statutes approved by the Ministry. There were also a number of attacks still being organised by the 'civil commandos'. In unions where the conflict between Peronist and anti-Peronist was particularly bitter many of the CGT's appointed interventors were effectively unable to take over from the anti-Peronist groups which had seized control of the union. All this led to a growing loss of confidence on the part of the Peronist leadership. At a crisis meeting of more than 300 Peronist union leaders on 26 October Framini had demanded of Cerrutti Costa the rectification of these violations of the 6 October pact.

Cerrutti Costa's reply to this was a decree regulating the election procedure. Essentially the decree removed the authority of all union leaderships, appointed three interventors in each union to take over while elections were held, and appointed an administrator of all CGT goods. The CGT response was to declare a general strike in protest, to start at midnight, 2 November. At this point the feeling within the government seemed to be moving inexorably in favour of the hardliners. Lonardi, himself, was not effectively in control of the government as the decline in his health became more drastic. Only Cerrutti Costa and General Bengoa were in favour of avoiding conflict at all costs. The conciliationist wing was, however, able to achieve a temporary victory in last-minute negotiations with the CGT which averted the strike.

The agreement represented a considerable compromise on the government's part and demonstrated the importance the conciliationist wing attached to the fragilely constructed union/government *modus vivendi*. Essentially it enabled Natalini and Framini to stay at the head of the CGT. In those unions with no internal conflicts the existing leaders could stay on and run the union with the aid of Ministry overseers until the elections. In those with internal problems a Ministry interventor would run the union until the elections; he was to be advised by a joint commission of rival tendencies. This crisis convinced the traditional, liberal wing of the government that only Lonardi's removal from the government, and with him the influence of the conciliationist Catholic nationalists, would ensure a thoroughly anti-Peronist application of the principles of the revolution against Perón.

Although there was no specifically union crisis involved in the events leading up to Lonardi's forced resignation on 13 November, the crucial point of attack of the anti-Lonardi forces continued to be the government's policy toward the unions. The radical and socialist press was full of scarcely veiled appeals to the armed forces to safeguard the democracy and liberty won by the overthrow of Perón. A carefully orchestrated campaign in this press continually gave prominence to the repression experienced by the non-Peronist unionists under Perón and their opinions on the continued Peronist leadership of the CGT and the proposed union elections. The basic theme was consistent. The CGT had to be intervened, the crimes of the Peronists investigated. Diego Martinez, a leader in the meatpackers' union prior to 1945, argued that: 'The whole set must be destroyed, we must dismantle the machine bit by bit. We have to enlighten consciousness, point out crimes, deals, fraud of union social funds before we can speak about elections.' The immediate solution he advocated was 'the handing over of all organisations to democratic trade unionists'.[10]

In the light of this attitude, the 2 November compromise between Peronist union leaders and the government confirmed the opinion of the socialists and radicals that a change of government was needed. They no longer saw any hope that they could convince the government of the foolishness of a course of action which would inevitably confirm the Peronist domination of the unions. With General Aramburu's assumption of the presidency on 13 November persuasion became unnecessary and the first attempt to integrate Peronist unions into a non-Peronist state collapsed. After renewed attacks from the anti-Peronist forces on many union locals, and after Aramburu's failure to answer a demand for the fulfilment of the 2 November pact, the CGT declared an unlimited general strike on 14 November. The same day the new government made the strike illegal and two days later intervened the CGT and all unions.

Determining factors behind the breakdown: the emergence of the rank and file

In order to understand the developments of the seven weeks following the overthrow of Perón we must look behind the surface gloss of agreements, compromises and conflicts. The guiding factor behind Lonardi's policy seems clear enough. He was prepared to contemplate on a general political level a possible Peronist victory at elections called within a year.[11] The only reservation was that it would be a 'Peronism purified of the vices that had led it to defeat. For him the only ones who had been defeated were the venal and corrupt leaders'.[12] The Lonardi sector was quite prepared to countenance continued Peronist domination of the working class and its institutions if, after a brief purge of those most involved in the corruption of the regime, the unions would respect the clearly demarcated spheres of government action and representation of the working class, and restrict their activity to the latter.

The nationalist wing of the opposition to Perón agreed with much of what Perón had achieved. They viewed Peronism as a bulwark against communism. With its emphasis on social justice within a framework of humanised capital, espousing national and communal interests as opposed to class ones, Peronism appealed to their, largely Catholic inspired, ideal of social harmony and order. The problem was essentially one of limits and excesses. If the unions recognised the need to stay within their own sphere, and if the corrupt demagoguery of those most closely compromised with Perón could be erased, then the Peronist-led unions had an important role to play in post-Perón Argentina as organs of social control and channels of expression of the working masses. Indeed, a constant theme of the pro-Peronist press that remained free in this period was the threat of a communist takeover of the labour movement if the Peronists were banned from labour activity.

From the union leaderships' point of view the issue of motivation and objectives is more complex. Certainly, they were prepared to make considerable sacrifices to adapt to the new situation. This can be seen in the way they opposed many spontaneous rank-and-file expressions of opposition and in the firm way in which they decreed 17 October a normal working day. Similarly they seem to have gone out of their way to avoid engaging in any activity which could have been interpreted as beyond the specifically union sphere of interest. Thus, for example, the publication of the Prebisch Plan in late October with its proposals which seemingly ran counter to the whole tenor of the trade unions' economic philosophy brought no single public statement from the CGT.

There seemed no reason in principle why a workable *modus vivendi* between government and unions could not have been arrived at. It was not intransigent loyalty to their deposed leader which stood in the way of such an agreement. It has also been suggested that the union leaders overplayed their hand and misunderstood the delicate tightrope that Lonardi and his followers were walking. Bengoa, the Minister of War, and a leading proponent of conciliation, spoke in his resignation letter to Lonardi on 8 November of the 'lack of understanding of certain groups' which was a major stumbling block to the realisation of Lonardi's basic theme of 'neither victors, nor vanquished'.[13] But was it a 'lack of understanding'? Did the union leadership overestimate its own strength and bargaining position and end up losing everything? Why, after making the concessions already mentioned, did they not give more to bolster up Lonardi?

Two factors should be kept in mind in assessing this issue. First, the fact that the CGT increasingly came to doubt, if not the intentions, then at least the ability to deliver of Lonardi and his followers. Framini's speech at the 26 October crisis meeting with Cerrutti Costa centred precisely on this issue. Despite Cerrutti's fine speeches occupations of union locals by civil commandos were continuing. The problem was that in many areas Cerrutti was powerless to act. The nationalist sector of the government did not in practice have sufficient authority within the police or armed forces to prevent such attacks. The growing number of arrests of middle-ranking Peronist union officials presented a similar problem; the sections of the police and armed forces who carried out these arrests were a law unto themselves.

This placed the union leadership in a very difficult position since there were concessions they could not make without weakening the very minimum basis of their power and they felt that the failure of the government to control such anti-Peronist activity would inevitably lead to a growing anarchy within the movement, and an erosion of their own position to a point where it would plainly be untenable. A line had to be drawn somewhere on the question of compromises if they were not to end up agreeing to their own elimination. It was, thus, something of a vicious circle since Cerrutti Costa and the nationalist sector were militarily and politically too weak to give the practical assurances that the union leaders needed to convince them that by continually compromising they were not eroding their position as union leaders. And, yet, without such concessions from the unions Lonardi and his supporters got weaker still in military and political terms.

A second, and even more crucial, factor that needs to be taken into account concerns the activity of the Peronist rank and file. This must be weighed in any attempt to understand the actions of the Peronist leadership and the collapse of the Lonardi interregnum. The Peronist union leadership was by no means free to do as it might have wished in these months. The extent of rank-and-file resistance to the coup against

Perón, and the harshness of the response to this resistance, were important determining factors in the events of these months. In spite of Di Pietro's disposition to accommodate, the initial reaction of stunned disbelief at the resignation of Perón soon gave way to a series of spontaneous demonstrations in the working-class districts of the major cities. In Buenos Aires, for example, on 23 September a massive demonstration which was trying to reach the central area of the Federal Capital was fired upon by the army and many demonstrators were wounded. There were also reports of continual small arms fire in the zone of Avellaneda.[14] In Ensenada and Berisso a large number of armed reinforcements had to be sent to occupy all strategic positions and points of acceses to the cities.[15]

Rosario – the 'capital of Peronism' – presented the most difficulties for the revolutionary forces. Already, on 24 September the *New York Times* had reported armoured cars opening fire on demonstrating workers; Reuters reported scores killed in these actions. This was clearly an exaggeration since the toll was reduced two days later, but it is clear that the tension and resistance to the new government in Rosario were considerable. Effectively the city had been at a standstill since the opening of the rebellion on 18 September. From then until the 23rd there had been continual demonstrations in the city centre by workers marching from the outer suburbs, in particular from the industrial belt to the south of the city where many of the large freezing plants were located. At night there was the continual sound of small arms fire and bomb explosions. All the factories were at a standstill.[16]

The difficulties confronting the rebel forces were increased by the fact that the infantry batallion normally stationed in Rosario, under General Iñiguez, was solidly pro-Perón and had to be confined to barracks. It was not until the newly victorious rebel batallions from Santa Fe and Corrientes could be sent on 24 and 25 September that the new authorities could begin the task of regaining control of the city. This took several days more. The 24th and 25th were days of serious street fighting with the use of trams and cars for barricades.[17] Workers in the railroad workshops declared a general strike and were joined by meatpackers and mill workers. On the 27th all bus and train services between Rosario and Buenos Aires were suspended. It was not until the army physically occupied the whole centre of the city, and issued an order that anyone found on the streets after 8 p.m. would be shot on sight, that order was restored.

The reimposition of formal authority by the revolutionary forces did not mark the end of rank-and-file resistance. Throughout October, as the battle for possession of the unions intensified, there were continuous wild-cat strikes to protest the attacks of the 'civil commandos' and the growing number of arrests. An activist's account of the atmosphere in Rosario in mid October is eloquent testimony to the underlying struggle taking place: 'The workers on the other hand were bursting with indignation and they were practically on a war footing, ready to throw themselves into the struggle at any moment ... Rosario gave the impression of a city occupied by an enemy, enveloped in an atmosphere of dumb rebellion, just waiting to explode.'[18]

Already by late October the embryos of what would later be known as the Peronist Resistance were appearing. In Santa Fe, for example, a Frente Emancipadora had already been formed and begun to coordinate Peronist union opposition.[19] The underlying resentment and feeling of rebellion described above found a channel of expression with the unofficial call for a general strike issued by various sectors of Peronism for the symbolic date of 17 October. Despite the CGT leadership's order that this should be a normal working day, large numbers of Peronist workers in fact ignored this appeal. The *New York Times* gave a figure of 33% absenteeism for that day.[20] All ports were brought to a standstill and the navy fruitlessly patrolled the dock areas looking for workers to coerce back to work.[21]

Similarly, the strike called by the CGT for 3 November and then called off was turned by the rank and file into another massive anti-government demonstration. Key industrial plants throughout the country were closed down.[22] 'Troublemakers' were assiduously tracked down. While a CGT claim that some 25,000 delegates were in prison seems an exaggeration, there is no doubt that the numbers were such as to considerably exacerbate the resentment and hostility of the Peronist rank and file toward the new authorities.

The nature of this rank-and-file opposition should be made clear. It was fundamentally spontaneous, instinctive, confused and leaderless. A participant in the events of the time has described how he and other Peronist workers went to ask union leaders at the La Blanca freezing plant in Avellaneda what were the measures being taken to oppose the coup against Perón: 'Instinctively we were trying to defend something we felt we were losing; we could do nothing else but go to our leaders and see what we could do in our plant, where there were more than 4000 workers. But the response of the leader was final: Perón is going on the scrap heap and us with him.'[23] This scenario was to be repeated consistently throughout these two months. The same observer who described Rosario as having a 'climate of rebellion' went on to add, 'but one had no idea in what way an insurrection could have been carried out, since there was not even a hint of organisation, nor could one glimpse the existence of any group which might have a certain authority'.[24]

Embryonic forms of organised resistance were already appearing but in general the most common channels of response were spontaneous, atomised initiatives, frequently taking the form of wild-cat strikes. Where a more generalised focus was at hand, such as 17 October or the initial CGT strike call of 3 November, then these were seized upon by the rank and file as means of showing their rejection of the entire process taking place in Argentina. In the absence of coherent, national leadership, however, these could scarcely be more than defensive protest actions.

This underlying phenomenon of rank-and-file resistance, present throughout this period, added a vital dimension to the entire process of bargaining and compromise between government and union leaders. In the light of this opposition it becomes clear that the 300 or so union leaders negotiating the future of the movement in Buenos Aires were by no means free to do as they pleased. Given the groundswell of opposition from their members they were always aware of the danger of being outflanked if they gave away too much. Framini at the meeting on 26 October made it clear to the government that 'the working masses had been prepared to show their strength' but had for the moment obeyed their leaders – the clear implication being that this obedience was contingent on their leaders putting an end to attacks on the unions.[25]

The Peronist union leaders were very aware of the threat to their credibility this posed, and the danger of their being by-passed if they could not gain concrete concessions from Cerrutti Costa sufficient to convince Peronist workers that the *libres*, the anti-Peronists, would not take over the unions. In the absence of such concessions they had to be seen to be giving some lead, even if this were only rubber stamping movements already initiated by the rank and file. The logical corollary of this situation was that however much they might personally favour compromise the union leaders patently could not *in practice* guarantee any such thing. As both 17 October and 3 November made clear, there were strict limits to their control of their members. This in turn alarmed, and strengthened, the ultras in the armed forces and made it even harder for Lonardi to give the sort of concessions that might have reassured the rank and file.

The Peronist union leadership in this period was deeply confused;

with its confidence profoundly shaken, and far from overplaying its hand in its dealings with the first post-Perón regime, it was in reality reacting to a series of pressures it was powerless to control. The final act, the general strike of 14 November, amply demonstrated this. Although not officially due to start until the 14th many workers had already struck on the 13th. There were already reports of clashes and deaths in Rosario on this day.[26] But while the strike call was used by Peronist workers as a channel of expressing their discontent, there was little concerted organisation from the national leadership and its calling had the signs of a last act of desperation. Juan M. Vigo in his memoir of this period described the situation in the following terms:

The order came down from Buenos Aires but nothing was done to ensure its fulfillment. Bureaucrats without any real notion of the power of organisation, accustomed to always having the support or neutrality of government, perhaps they thought that things were going to happen as before.[27]

The response to the strike call by the average Peronist worker was considerable. On 15 November the government officially admitted absenteeism in Buenos Aires of 75% and 95% in the principal industries.[28] Lack of national leadership and the force of repression doomed the strike, however. The new president, General Aramburu, had threatened strikers with arrest. 'Strike agitators' would face from three months to three years in prison. The *New York Times* reported the arrest of over a hundred delegates in Buenos Aires and the beating up of many others as they stood outside the factory gates urging workers to strike.[29] By the end of the first day over a thousand strikers had been arrested. On the 16th the government intervened the CGT and all its member unions, arresting many leaders. On the same day the strike was lifted, though many workers had already started to drift back in view of the repression.

Thus the breakdown of the Lonardi interregnum left a Peronist working class that was defeated, confused, but which had also shown its disposition to spontaneously defend 'something it instinctively felt it was losing'.

For the union leaders the two months represented a watershed, the passing of an era. From the beginning they had shown an inability to act decisively, a form of paralysis of the will to do anything. Alberto Belloni's description of them, cited at the beginning of this chapter, captures the rank-and-file activists' judgement of their leaders. Miguel Gazzera's condemnation is, perhaps, even more final, if only because he was himself a union leader at this time: 'We were satisfied with what we had already lived through, and tasted and enjoyed. We were inexorably finished, totally exhausted.'[30]

Aramburu and the working class: first elements of a policy

There had, therefore, been, from the beginning of the military revolt against Perón, a considerable degree of resistance of the Peronist rank and file to the new authorities. This opposition had primarily focused on the takeover of union locals by the *libres*, and the arrests that were already occurring of both leaders and activists. It had chiefly reflected a generalised sense of fear, uncertainty and confusion and had crystallised around issues such as the anti-Peronist offensive to wrest control of the union structure. In general, in the brief period of Lonardi's government this anti-Peronist offensive had not reached the shop floor.

This was to change immediately and drastically with the new provisional government of General Pedro Eugenio Aramburu and Admiral Isaac Rojas. The new government's policy was based on the assumption that Peronism was an aberration that had to be erased from Argentine society; a bad dream that had to be exorcised from the minds of those enthralled by it. Concretely the new government's policy toward the working class and its institutions was threefold. First, there was an attempt to legally proscribe a whole stratum of Peronist trade union officials from further union activity. This was in line with the new government's intervention of the CGT and its member unions and appointment of military overseers in them. This was to prepare the ground for the creation of 'democratic bases in the unions and the election of leaders with moral authority'.[31] Second, there was a consistent policy of repression and intimidation directed at grass-roots union organisation and rank-and-file activists. Finally, there was a concerted government and employer attack on the issue of productivity and rationalisation which went hand in hand with an attempt to hold back wages and restructure the functioning of the collective bargaining system.

The first line of policy was the easiest to implement. Apart from the hundreds of national union leaders arrested by Aramburu when he declared the general strike of November illegal, there was also the fact that many thousands of middle-rank officials dropped out of activity. The prevailing mood of inertia and confusion described in the previous chapter hardly stood them in good stead to cope with the rigors of the period they were now entering. A special commission was set up by the government to investigate the crimes and irregularities committed by the Peronist union leaders. The new authorities also passed decree 7107 of April 1956 which excluded from union activity all those who had held a leadership or representative position in the CGT or its unions between February 1952 and September 1955. This ban was extended to cover all those who had taken part in the CGT congress of 1949 which had approved new statutes proclaiming the CGT the 'faithful repositary of Peronist doctrine'. In addition, all those officials of the now illegal Peronist party were also included in the prohibition, as were all those being investigated by the special commission. This decree was modified later in the year but a large number of former union officials still remained proscribed.[32]

A far more crucial and complex problem concerned union organisation on the factory floor and its domination by the Peronists. Immediately following the intervention of the CGT the Ministry of Labour had declared all internal commissions dissolved and lacking in authority. In many factories the delegates were being appointed by the Ministry of Labour as early as mid November 1955.[33] The Junta Asesora Gremial, set up to advise the CGT overseer, Captain Patrón Laplacette, discussed the problem in late December 1955. They generally agreed that the Ministry's solution of appointing the oldest, non-Peronist workers as delegates was unsatisfactory because the oldest workers were usually regarded as the least militant and were thus not respected by those they were supposed to represent.[34] Patrón Laplacette eventually decreed that the overseers in each union should appoint the delegates. In practice, however, employers simply took matters into their own hands in many establishments. In La Bernalesa, for example, a major textile plant in Greater Buenos Aires, all of the 120, mainly Peronist delegates were fired.[35] Even the union commission of the Socialist Party felt called upon to send a note to Aramburu warning him of the dangers of such actions and insisting that no worker should be fired without receiving a hearing from the Emergency Arbitration Tribunal set up by the government.[36]

The impact of Peronism on the shop floor during the Perón era

This policy of controlling and weakening the internal commissions was intimately linked to a major concern of the new government's economic policy – an increase in the productivity of Argentine industry. This concern was not a new one for Argentine government and employers. It had underlain much of the increasing tension between employers and unions in the last years of Perón's government. In order to under-

stand the importance of this issue in the emergence of working-class resistance to the post-1955 status quo we must first examine attempts
made in the 1945–55 period to restructure the balance of power on the
shop floor and thus lay the basis for effective rationalisation. The
increased social weight achieved by the working class and its institutions in the wider society during the Peronist regime was inevitably
reflected within the workplace. In general this meant a shift of power
within the workplace from management to labour. It was this shift
which provided the lens through which much of the rhetoric of Peronist ideology was filtered. Formal slogans concerning 'the dignity of
labour', 'the humanisation of capital', 'the social responsibility of the
employer', were interpreted concretely by the worker in terms of the
ability he had under Perón to control, to a greater or lesser degree, his
life on the shop floor, to at least limit the prerogatives of management in
this area. This whole area of shop-floor relations was to become the
focal point of management and state concern after the economic crisis
of 1951/2, as they linked the theme of Argentina's further economic development with the issue of increased productivity.

In economic terms increased labour productivity was considered
vital in achieving the capital accumulation necessary if Argentina was to
move toward a new stage of economic growth based on the production
of heavy machinery and intermediate consumer durables envisaged in
the Second Five-Year Plan drawn up by the Peronist regime. Technically, in the conditions of economic recession of the early 1950s such an
increase in productivity could not be generated principally by the introduction of new machinery. Instead it was assumed that in the short
term at least increased labour productivity would have to come from
increasing output per worker from existing machinery.[37] However,
from the employer's and state's point of view, the problem was not primarily economic or technical but, rather, social in nature. It lay precisely in the unsatisfactory balance of forces generated on the shop floor
by a self-confident working class and a strong, state-backed labour
movement.

Concretely, the employers developed a three-pronged strategy designed to counter the effects of the expanded working-class power
within the workplace. First, from the early 1950s employers increasingly tried to revise existing incentive schemes by resetting bonus rates
with the aid of work study, lowering fulfilment times – in a word a
speed up of production. Where such schemes did not already exist
employers increasingly attempted to introduce them in their factories.
Behind this concern to introduce incentive schemes to intensify pro-

duction lay a basic preoccupation among employers and the state about 'anti-social' work habits. Given full employment, an expanding state-backed union movement and a high level of self-confidence, workers not unnaturally tended toward a more liberal definition of legitimate work intensity than that which prevailed in the pre-Perón era. Relatively high basic wage rates together with the fringe benefits built into the new contracts considerably reduced the traditional economic compulsion on workers to intensify work effort and follow 'healthy' work habits. While employers had acquiesced in this during the expanding economy of the immediate post-war period, by the early 1950s they were determined to tighten up on work habits and labour intensity.

The second area of employer concern was the existence in many of the contracts signed in the 1946–8 period of clauses regulating work conditions. These clauses, won by an insurgent labour movement in the strike wave of those years, limited management's rights concerning labour mobility and job demarcation, and guaranteed social benefits such as sick leave with pay. The symbol of the new balance of power on the shop floor and a main target of the employers' complaints was the internal commission of shop-floor delegates. The contracts signed in the early years of Perón's first government contained clauses guaranteeing management recognition of the commissions and assuring delegates stability of employment both during and after their terms of office. While their basic function was to oversee the implementation of the contract provisions, by the early 1950s they had come to assume a wider role of articulating working-class confidence and limiting management prerogatives in the production sphere. They were perceived by employers as a major obstacle to effective rationalisation and the imposition of labour discipline. José Gelbard, the employers' leader, had, indeed, vigorously complained at the Congress of Productivity, March 1955, about the position which the 'internal commissions assume in many factories where they alter the concept which holds that the mission of the worker is to do a fair day's work for a fair day's pay ... neither is it acceptable that for no motive the delegate blows the whistle in a factory and paralyses it'.[38]

Argentine employers encountered considerable resistance to the implementation of this strategy. Indeed it was this resistance, which rarely surfaces in official documents, which led the employers to enlist both the state and the union hierarchy in an official productivity campaign launched in 1955. In this sense the Congress of Productivity, which was the culmination of this campaign, was an attempt to implement officially, with the aid of Perón's personal prestige and the weight of the state and union apparatus, a policy which employers had not been able to push through on an *ad hoc* basis on the shop floor in the preceding years. Working-class resistance to this was focused on two levels. One was as a response to the concrete effects of the employers' offensive – resisting increased work loads, the lowering of fulfilment times, speed up of the line or the defence of a victimised delegate. Worker opposition generally took the form of a refusal to cooperate rather than overt strike action.[39]

More fundamentally, though, the employers' intentions regarding productivity and rationalisation clashed with some crucial working-class cultural and social assumptions which had emerged from their experience of the Peronist regime. Thus, they questioned, in a most basic sense, the *legitimacy* of many of the presuppositions of the employers' policy. It is clear, for example, that large sectors of the working class rejected the legitimacy of *any* form of payment-by-results incentive schemes. The almost obsessive insistence of the employers at both the Confindustria congress of 1953 and the Congress of Productivity on the basic need to accept such schemes indicates their concern to assert, over and above the validity of the specific mechanisms involved in rationalisation, the legitimacy of the *idea* of incentive schemes as the basis for establishing the relationship between pay and work. While it is true that incentive schemes were increasingly attractive as a means of gaining wage increases in a period of inflation and government-controlled wages policy, the constant pleas of employers for the acceptance of payment-by-result schemes indicate that they were still an unacceptable device in the minds of many workers.

This generalised resistance to the notion of incentive schemes and rationalisation plans was rooted in the development of a shop-floor culture in the Peronist era which translated the new social and political position of the working class within Argentine society into a series of often informal assumptions and assertions concerning what employers could and could not legitimately demand of their workers within the production process. Within this context it is clear that Argentine workers considered the legitimate way to increase living standards to be the adequate updating of basic hourly rates contained in the contracts, many of which had been frozen since 1950.[40] Time wages based on good hourly rates, together with the fringe benefits such as increments for experience, family allowances, etc., which had been introduced into the contracts of the 1946–8 period, were considered a crucial gain by the working class. They were a concrete expression of what *justicia social* represented for workers; the ability to earn a good wage without being subjected to inhuman pressures within the production process.

In a similar fashion, the clamour of the employers for the revision of the clauses in the labour contracts which regulated work conditions encountered a generalised opposition from workers. While for management these clauses represented a major obstacle to effective rationalisation, for workers the work practices and provisions enshrined in them provided a vital safeguard in terms of the quality of life in the factories. These clauses were symbolic of a crucial part of what the Peronist experience meant for workers. They expressed, in a very concrete way, the change in the socio-political position of workers in the broader society as this transformation was experienced at a most basic level of class relationship – the relationship between employer and worker within the workplace. They were, so to speak, the small print of everyday reality which lay behind the vaguer abstractions of Peronist rhetoric. They embodied what workers had come to regard as a rightful and essential regulation on their part of the functioning of the labour process and as such there was a tendency to regard them as not open to legitimate negotiation between management and unions.

This generalised ideological resistance of workers to the employers' strategy was both of a limited and ambiguous nature. It never involved a critique of the criteria underlying capitalist production relations. The opposition to rationalisation was never extended to a general challenge to 'management's right to manage its plants'. There is little evidence, for example, of any demand for workers' control emerging out of the battle against Taylorism. Evidently the general acceptance of the legitimacy of capitalist production relations and the authority relations contained within them was itself a reflection of certain of the basic tenets of Peronist ideology.

We must be careful, however, not to ascribe the limitations of the working class's challenge to capitalist authority solely to the weight of the Peronist state's ideological manipulation. If, as we have already suggested in the preceding chapter, the desirability of general social harmony preached by Perón spoke to an important perception within the working class, then we may also suggest that a recognition of the mutual interests of capital and labour to cooperate within the production process was also an intrinsic part of working-class culture at this time. This implied that management's right to exercise control and authority was generally recognised, as was the existence of a generally accepted ethical ideal that the relationship between employers and workers should be consensual. This would seem to have been reinforced by a genuine internalisation by workers of pride in Argentine industrial performance which symbolised the regaining of national self-esteem under Perón.

What had made the issue so complex and fraught with problems for both management and the Peronist state, however, was that while there might be genuine abstract agreement on the ethical desirability of harmony and consensus, the translating of such agreement into the concrete reality of shop-floor relations involved competing versions of what this ideal scenario should comprise. Certainly, from the working class's point of view, their notions of where the legitimate parameters of managerial authority were to be drawn were deeply influenced by the development of the shop-floor culture to which we have referred and, more generally, by the changed status of workers within national society. This meant that despite the general endorsement of employer authority, in everyday practice within the factories worker resistance on these issues *did* represent an implicit challenge to fundamental aspects of capitalist organisation of production. Despite the lack of an explicit challenge to managerial control, the concrete effect of workers' insistence on their definition of what were acceptable effort and work practices within the workplace was to challenge employers' authority within their factories.

By the end of the Peronist regime employers had gained few positive results in terms of nationally enforceable agreements between themselves and the unions on these issues. The union leadership, aware of their members' hostility, signed the National Agreement on Productivity at the end of the Congress of Productivity but this was largely a symbolic declaration of intent, the minimum they could do, given the amount of personal political capital Perón had invested in the campaign. One of the reasons for this failure was simply the extent of shop-floor resistance. Perón's growing dependence on the working class and the unions in the face of the disintegration of the original Peronist coalition, meant that there was a limit as to how far the state could exert pressure on behalf of the employers. This failure was to continue to haunt Argentine employers. In April 1956 the Chamber of Metal Working Industries echoed the same complaint that José Gelbard had uttered to the Congress of Productivity a year earlier: 'It is urgently necessary to reestablish healthy discipline in the factories, which at the moment are something like an army in which the troops give the orders, not the generals.'[41]

Rationalisation and repression on the shop floor: the *Revolución Libertadora* reaches the workplace

Once the Aramburu government had dealt with the issues of the power of the delegates it turned its attention to the problem of productivity. Decree 2739, February 1956, which authorised an emergency wage increase of 10% while longer-term agreements were being negotiated, dealt with the issue. Article 8 authorised labour mobility within a factory if this was considered necessary for greater productivity. Paragraph (d) of this article allowed employers to reach special arrangements with their workers concerning new production systems, over and above the conditions contained in the existing contracts. Existing clauses relating to conditions and job classifications were to be extended, 'with the exception of those conditions, classifications and clauses which, directly or indirectly, operate against the national necessity of increasing productivity; all these clauses are to be considered as abolished'.[42] Thus, very clearly new agreements on wages were to be tied to productivity issues. Patrón Laplacette commented a few days after the decree that 'the government proposes to carry out in practice the conclusions arrived at by the Congress of Productivity, which Perón's government limited itself to enunciating, without taking any appropriate measures to ensure their realisation'.[43]

It was as a reaction to these policies and what they meant concretely in terms of worsened working conditions and weakened union organisation at the factory and national level that major sectors of the working class embarked on the long defensive struggle that became known in Peronist working-class culture as 'the Resistance'. Partly it was a defensive response to outright repression and harassment of shop-floor workers. Almost any worker who could be considered a 'trouble-maker' was vulnerable and exposed to management caprice and victimisation. The factory delegates were particularly vulnerable. Indeed the situation was so bad that the Socialist Party felt called upon to send Aramburu a memorandum in June 1956 complaining of the government's counter-productive policies. In its opinion, 'the working class considers that a process of revenge by the bosses is taking place, which they see as being encouraged by the government's policy which has not been to fulfill its promises of guaranteeing stability, since in many places there have been mass dismissals, particularly of factory delegates'.[44]

The police cooperated fully with the employers in this policy. A pamphlet issued by rank-and-file metal workers spoke of one of the commonest stratagems used by employers:

The employer who wishes to rid himself of any worker capable of demanding his rights and the fulfillment of laws and guarantees calls in the police and they, through the *Sección Orden Gremial* of the Federal Police, construct a suitably

vague charge which attributes to the worker the intention of sabotaging production. Simultaneously they arrest him and keep him incommunicado, send-
ing him to the section which corresponds to the place where he would have
committed the supposed crime ... it doesn't matter that the person charged
may be released immediately. The intimidatory action has fulfilled its purpose
and the boss has been able to fire him 'with just legal cause'.[45]

Harassment within the unions was common, too. Local overseers
were often socialists, radicals or syndicalists active in the pre-1946 era
who now took advantage of the changed circumstances to settle old
scores. Within the factories, too, at the level of local supervisors there
was much scope for personally motivated retribution. In the ship-
repair yards of Rosario, for example, all chief engineers and heads of
workshops were replaced by the new government. The new head
engineer was in the words of an activist in the yards at this time, 'a very
"gorilla" type of socialist who had been persecuted and hard hit by the
Peronists. He arrived in the yards with a very vengeful attitude and surrounded himself with supervisors who had the same attitudes.'[46]

This changed relationship of forces on the shop floor was a vital precondition for the implementation of the government's productivity
policy. Decree 2739 became the employers' bible as they sought to
remove 'hindrances to productivity' allowed for in Article 8. Taken in-
dividually many of these 'hindrances' were small issues, but cumu-
latively they represented far more. They were a crucial touchstone in
workers' minds by which they could assess the changed circumstances
since the fall of Perón and by which they could gauge the concrete implications for their working lives of the change in political leadership of
the country. In this sense they were, perhaps, of greater importance in
confirming the Peronist loyalty of the majority of workers than the
straightforward issue of wages.

A typical example of such small, but symbolic, issues was the conciliation procedure clause contained in most contracts of the Perón era.
The Chamber of Metal Working Industries in the memorandum
already referred to had complained: 'To resolve any demand from a
worker both he and the internal commission, sometimes consisting of
as many as five people, are allowed to attend the meeting with management. And all of them have to be paid the wages they lose. The attendance of the claimant, together with one official should be sufficient.'[47]
With the weakened power of the internal commissions the employers'
wishes became common practice, thereby weakening an individual
workers' guarantee of a fair hearing in any dispute he might have with
management.

In a similar fashion the safeguards contained in contracts in terms of job classifications and salaries were now attacked as an unproductive restraint on labour mobility and the employers' right to place workers where they wanted within their factories. In many cases Article 8 was taken as specifically prohibiting such safeguards. Employers complained, too, of the rights workers enjoyed when taken ill at work; the right to be sent home with pay, etc. This, too, was now limited.[48] Even smaller changes, though arguably of greater immediate significance for workers, took place from workplace to workplace. In the Rosario shipyard, for example, the free pint of milk given to workers engaged in the unhealthy task of cleaning the engine rooms was withdrawn, as was the provision by management of special clothing and protective masks.[49]

Clearly, then, the radical shift in the balance of power at the national political level could not help but be reflected within the factories. However, once more the employers were to be disappointed in terms of longer-term results. While there were extensive removals of many 'hindrances to productivity' there was no all-embracing, across-the-board implementation of rationalisation schemes, no extensive renewal of contracts in an overall sense which would have legally enshrined new arrangements at a national, industry-wide level. In part this was due to government ambiguity when actually interpreting the law. The Arbitration Tribunal and Ministry officials were not uniformly favourable to the employers in this respect and seem to have balked at the introduction en masse of new clauses concerning productivity arrangements into existing contracts. Underlying this ambiguity on the government's part, and indeed limiting the effectiveness of the productivity offensive, was the working-class resistance it provoked. Whatever the limitations on the overall introduction of new work schemes, the cumulative effect of the removal of clauses governing conditions, and the attack on shop-floor organisation, was such that workers clearly viewed the period as one of unrestrained management abuse. As one union newspaper put it:

The employers thought that they could ignore the conquests of the workers because of the military intervention of our union. In particular they attempted to ignore and weaken the internal commissions ... all this inexorably suggests to us that we are faced with an uncontrolled and unjustified *revanchismo* on the part of the employers.[50]

The organisation of the Resistance in the factories

It was precisely to defend themselves against this government-backed *revanchismo* that workers began the process of reorganisation in the factories aimed at maintaining the conquests obtained under Perón. It was a fundamentally spontaneous and localised process. A rank-and-file activist described the process in the following terms:

It was an embryonic and gradual process which arose from the very roots of the labour movement and which was not dominated by the old bureaucrats but neither did it install a fixed leadership either locally or nationally ... we were a little like islands. I remember that in Rosario we in the Asociación de Trabajadores del Estado, began to form a semi-clandestine grouping and most of us were youngsters who had no active participation in the union before 1955 and we had very little connection with other unions. I recall that apart from meeting in private houses the only communication we had with other union people was with the tramdrivers, the ATE local of Puerto Borghi and the woodworkers.[51]

These semi-clandestine groupings, often meeting in private houses, based their activity on very concrete issues. In the case of the group mentioned above one of the first grievances they organised around was the withdrawal of the six-hour workday for unhealthy work and the provision of protective clothing. Even more common as a rallying point and organisational focus was the defence of shop-floor delegates. In CATITA, a large metal-working plant in Buenos Aires, there had been a successful strike in December 1955 to defend delegates whom management wished to dismiss.[52] In the Lisandro de la Torre meatpacking plant in the Federal Capital the first mobilisation and strike in April 1956 involved the arrest of three delegates by the military interventor. An unofficial committee of rank-and-file union members led the strike for six days and secured their release.[53]

Not all struggles were as successful as these, but by May and June 1956 there was growing evidence of the increasing confidence and organisation of semi-clandestine committees. In both the Swift meatpacking plant of Rosario and the Swift plant in Berisso unofficial committees organised similarly successful strikes around the same issue.[54] The unofficial committee which had organised the Lisandro de la Torre strike was by June officially recognised by the interventor as the representative of the workers. Of course, this was by no means a uniform process; much depended on the state of union organisation in a factory before the September revolt. The meat workers had been one of the best organised and most militant unions under Perón. They were also in a crucial sector of the economy. Evidently workers in less important sectors and with less of a tradition of militant organisation were

likely to find the task of largely clandestine reorganisation more difficult. Even in the meatpacking plants the process of organisation of unofficial committees was largely a plant-by-plant one. However, by mid
1956 this process was gathering momentum and similar committees
were being given *de facto* recognition by military authorities in other
unions.[55]

The recognition by the military authorities of these unofficial committees reflected their growing acceptance of their failure, in the face of
this sort of response from the factory floor, to effectively eliminate the
internal commissions or eradicate Peronist influence from within them.
A similar lesson was driven home by the election for delegates to sit on
the wage-negotiating committees. These elections started in March
1956 and despite electoral manoeuvres by the interventors to try and
ensure an anti-Peronist majority on these committees, in most unions a
majority of Peronist delegates were elected. In Alpargatas, the biggest
textile plant in the country, over 12,000 workers voted for Peronist
candidates against 400 for the socialist list.[56] Where the manoeuvres of
the interventors were such as to make free elections to the negotiating
committees impossible, the unofficial committees organised massive
abstentions and 'blank vote' campaigns.

The trend shown by the elections to the wage committees was confirmed by the elections for the internal commissions called in August,
September and October. The very calling of such elections was itself an
admission by the authorities of their failure, in the light of the growing
number of unofficial committees, to impose military-appointed
workers' representatives. By October the Chamber of Shoemaking
Industries was complaining to the Minister of Labour that 'in the majority of factories all the representative posts are falling into the hands
of undoubted adherents of the deposed regime, whose attitudes hinder
the normal carrying out of tasks in the factories'.[57]

This confirmation of the Peronist domination of the working class at
the shop-floor level was rooted in the struggle to defend immediate
gains. In an important sense there had never been any question about
this, never any period of wavering when it had seemed possible that the
allegiance to Peronism might be effectively challenged and replaced. A
Peronist worker, quoted in the preceding chapter, had said that 'we instinctively defended something we felt we were losing' when describing
the initial working-class response following the September coup. The
Aramburu–Rojas government immediately made that 'something' concrete. The attacks on the internal commissions, the general *revan-*

chismo on the shop floor, the offensive against working conditions, all spelt out very clearly and immediately what was being lost and the contrast with the Perón era. The policy of the new government and the employers directly reinforced the identification of Perón and Peronism with these concrete, daily working-class experiences. This was underlined, too, by the attitude of the other potential rivals for working-class allegiance.

Socialists and communists in the Aramburu era

The socialists were in a particularly ambiguous position. They regarded the *Revolución Libertadora* as a revolution to restore democracy and end Perón's tyranny. As such it was not the revolution of any one class but rather represented the united aspirations of all democratic forces. The socialist press frequently reminded the employers and government that the revolution was not intended to be anti-working class and that attacks on wages and working conditions were a betrayal of its ideals. Yet, they also realised that left to itself the working class would continue in its majority to be loyal to Peronism. In the light of this they had to recognise the need for limitations on Peronist activity, both politically and in the unions. This led to an ambivalent attitude vis-à-vis the government's measures affecting the working class and the unions. On the one hand, they openly criticised the military for being a party to employer attacks on basic conditions and rights. On the other hand, they also condemned the government when it recognised Peronist-dominated rank-and-file committees dedicated to defending these rights and conditions. Like many other professed democrats at this time the socialists were caught in a vicious circle: in the absence of the hoped-for realisation by the workers of their error in supporting Perón, it became clear that the implementation of the democratic principles they espoused would confirm the loyalty of the working class to Peronism – the very antithesis, in their eyes, of freedom and democracy.

More than this, the socialists and other non-Peronist militants were unable to come to terms with the implications of the experience of ten years of state-backed unionisation and improvements in wages and conditions. For them all this had been a diversion from the healthy development of the labour movement; the result of workers with an insufficient intellectual level being misled by a corrupt demagogue. The gains achieved were, therefore, tainted in a moral sense by their association with a paternalistic and undemocratic government. This led in practice to the association of the socialists with the government and employers' policy. This was clearly symbolised in the figures of prominent socialists at the head of intervened unions.[58]

Clearly, this was a particular problem with leaders from the pre-1946 era. However, even rank-and-file socialists were often at a loss to identify themselves with the kind of elemental, largely spontaneous working-class struggles that were taking place. They represented a different tradition and notion of organised working-class activity. A socialist militant complained, for example, about a wild-cat strike that had broken out among bus drivers in Buenos Aires: 'A union strike must be carefully planned and decided on; generally speaking it should be announced by public meetings and preliminary declarations which should hope to achieve what is being demanded at the first go.'[59] Imbued with this sort of attitude there was little common ground such militants could find with Peronist workers in the unofficial committees.

The Socialist Party maintained officially throughout this period an attitude of moral superiority, complaining continuously and admonishing the working class for its failure to realise that its true interests lay outside Peronism. Their policy oscillated between in practice endorsing military government policies and proclaiming the need for the moral regeneration and reeducation of Peronist workers. An editorial in *La Vanguardia* lamented:

The authentic working class has not so far been able to be helped morally by those who had the virtue to keep themselves above the demagogic contamination and low electoralism (of the Perón era). Although it is difficult to say why, the labouring masses have not yet been able to be freed from such regressive and pernicious influence.[60]

While the communists shared many of the same basic attitudes towards Peronism and its influence on workers they in general adopted a more realistic approach. Although involved in some of the initial attacks on Peronist unions in September they had soon adopted a line of working with Peronist workers in the factories to defend conditions and delegates. The problem this presented to the communists was that since they were fighting alongside the Peronists on essentially the same terrain they had little practically to distinguish themselves from the Peronists or to offer Peronist workers by way of inducement to change allegiance. Although they worked alongside Peronists in many unions in this period and were accepted by rank-and-file Peronists as allies in a way very few socialists were, they never posed a threat to Peronism's hold on the majority of workers. Once the realm of immediate shop-floor struggle was left behind, the Communist Party as such was treated with considerable suspicion. This partly reflected memories of the party's former anti-Peronism and partly suspicions of the party's overall political strategy at this time which seemed designed to attain acceptance of the party as an essential force in the 'democratic' camp. Many Peronist workers suspected that the hardline adopted by the party in the union field was negotiable in return for an opening in the political arena.[61]

By the end of 1956 the government had reluctantly come to accept the impossibility of simply erasing Peronism from the unions by legal decree or simple repression. It was also convinced of the lack of viability of alternative candidates for working-class leadership. The policy which emerged from this realisation was in general the maintenance of a continued hardline coupled with an attempt to minimise the completeness of continuing Peronist dominance in the unions. Measures were taken to weaken any future union movement; minority representation was guaranteed, more than one union was to be allowed to represent workers in a single industry, local CGT bodies were to be autonomous from the central confederation. Above all the Aramburu government attempted to secure a significant, though minority, portion of the union movement for anti-Peronists in the union elections held from October 1956 on. With enough government intervention and manipulation by the military interventors in the election process the Peronist advance might be held within acceptable limits. The policy was scarcely successful. The results of the first elections held in October simply confirmed the trend already shown in elections for the internal commissions and wage committees.[62]

The wages struggle during the Aramburu government

The incomes policy of the Aramburu government was initially based on the assumption that inflation arising from the devaluation of the peso that was a major part of the new regime's strategy would be no more than 10%. The wage award decreed in February was based on this assumption. However, devaluation combined with the relaxation of government controls on prices pushed inflation well over this figure. Employers used the new political circumstances to readjust profit margins which they considered to have been held down by years of government control by the Peronist regime. The wage committees which began to meet in the winter of 1956 were, therefore, faced with almost total intransigence on the part of the employers. Offers were generally percentages on the basis of 1954 rates, and nearly always they were contingent on the prior acceptance of rationalisation clauses. Most workers were already earning well above basic rates and so the increases offered would have given them very little. The result was increasing conflict. In the end most conflicts were resolved by the arbitration tribunal set up by decree 2739.

The results were uneven for workers. Workers certainly gained little in real terms; while real wages may have increased slightly in 1956 they declined sharply in 1957 when inflation reached 25%.[63] There was, however, a clear redistribution of income in this period away from the working class and since there was little evidence of increased domestic investment 'a strong presumption existed that the main result of income distribution in this period was to reduce the share of wage earners in favor of the more well to do'.[64]

Indeed, the significance of the wages issue under Aramburu lay rather more in the area of perception than in the straightforward rise or fall of real wages. Real wages had after all declined at times under Perón, particularly in the early 1950s. What gave the issue an added significance in this period was the degree of social antagonism and bitterness involved. Concessions on wages were prised from a reluctant management usually as a result of a bitter struggle. Where prolonged strikes occurred they invariably involved the government since they were declared illegal and the government took upon itself the task of breaking them. The bitterness which resulted was all the greater since the wages battle took place within a general context of steady, if unspectacular, economic growth. This not only increased the perception of the majority of workers of the injustice of the government's wages policy but also emphasised the direct role of the government in holding down living standards. The decline in real wages and the redistribution of income was not the result of a general economic crisis and increased unemployment. The strike statistics themselves bear witness to the capacity in purely labour-market terms of the workers to defend their wages. The decline in living standards was rather the result of a political defeat, the overthrow of Perón, not an economic one. It was the direct result of government attack on the unions and a government-backed wage freeze. The government and employers imposed by legal means and the power of the state what they could not impose through the discipline of the labour market.

The wage battles of late 1956 helped to consolidate the growing resistance movement. The most serious strike from the government's point of view, and in many ways a symbol of the bitterness of industrial relations in this period, was the metal workers' strike of late 1956. Sparked off initially by the employers' offer of only 20% increases on top of 1954 basic rates, the strike lasted more than six weeks and centred increasingly on the release of arrested workers and the reinstatement of thousands who had been dismissed. During the strike government planes and trucks distributed notices urging shop keepers in the working-class suburbs such as Avellaneda and Lanus not to give credit to strikers. Loudspeaker vans patrolled these neighbourhoods naming strike leaders and urging strikers to return because other workers were going back. Tanks and troops patrolled streets in these suburbs; the police entered bars at random and ejected metal workers.[65] Most of the metal-working plants were occupied by the army which carried out ostentatious manoeuvres in the surrounding areas.

The strike was run by rank-and-file committees who established an impressive organisational structure and ran the strike on the basis of frequent delegate and mass meetings, and set up a number of committees to mobilise community support. While the strike was lost in terms of concrete wage demands it was not regarded as a demoralising defeat in the personal reminiscences of workers, nor indeed in the rank-and-file leaflets of the time. Rather, it came to symbolise class pride in the ability to organise and confront employers and the state. This feeling of pride and communal solidarity was mixed with a deeply felt sense of bitterness. The workers who ran the strike were hunted men who lived on the run. Eventually the strikers were driven back to work with an improved pay offer but without the release of those arrested or guarantees of reinstatement. In fact, mass dismissals continued in the metal-working industry as workers returned to work. In some plants between 50% and 70% of workers were being fired. In CAMEA, one of the largest companies in Buenos Aires, the employers demanded that workers first sign a petition asking for reinstatement; when they refused all 1300 were dismissed.[66]

This strike was the worst example in this period of government and employer intransigence but it was not atypical. In the latter part of 1956 strikes in construction, shoemaking, printing, textiles, meatpacking and shipbuilding were all declared illegal and the strikers subjected to similar treatment. Anger at the ferocity of the repression and pride in working-class resistance were to remain a crucial part of a militant culture which emerged from the period. Raimundo Villaflor, a member of the metal workers' delegate committee in Avellaneda, described years later how the twenty-nine members of that committee were eventually tracked down by the police:

As the twenty-nine were taken out to be loaded into the police trucks bystanders began to protest and so the police told them that we were thieves. What a joke. A band of twenty-nine thieves. So the delegates yelled back, 'We are not thieves, we are workers.' But they carted us off just the same.[67]

Workers had suffered inflation under Perón and hard times but they had rarely been hunted down and treated like thieves.

3

Commandos and unions: the emergence of the new Peronist union leadership

We didn't have arms, we couldn't speak, nor vote, nor do anything. Neither did we have any explosives; sabotage was the only way we had of standing up to that lot who were screwing us. We didn't have freedom of press – nothing. All we had was Decree 4161 which said that even if we mentioned Perón we could go to jail. We couldn't even have a photo of Perón in our homes. So we resorted to the *caños*.

Juan Carlos Brid

Old and new union leaders

Those who led the strikes of 1956, and who had been elected in the unions where normalisation had been allowed, were largely new figures thrown up in the course of the factory struggles since the fall of Perón. In the vacuum created by Decree 7107 proscribing many former Peronist trade union officials, the activists who had distinguished themselves in the daily actions on the shop floor naturally came to prominence. Their attitude to the former union leaders is well demonstrated by Sebastian Borro's contemptuous dismissal of the older leaders in his union, the meatpackers, who 'shouted Viva Perón a lot but didn't use to do anything ... they knew nothing about struggle from below. When we began our struggle in the *frigorífico* we were nearly all new people. There were perhaps two or three older leaders who hadn't disappeared completely.'[1]

Not all of the former leaders disappeared from the scene or suffered the same degree of opprobrium. Some had from the beginning adopted a position of intransigence and maintained a standing amongst their rank and file. Augusto Vandor of the metal workers, Miguel Gazzera of the pasta makers and Amado Olmos of the hospital workers were examples of younger leaders who had emerged as significant figures in their unions in the latter stages of Perón's regime and now from prison continued to influence their unions. Where a former leader had maintained his standing the new leaders elected in 1956 and 1957 often considered themselves as temporary replacements until the former leaders could occupy these positions themselves.

Those former leaders who wished to continue influencing the unions, and the Peronist movement in general, began in the course of 1956 to organise themselves. By 1957 there were four main groupings: the CGT Única e Intransigente, the Comando Sindical, the CGT Negra, and a body simply known as the CGT. Most of these groups had at best a very limited influence over the Peronist rank and file. Their influence was somewhat increased when they united into the CGT Auténtica in July 1957. The secretary general of this organisation was Andrés Framini. Framini was in fact typical of the sort of residual influence the CGT Auténtica exerted. A leader of the textile workers since the early 1950s his intransigent position since November 1955, and his imprisonment, had refurbished a somewhat tarnished reputation among Peronist workers.

There was friction between these groups and the newly emerging leaders. This was partly a reflection of different temperaments, different types of people and different union practices. The new leaderships who had largely arisen from a spontaneous and *de facto* democratic struggle on the shop floor tended to carry over the practices derived from this experience into the newly normalised unions. Very few of them had had much formal experience in the Peronist union hierarchy and they owed their leadership positions now overwhelmingly to activity in the daily resistance to management and government policies. There was therefore a close identification between the rank and file and these new leaders and this was reflected in an enhanced degree of democratic union practice. Sebastian Borro, the leader of the meatpackers in the Lisandro de la Torre plant, recalled:

We gave participation in the assemblies to everyone. A general once said to me, 'You allow communists to speak in your meetings.' I replied, 'In my union I practice union democracy. All members have the same rights and obligations. I as elected leader respect their rights and they must fulfill their obligations.'[2]

Alberto Belloni recalled, too, that his union in Rosario regularly held meetings with more than 300 participants even before the union was formally normalised.[3] This increased participation in union affairs not only reflected a different attitude on the part of the new leaders but also a desire on the part of the workers themselves to take a more active role. The very nature of the struggle at this time reinforced this. Faced with a hostile state and with much of basic trade union activity condemned to semi-legality, with very little formalised bureaucratic structure to utilise, there was an inevitable increase in rank-and-file involvement. In addition to feeling threatened by this new spirit, the former leaders resented having to stand on the sidelines and watch their unions move increasingly beyond their grasp. This feeling increased as, throughout 1957, more formalised structures arose to give some shape to the largely spontaneous upsurge of 1956.

The Intersindical and the 62 Organisations

In early 1957 a *Comisión Intersindical* had been set up by some of the normalised unions to agitate for the complete return of all unions through free elections, the return of the CGT, the lifting of all legal restraints on participation in union affairs and the release of all those imprisoned for union activities. The initial driving force behind the Intersindical had come from the communists but it was soon seized on by others as a first legal structure around which to organise some form of pressure on the government. By April 1957 it claimed the affiliation of thirty-five unions and five federations and throughout the winter of that year, as more of the big industrial unions like the textile workers, metal workers and meat workers were won by the Peronists, its influence increased.[4] The original communist influence on the organising committee diminished and by July it was dominated by the Peronists. On 1 May 1957 the Intersindical called a demonstration to celebrate international workers' day; this was the first legal demonstration by workers since November 1955. On 12 July it organised a general strike to demand the release of all union prisoners and the complete normalisation of the unions. Unofficial estimates calculated that some two and a half million workers were affected.[5]

The growing influence of the Intersindical fuelled the latent antagonism between old and new Peronist union leaders. For the former union leaders the power of the Intersindical represented a direct challenge to their hopes of regaining their old positions since the very legality under which it operated confirmed the legitimacy of the new leadership. In the clandestine councils of the Peronist movement – in particular in arguments presented to John William Cooke, Perón's personal delegate – they maintained that the Intersindical had to be fought since many of the newly elected leaders emerging under its protection were only 'lukewarm' Peronists elected in fraudulent elections. Moreover, they argued, the Intersindical would not alter the government's determination to do everything in its power to weaken Peronist influence in the unions, only handing back the unions as and when it thought fit.

The new leaders, on the other hand, argued that it was essential to use the Intersindical and the legality it enjoyed. With many unions still to be won back from government and non-Peronist hands an organisation of this type could help limit the effectiveness of government fraud and manipulation. Moreover, to ignore it would would be to leave the way open for its use by anti-Peronists.[6]

It was only with the emergence of the Intersindical that a certain coherence began to be possible in the organisation of the Peronist forces in the unions. The struggle in 1956 had been localised and atomised, with activists in one union scarcely knowing what was taking place outside their union, or often outside their workplace. The space conceded by Aramburu as he tried to move from a policy of outright repression to some more realistic solution to the 'working-class problem' was seized on and used by the new leaderships to consolidate and organise the positions won in the course of 1956. This also gave the Peronist movement in clandestinity a greater coherence since it provided it with an institutional framework lacking since the proscription of the Partido Peronista and the CGT in November 1955. It was, for example, only really with the appearance of the Intersindical that orders from Perón began to reach the union leadership, and through them the rank and file, in a consistent way. It was, likewise, largely through the unions that the Peronist campaign for a blank vote in the Constituent Assembly elections of July 1957 was organised.

This organisational progress was confirmed and increased with the setting up of the 62 Organisations. This organisation emerged out of the congress called to normalise the CGT in September 1957. The military head of the CGT, Captain Patrón Laplacette, had attempted through the purging of voting lists in some unions where the anti-Peronists had strength to ensure a considerable anti-Peronist presence in the congress. By September socialists and other anti-Peronists were in power in the shop worker, bank worker and civil servants' unions, in addition to those unions won by these forces in the 1956 elections: principally the print workers, the municipal employees and garment workers. In addition they controlled many sections of the Unión Ferroviaria, the main rail union. By grossly inflating the membership figures for these unions Patrón Laplacette hoped to guarantee them a majority of the delegates sent to the congress.[7] When this was seen to have failed and the anti-Peronists found themselves in a minority on the commission reviewing delegate credentials they abandoned the congress. Those unions who remained in the congress, chiefly Peronist but with some communist-influenced unions too, numbered some sixty-two organisations and thus constituted themselves as a body with that title. The communists soon left and formed a body of nineteen unions which they controlled. The anti-Peronist unions which had left the congress formed a grouping known as the 32 Democratic Organisations.

The emergence of the 62 Organisations was an important development since it not only confirmed the dominant position of the Peronists in the unions but also provided them with a completely Peronist legal organisation with which to operate and pressure the government in the wider union and political field. It also confirmed what in practice two years of struggle since the fall of Perón had shown: that the unions were the chief organising force and institutional expression of Peronism in the post-1955 era. The 62 Organisations, reflecting the growing confidence of rank-and-file workers, adopted a very militant policy, organising a general strike on 27 September, and another on 22 and 23 October, in protest at the government's economic and union policy. The government responded with a renewed wave of interventions and arrests of union leaders. In December 1957 a public meeting called by the 62 Organisations was broken up by the police, the speakers arrested and their unions intervened once again. This affected key industrial unions such as metal workers, textile workers and meat workers, but the government was unable to break the power of the Peronist unions to act as an organisational force for Peronism as a whole. This was to be clearly demonstrated by the role played by the 62 Organisations in organising the working-class vote for Arturo Frondizi in the presidential elections of February 1958.

Sabotage and clandestine groups

The popular repudiation of the military government and its policies utilised channels of expression which were outside the specifically union sphere. The term 'the Resistance', which became a crucial reference point in Peronist political culture, carried within it a wider meaning than that arising from the process of defending conditions and organisation in the factories. In the folklore of the movement, which was itself an integral part of the ideology of the working class in the post-1955 era, resistance in the factories was inextricably bound up with resistance on other terrains. This involved a heterogeneous mixture of different types of activity; the Resistance included in popular Peronist consciousness a diverse set of responses ranging from individual protest on a mundane level, through individual sabotage to clandestine activity and beyond to attempted military uprisings. All these responses tended to be mixed in a very diffuse set of images which were later to be encapsulated by a new generation of Peronists within such phrases as 'popular warfare', 'national popular resistance' and which carried with them a whole mythology of heroism, dedication, suffering, shared comradeship and loyalty to an ideal which was to be a crucial element in the development of Peronism in the years to come.

The first and most immediate response to the new provisional government took the form of what could be called a spontaneous terrorism. In the first half of 1956 a wave of attempted sabotage actions took place. A typical newspaper report of such an action told of how a group in Paraná, in Entre Rios province, had been arrested for a series of actions which included painting slogans, trying to set fire to a cereal deposit of a large grain merchant, the burning of railroad wagons and the attempted burning down of a Radical Party local. Those involved were a truck driver, a railroad employee, and two others, all of 'humble origin'.[8] Similar reports filled the press each day. A particularly vulnerable target was the rail system. In Tacuarí, in Buenos Aires province, in early February 1956 'of a convoy of 27 wagons the seven front ones and the engine jumped the tracks'. Two rail employees were arrested.[9] This was to be an almost daily occurrence together with attacks on another favoured target, electricity power stations.

At the same time an increasing amount of sabotage inside the factories was occurring. A typical complaint of employers was that of the owner of a glass factory in Berazategui who complained of constant damage to machinery and low production levels.[10] In the month of February the Frigorífico Wilson in Avellaneda suffered three incidents of sabotage, one of which closed the plant for several days.[11] The situation was so bad that the Dirección Nacional de Seguridad felt called upon to warn the population that,

The law qualifies as sabotage and punishes with up to life imprisonment anyone who destroys, disorganises or puts out of action in whole or in part documents, objects, materials, installations, services or industries of whatever type ... and warns the population that the police have been told to use their arms whenever it is necessary to stop sabotage.[12]

The breadth of the warning was an indication of the range of actions taking place. It is difficult to know precisely how structured these actions were. It seems probable that the sabotage in the factories was largely the spontaneous work of individual workers – the almost literal throwing of a spanner in the works, the dropping of a lighted cigarette in the paint shop. A typical court case at the time involved a textile worker accused of destroying miles of cotton yarn and thus paralysing the night shift in his factory.[13] In a similar case two metal workers were accused of destroying machinery vital to the entire production process in their factory.[14] Perhaps even more commonly there were other forms of indirect sabotage of production used by workers as a way of registering protest. The owner of a shoe factory in the Matanza suburb of Buenos Aires complained to the police that the quality of his product had declined dramatically.[15] In the food-processing industry a common device seems to have been to sabotage canned food by putting ground glass in the tins; there were also numerous other reports of adulterated food.

On the other hand it is also clear that the germs of a very chaotic, localised organisation were present from early 1956. In many areas groups of workers, often from the same factory, did start to meet regularly and plan actions. This was particularly the case with railroads. In March a group of ten rail workers were accused of having planned and carried out a series of sabotage actions on the Belgrano railroad in Greater Buenos Aires.[16] Juan Vigo, an important figure in the resistance groups at this time, estimated that by April 1956 there were over two hundred 'commandos' in Greater Buenos Aires, with perhaps some ten thousand participants; though he added that 'the control one had over these ten thousand men was very relative'.[17] Many of these 'commandos' were, at this stage, made up entirely of workers and were based on a particular factory or group of factories. Vigo describes a typical group of this type centred on the suburb of Ramos Mejía. Its leader was a prominent leader of the leather workers' union and their strength lay in this union, the textile and the metal-working industries, and the local electricity station.[18]

It is evident, however, that there were innumerable clandestine cells which consisted primarily of friends who lived in the same *barrio* and whose influence and actions were very much more circumscribed. Any coordination with similar groups, even in the same neighbourhood, would have been tenuous at best. These cells dedicated themselves largely to the painting of slogans or the distributing of leaflets; since this was illegal if it contained any mention of Perón's name or Peronist slogans it carried its own risks and was considered a legitimate form of protest. It was also the case that many of the cells were not made up specifically or even predominantly of union members. Many included a cross section of social classes. A cell uncovered in Pergamino in the province of Buenos Aires included a doctor, the sub-inspector of local police, a building contractor and a former leader of the local CGT.[19] In Junín a cell was made up of the ex-mayor, a pilot and the foreman of the local railroad workshop.[20]

There was also in 1956 an increasing use of bombs against both military targets and public buildings. This form of action required planning in execution and a certain expertise in bomb making. Actions such as the bombing of the Fábrica Militar in Villa Martelli, or the attempt on the weapons deposit of the Colegio Militar, had to be well planned and required a minimum of back-up organisation.[21] This was particularly so because of the nature of the bomb-making process employed. In these years very little dynamite was used since it was extremely rare in Buenos Aires; most bombs were crude constructions made up of very basic chemicals in improvised containers. They were known as *caños* and were to become an integral part of the mythology of the Resistance. Partly their place in this mythology was due to the process of production which was eminently amateur and social. There were very few experts at hand with any knowledge of bomb making or weaponry in general and the bombs made in 1956 were the result of trial and error and based on very little actual expertise and made with considerable risk to the participants. To acquire the materials needed a network of people prepared to steal them, usually from pharmacies or factories. A bomb-making operation needed at least six people to operate efficiently. Thus the whole process came to be symbolic of the Resistance in general; it summed up a series of virtues associated in Peronist folklore with the Resistance period – non-professionalism, self-sacrifice, the active participation of ordinary people and the lack of an organisational, bureaucratic elite.

The general motivation behind these different forms of resistance to the military regime could evidently be described as a rejection of the new political regime and what it implied in social and political terms. Behind actions such as bombing and sabotage, however, there also lay an overwhelming sense of desperation. Sabotage, whether in a factory or carried out against a public building, was almost literally the only avenue open to most Peronists to express their rejection of the status quo. Peronists who felt the need to fight back turned to some form of sabotage as a means of expressing their anger and sense of loss, and of asserting their ability to do something about this. Juan Carlos Brid, a veteran of resistance 'commandos' described this sense of frustration in the comment cited at the beginning of this chapter.

The perspective that these actions were placed in was appropriately cataclysmic. Militants expected the new regime to collapse from one week to the next. Rumours abounded of Perón's imminent return; the legend of the *'avión negro'* in which Perón would return to lead his people against the tyranny circulated widely. Innumerable fly-sheets circulated giving advice concerning what to do to hasten the return of Perón. One advised all Peronists to withdraw their money from the banks, not to buy more consumer goods and to stockpile food. This sacrifice would lead to the return of Perón.[22] The leaflets always ended with the assertion that 'the hour is near', 'Perón will return'. A crucial element in this perspective was the belief that large sectors of the armed forces remained loyal to Perón and were awaiting the order to rebel. This rebellion, it was assumed, would be coordinated with the general strike and paralysis of the country.

While this outlook clearly corresponded to an emotional need, it had two immediate effects on the resistance movement in the first half of 1956. First, it made worse an already chronic lack of security in most groups. If the revolution was due next week there was hardly any need felt for longer-term perspectives or security. Second, many resistance groups focused their activity and aspirations on finding sympathetic military figures. This again tended to obviate the need for longer-term organisation. There was no shortage of sympathetic military figures; Juan Vigo bemoaned the fact that there was always some 'retired officer willing to promise the revolution for next week or even for tomorrow'.[23] This all tended to wreak havoc on any attempted coordination of the many disparate groups. A report in *La Razón* in March 1956 described a not untypical case of a resistance group which had been broken up in Córdoba, 'all those arrested were workers who had let themselves be convinced by rumours which said that Generals Bengoa and Uranga had taken up rebellious attitudes'.[24] It was only with the defeat of the rising led by General Valle in June that the search for military saviours abated somewhat and with it the cataclysmic perspective.[25] By mid 1956, too, a weeding-out process had taken place – only the best-organised groups had survived and lessons of tactics and security had been learned.

Divergence in the Resistance

From mid 1956 on most of the energies of working-class Peronist activists went into the recuperation of the internal commissions and later the unions. Inevitably the crucial area of the Peronist Resistance was bound to be that which most directly affected the lives of working-class Peronists. The other forms of activity centred around the commandos did, however, continue and the line which separated them was often difficult to draw. Indeed Perón himself had, from the beginning, envisaged an overall strategy which did include the different levels of activity and to which he gave the name civil resistance. His ideas about this strategy were first laid out in the 'General Instructions for Leaders' which were drawn up in December 1955 but which probably first reached the eyes of resistance leaders in March or April of 1956. The overall strategy the Peronist movement was to follow was, according to Péron, a 'war of guerrillas' in which the civil resistance played an important part. All attempts at confronting the military regime where it was strongest, on the purely military level, were to be avoided. Far more effective, said Perón, were the thousands of small actions which would gradually wear down the military and undermine its will to continue in power. In the social arena the resistance should keep the workers in a constant state of upheaval with strikes, go slows, low productivity. On a more individual level thousands of both passive and active actions should be undertaken. Active resistance could include sabotage; passive resistance included rumours, leafleting, painting slogans. All these myriad acts of resistance would eventually make the country ungovernable and prepare the ground for the revolutionary general strike which, Perón considered, would be the signal for the national insurrection. Vital at this stage would be the commandos who, together with loyal sectors of the armed forces, would be crucial in guaranteeing the success of the insurrection. The commandos must organise and train for this with actions such as attacks on military and government installations.[26]

The strategy outlined in these general instructions was realistic if one leaves aside the always problematic notion of the revolutionary general strike and subsequent insurrection. The basic notion of the civil resistance did take into account the different levels of commitment and activity. Moreover, the instructions did have the salutary affect of placing sabotage and clandestine actions within a less cataclysmic perspective, to see them as parallel to forms of union activity and with a similar goal – the *desgaste* (exhaustion) of the regime.

In practice, however, from the middle of 1956 there was a growing differentiation between the commandos engaged in sabotage and other clandestine activities and the resistance movement in the unions. This was reflected in an underlying tension that grew up concerning the relative functions of the newly regained unions. Initially, in the early part of the year, people like Vigo had found it difficult to convince others of the need to organise in the factories and the unions.[27] This extreme attitude did not persist but a difference in emphasis did remain. Thus in August 1956 a semi-clandestine newspaper connected with activists fighting in the unions found it necessary to discuss the relative merits of terrorism and union work and to champion the latter: 'There is no way we can successfully confront this organised force of our enemies except through the organisation of the workers themselves. To reorganise ourselves in the factories is therefore the fundamental task. Our factory organisation must be reconstituted.'[28] In theory, of course, there was no disagreement. Those involved predominantly in the commandos recognised the need to regain the unions. But this recognition was tinged with a certain suspicion. Memories of the inertia of the union movement at the fall of Perón lingered. A participant of the time has described the attitude which was shared by a not inconsiderable number of militants at this time:

We all thought that the unions had to be regained to the extent that they could serve the interests of the revolution. We thought that the unions had to give their all for the revolutionary movement because if not they were not worth worrying about ... to regain the unions was worth it to defend the rights of the workers but fundamentally it was of value in so far as it helped the revolution. Because to have a union just for the sake of having it was pointless.[29]

Much of the tension was unspoken, particularly in 1956 when the idea of integrating the unions into the governing system seemed absurd in the face of consistent government attacks. It should be emphasised that there was never at this time anything like an open split over this issue. Indeed there was often a good deal of overlapping in personnel, and in many cases material support for the commandos came from union-based groups. Often a well-functioning union grouping could provide forms of solidarity and support to clandestine groups. Sabotage was an integral part of workers' struggles in these years. A particularly bitter union struggle was almost unimaginable without its attendant bombings and arson.

In practice, however, those with the closest ties to the commandos were the old union leaders rather than the new union groupings. Those around the CGT Negra had been involved with Valle's attempted uprising and they were to call a general strike in December 1956 to coincide with another promised rebellion. This was a disaster and led to the arrest of many unionists connected with the enterprise. It was they, too, who influenced those younger enthusiasts in the unions who did join the commandos. Once again, however, the differences were implied, unspoken and perhaps unnoticed for much of this period. The men of the union-based resistance, in a general and ill-defined way, regarded insurrection and the general strike to bring back Perón as the ultimate goal of their activities in the unions. They had, for example, rejected the original call of the communists in the Intersindical for a general strike to demand the release of prisoners; a general strike was only worthwhile, they had maintained, if it were demanding the return of Perón. Indeed they regarded themselves as just as intransigent as those of the armed resistance and combatted as fiercely as they the neo-Peronist politicians who had emerged and who were trying to attract workers into their ranks with less than the complete return of Perón.[30]

Ultimately, however, it remained true that the strategic prospects for the two forms of resistance were distinct and of a fundamentally different order. This was to become increasingly apparent throughout 1957 and although largely hidden for as long as the military regime lasted, the implications were apparent for the perceptive to note. One of these was John William Cooke who was by early 1957 in exile in Montevideo acting as Perón's chief delegate and in constant contact with him in Caracas. His letters to Perón throughout 1957 bear witness to an, at times vaguely expressed, but ever present, unease about the strategic future of the Peronist movement.

In particular, Cooke was preoccupied with what he saw as the disjuncture between what he considered to be Peronism's crucial strategic project – the insurrectional seizure of power to implement a social revolution – and what he recognised as the tactical adjustments forced on the movement by the changes in the political conjuncture. This disjuncture partially corresponded to the gap between subjective desire and reality. Cooke, and Perón himself, constantly affirmed that insurrection was the only meaningful strategy for Peronism. This insurrection had as its goal a social revolution: 'We are not against this or that policy, we are against a social system.'[31] For this reason the movement had to maintain its intransigence. In Cooke's words, 'a movement like Peronism nourishes itself on absolutes. It is the glory and the inconvenience of national liberation movements. They must arrive uncorrupted, they must be above politicking, at the margin of the common game played by the political parties.'[32] And yet the conditions appropriate for launching this insurrection stubbornly failed to present themselves. Time and again Cooke had to bemoan to Perón the fact that the basis for launching the revolutionary general strike did not exist. In June 1957 we find him writing:

The general repulsion felt for the tyranny provokes protests, incites terrorism and foments rebelliousness. This state of mind is not translated, however, into a total civil resistance such as we desire. There are activist groups who place bombs and carry out sabotage: this is creating a mentality for action and is exciting many expectations. But as you pointed out people only very timidly back these up with others ... this discontent against the government must be channelled into insurrectional activity which will lead to a popular rising.[33]

Not only did the conditions for such a rising fail to materialise, the likelihood that they would steadily receded throughout 1957. The very success of the Resistance, especially in the unions, was changing the context within which the movement had to operate. The government was retreating and opening up possibilities of semi-legal, or indeed fully legal, activity within the existing structures. Cooke recognised that the movement could not ignore the new tactical possibilities opened up for it and retreat into a revolutionary purism which would only leave the field open for those wishing to divert it into the mire of traditional politics. He wrote to Perón: 'The present semi-legality, with its slackening off of persecution, has made the soft stratum of Peronism flourish.'[34] The problem was not, however, really one of 'soft' elements taking over. Rather it was a problem of what social reality might impose on those elements who were intransigent. Concretely the problem was most clearly posed for the newly regained Peronist unions. With their confidence increased by the wages battles of late 1956, workers were seeking channels of expression outside the purely defensive, union sphere. They saw such a channel in the Intersindical. For Cooke the danger was that the Intersindical would come to be seen as an end in itself and not a simple instrument of struggle. A similar issue was at stake in the CGT congress of September 1957 and indeed in the debate over whether government-sponsored union elections should be contested at all.

The solution to the problem for the commandos was simple and amounted to what Cooke had meant by a retreat into purism: the maintenance, *tout court*, of an intransigent refusal to have anything to do with the openings in the institutional system. The newspaper, *Soberanía*, a mouthpiece for these groups, maintained that the problem of how to deal with fraud in the CGT congress was irrelevant – Peronist trade unionists should simply have nothing to do with any government-inspired CGT congress.[35] Two important figures in the clandestine groupings, Lagomarsino and Marcos, sent Cooke a forty-page document denouncing the takeover of the Intersindical by the Peronists as a break with the intransigent position.[36] This was a solution Cooke rejected. In a long plan of action presented to Perón in August

1957 he argued that simple intransigence was no longer a feasible position. The great intransigent slogans of the Resistance had to be given a 'tactical translation' and thus correspond to the Peronist masses' desire to act concretely and positively. New semi-legal structures had to be created for the movement. According to Cooke these new structures would enable practical activity which would culminate, when the circumstances were appropriate, in an insurrection.

While Cooke's plan of action was theoretically plausible it was open to objections. Specifically, it avoided the problem of the fundamentally different nature of unions and commandos, and their consequent different strategic possibilities. The unions were fundamentally social institutions rooted in the very existence of an industrial society and as such they had an instrinsically functional role in that society. Their existence as organs of working-class activity and organisation endowed them with a certain degree of immunity to changes in the political situation; a certain durability and resistance to political attack. The commandos, on the other hand, were eminently political organisations very much dependent on a specific set of circumstances for their existence and future perspectives. Unlike the unions they corresponded to no intrinsic social or economic working-class need. In the absence of this it was impossible for the clandestine groups to achieve a long-term basis for survival in the one area where such a basis might have been possible, in some sort of organic relationship with the unions. They needed the possibility of concrete action and practical success. The further away such possibilities got the more likely it was that the semi-legal and legal structures, especially the unions, would be caught up in their own dynamic and logic. There was a limit as to how long the clandestine sectors could be kept in reserve before they ossified, starved of any genuinely realisable perspective and, thus, inevitably subordinated to the legal sectors of the movement.

This conflict remained for the most part latent in this period. Within the context of a military government, which even as it granted a certain legality to the unions still maintained a policy of repression and violent anti-Peronism, the potential conflict between legal and clandestine sectors was barely noticeable. Yet the implicit tension was present. It was especially present in the whole debate concerning the presidential elections of February 1958. Should Peronists vote and if so should it be for a candidate like Arturo Frondizi? While Cooke and Perón maintained a rhetorical stance opposed to any participation in the elections, the attractions of a positive vote were not lost on them. However, they were concerned that the *capa blanda* of Peronism would be revitalised at the prospect of elections. This was, though, once again not the real problem. The neo-Peronist politicians who would attempt to benefit from an electoral opening had little real standing with the Peronist working class and if Perón had ordered another 'blank vote' it would have been respected by the majority of working-class Peronists.

The problem was, rather, what credible alternatives could be offered to voting for a non-Peronist candidate. Cooke seems to have vaguely hoped that the dilemma would be resolved by an insurrection before the February elections; he was particularly hopeful about capitalising on the strikes led by the 62 Organisations in late 1957. Yet, he was forced to recognise that insurrection remained only a very vague possibility in the minds of most Peronists. The strikes did little to convince unionists of this viability. Indeed after the police raid on the 62 Organisations' rally in late December the main Peronist-led industrial unions were intervened and the 62 Organisations were forced to deny any political content to their activities. The secret negotiations begun with Frondizi's representatives at this time were tacit recognition on Perón and Cooke's part of the failure of the insurrectionary option.[37]

The maintenance of intransigence, the need to cast the 'blank vote' in the upcoming elections, became the rallying cry of the commandos, the clandestine groups. In the absence of any even medium-term prospect of organising an armed rebellion this could be no more than a gesture of faith, a reaffirmation of values and a rejection of the anti-Peronist status quo. Objectively such a position had little to offer union militants. On the other hand, there were concrete advantages to be gained from voting for Frondizi. A victory for the 'non-continuist' candidate would help consolidate the positions prised from the military regime.[38] The interventions following the December rally had driven home the fragility of their newly regained positions.

There was, moreover, the possibility of consolidating union power still further with the reconstitution of the CGT. Frondizi was particularly insistent in his election propaganda on this theme. There was also the issue of the legislation the military had introduced to weaken centralised union organisation. Decree 9270, for example, had allowed minority representation in union leaderships and the establishment of several unions in one industry all with equal bargaining rights. All political activity by unions had also been prohibited by this decree. Much of this legislation had in practice been very difficult to enforce but it remained a reminder of the arbitrariness of the military regime and its fundamental antipathy to the concept of a strong, centralised union movement. Evidently a candidate such as Frondizi, who promised to hold free elections in all unions where they had not yet been held, who called for the return of the CGT and the reconstituting of a strong collective-bargaining system akin to that which had existed under Perón, held a strong attraction for the unions sector of Peronism.[39]

Many union militants could not, however, bring themselves to accept the argument of voting for Frondizi, who had a long anti-Peronist past prior to 1955. Sebastian Borro recalls how difficult it was for the ordinary Peronist to conceive of Perón giving such an order and the effort needed from the union leaders to convince the rank and file. In Rosario the 62 Organisations needed ten sessions before they would agree to back such an order.[40] On the whole the new Peronist leadership accepted, though, the logic of Perón's order – the need to prevent the consolidation of the most virulent anti-Peronism. Their leadership and influence were crucial in gaining the mass of Peronist voters for Frondizi. Nevertheless, over 800,000 Peronists disregarded the order and reaffirmed their intransigence by abstaining or blank voting.

4

Ideology and consciousness in the Peronist Resistance

> For us the return of Perón meant so many things; the return of dignity and decency for those who worked, getting the boss off our backs, the return of happiness, the end of so much sadness and bitterness in the hearts of ordinary men, and the end of persecution.
>
> Anonymous worker

The period of the Aramburu government and the Peronist resistance to this government was regarded throughout the 1960s and into the 1970s by the Peronist left and others as a highpoint of militancy, an exemplary period of working-class combativity. The very term 'the Resistance' came to embody radicalism, to imply a left-wing movement, a somewhat revolutionary notion. The basis for such an assessment has been outlined in the prior chapters of this section. Purely in terms of strike statistics the years 1956 and 1957 were unrivalled until then in Argentine labour history. Over 5 million days were lost in the Federal Capital alone in 1956 and over 3,300,000 in 1957.[1] These strike figures reflected not simply a battle on wages issues but were also symbolic of daily struggles within the workplace to defend conditions and organisation won during the Perón era against a concerted state and employer attack. The Peronist union movement had been revitalised in the course of these struggles and was now largely led by a new generation of leaders thrown up by the rank and file, a leadership which maintained a greatly enhanced union democracy and participation. How can we begin to characterise the ideology which emerged from this general context among rank-and-file Peronist workers?

The reaffirmation of traditional tenets

Analysing the clandestine union newspapers, participant memoirs, and pamphlets we can isolate a number of strands which represent the continuing influence of traditional ideological tenets to be found in the formal discourse of Peronism in power. First, there is a strongly voiced economic nationalism, the defence of the national patrimony. One sees this as a constantly reiterated theme from the very beginning of the post-Perón period. One of the first mimeographed sheets which began to circulate in the Rosario area, put out by workers in the Puerto General San Martín, gave the warning that, 'at present they want to drag us back to a pastoral state, to a situation where the only wealth comes from farming and cattle breeding'.[2] One of the principal targets of this economic nationalism was the economic policy of the military government. The agreement with the International Monetary Fund, the liquidation of state control of foreign trade, the decontrol of imports and the relaxation of price controls, especially on agricultural goods, all confirmed the image of a pro-imperialist regime bent on taking Argentina back to the golden age of the cattle-exporting economy. The shift of resources to agriculture as a whole, achieved through the devaluation of the peso, added to this.

Perón's books and pamphlets took up the same theme with great persistence, as did the organs of the Resistance. A clandestine newspaper from Rosario, *El Cuarenta*, gave as the reason for its title the fact that, 'We are anti-oligarch and anti-imperialist and for us 40 is the number of the article of the 1949 constitution which guarantees the right of our people to the natural riches of its subsoil, prohibiting their handing over to imperialism.'[3] José Rucci, at this time a delegate in the metal workers' union, wrote an article in *Palabra Argentina*, in which he voiced what seems to have been an overriding perception by working-class Peronists of this issue:

Argentina seems not to know that we are living in a metal-working civilisation, very far indeed from the pastoral and semi-colonial economy of our ancestors and which a dozen or so oligarchic families are trying to reimpose on us; they want to hold up the historical forces of the country, its technological development and the march of a nation towards an industrial civilisation.[4]

Working-class Peronists associated the pre–1955 era with a time of national development which had gone hand in hand with a policy of social justice. As such they saw the policy of the military government as fundamentally anti-national, anti-industrial and anti-worker. They saw an interconnection between these aspects. A statement issued by a delegate conference during the metal workers' strike of 1956 bears witness to this:

What we are seeing is the creation of an anti-national and anti-worker front: the representatives of the state and foreign capital united in a common design to annihilate Argentine industry and crush the union organisation of the working class ... in a semi-colony like Argentina the battle for economic liberation can only be fought on the basis of a respected and organised working class which will sustain the country in the face of the big international enterprises.[5]

The defence of economic gains made under Perón and of working-class organisation, it hardly needs to be added, was another element found in the ideology of the Resistance. This was conceived in terms of the traditional Peronist notion of 'social justice', which together with 'national sovereignty' were two cornerstones of state ideological rhetoric under Perón. Economic nationalism and anti-imperialism had as a corollary an affirmation of traditional concepts such as the common interest between employer and worker in the protection of national industry. Similarly, 'social justice' was accompanied by the concept of humane, socially conscious capital and its speculative, exploitative opposite. José Rucci, in the article referred to above, had warned employers that 'we know how to distinguish between national industry and exploitative, speculative and oppressive capital'.[6] A closely allied notion was that of the fair profit that this humanised capital was entitled to earn. Rucci's main complaint about the employers in the metal industry was, in fact, that their profits were excessive and therefore exploitative.

In a similar vein a textile workers' leader, Juan Carlos Loholaberry, voiced a common perception when asked his attitude to the socialist concept of the abolition of classes. He replied that Peronists could not be opposed to private enterprise but rather wanted to ensure that it contributed to the public good: 'As for social classes, they conform to a natural order of things which is impossible to change. Thus we do not propose that they be abolished, but that they all aim for a single goal: social welfare.'[7] Part of this, too, was an implicit notion of a special role for the state as the ultimate guarantor of the implementation of these formal concepts: the ensurer of social harmony, the moderator of excessive class interests, the protector of national sovereignty. There was, also, often a strong paternalistic tone to this affirmation. At times implicitly, though often explicitly, Perón was identified with the state. 'La vuelta de Perón' became a guarantee that the state would remain committed to playing its guiding role in society.

Elements of a counter-discourse

Yet if these traditional elements of formal Peronist rhetoric were a powerful presence in working-class discourse, there were also other elements present in this discourse, fragments of what one author has described as 'counter-discourse.'[8] Many of these elements were symbolised in working-class struggle itself. The context of direct confrontation with employers and with the forces of the state, and the intensity of that confrontation generated and implied certain values and moral choices which were drawn from, and themselves encapsulated the meaning of concrete social experience. Strikes, as we have suggested, represented more than the quantitative indices tell us. They also had their peculiar tone and quality which imparted a particular character to the consciousness of those workers who experienced them. A thorough bitterness pervaded all aspects of class relations in this period and surfaced particularly during major strikes. The metal workers' strike of November/December 1956 was, as we have seen, a notable example of this. The strike like many others in this period became symbolic of the concrete solidarity and sense of unity workers felt. Far smaller-scale daily conflicts – often over issues of shop-floor organisation, defence of delegates, defence of traditional work norms – reaffirmed these values of pride, solidarity and self-confidence. Sabotage activity was itself affirmative of very concrete values. Though by no means a purely working-class expression, this form of action had a clear influence on working-class perceptions. Sabotage in the factories was not simply a negative rejection of a particular employer. It also represented an affirmation of a worker's ability to confront, in at least a minimal way, a social, economic and political situation he rejected. It affirmed his presence as a social actor.

This lived experience had, then, its own implicit meanings and values, which we often find more explicitly articulated in the clandestine newspapers, personal testimonies, *barrio* broadsheets of the period which emerged from, and speak to, this realm of practical consciousness. One finds, for example, among these diverse rank-and-file sources a widely expressed anti-politicism. As one participant in the events of the period recalled: 'During the Resistance we despised all things political. For the Peronists political meant the same thing as electoral and to call someone a politician was regarded as a kind of insult. Those of the Resistance thought that only *gorilas* were members of political parties.'[9] This deeply imbued suspicion of the political system and politicians was clearly closely related to the post-1955 political situation in Argentina. The credibility and legitimacy of a political system that used a rhetoric of democracy while outlawing the political expression of the majority was evidently fragile. There was more to it than this, however. Related to this was a clear scepticism concerning the political slogans of official ideology. 'Democracy', 'justice', 'liberty', the 'rule of law', were frequently referred to contemptuously – not in favour of authoritarian, anti-democratic notions, but rather in relation to the hypocrisy of official political rhetoric. A mimeographed newspaper put out by militants in the Puerto General San Martín, to which we have already referred, voiced a typical perception in this respect:

It is not necessary to be intelligent, it's enough to be a little sensitive to understand that this 'Liberty' is too stained with blood of the people; it is a repudiated liberty which needs the force of fear, vigilance and death to sustain it ... we are democrats but not of a democracy in which liberty, justice and law are instruments which oppressors use to maintain their privileges. We recognise that only one true and authentic democracy exists: social democracy.[10]

A corollary to this political scepticism was an affirmation and pride in their existence as workers, which was not infrequently expressed in terms of a concern for working-class self-reliance and autonomy. This reflected a clear feeling of isolation and abandonment by other, previously allied, social sectors: 'Political leaders have defrauded us, politicians have fooled us, intellectuals have forgotten us.'[11] This lament was directed as much against Peronist politicians as any others. Rarely, however, is this left as a simple lament. At the very least a political or moral lesson is usually attached to it: 'Until when will we be the voting fodder on whom the opportunists, the adventurers and the daring clamber their way to the top?'[12] The implicit lesson drawn here was that the fate the working class was suffering was due to its own failings, its lack of autonomy, its permitting itself to be used. A union grouping of militants who simply call themselves the Agrupamiento Sindical Argentino issued a leaflet in May 1956 which circulated in the factories of Greater Buenos Aires. One of its principal assertions was that: 'The conquests that we have achieved must be maintained and extended by the conscious action of the workers, without official protectors who compete to redeem what they suppose is our incapacity or our ignorance. Nobody will do for us what we are incapable of doing for ourselves.'[13] To remedy this situation the workers must convince themselves of their worth, their presence as *the* fundamental class in society. The militants who produced *Crisol del Litoral*, for example, frequently returned to this, often in a tone which implored workers to listen: 'The social dynamic lies in us, in our breasts, in our muscles, in our hands.'[14] An identical plea for recognition of their own worth and potential control of society can be found, too, in many other rank-and-file materials from this time. One from a group simply entitled Agrupación Obrera in the suburb of Lomas de Zamora began by stating that:

> The Revolution carried out by the oligarchy which always dominated our society ... is underestimating the power and the value of the workers ... but have they thought what their money is for? Money is only of use to buy goods for use or consumption. Who makes with their energy all, absolutely all, the goods? WORKERS!!! Neither sailors, nor soldiers nor public employees nor priests nor shopkeepers make goods ... they only consume ... while those who produce, the workers, never earn enough to be able to enjoy the goods they make ... Perón understood this undeniable truth ... he knew and knows that you are the basis of everything: the houses, skyscrapers, machines, roads, ports, boats, machines, everything, everything is made by you. Capital is dead, it has no value without labour which transforms capital into a product. What use is money in the banks if this is not used to create goods which represent wealth? No use! What use is there in having millions in bills if there is no food to buy? Capital without you is a corpse which is rotting.[15]

The leaflet went on to outline the strategy to be drawn from this – a total general strike, a refusal of the workers to produce, consume or distribute for five days. This would teach the oligarchy what they were worth without the workers and increase the chances for Perón's return.

This strange mixture of anarcho-syndicalism, Marxist economics and personal devotion to Perón should not be passed over simply as a confused, if colourful, anecdote. It is, I would suggest, a summation and condensation of the experience of a significant sector of the working class prior to 1955, an affirmation of that experience and the drawing of lessons from that experience for the post-1955 situation. Potentially, too, this was done in a way which challenged implicitly many of the assumptions of formal Peronist ideology. This is not, it must be emphasised, to deny the complexity and ambiguity of this process. Official Peronist discourse had itself adopted after its removal from power a more radical posture and this certainly helped legitimate rank-and-file notions concerning working-class autonomy. But clearly there were also elements present which even a radicalised official Peronism would find hard to absorb. Moreover, the organisational forms this working-class self-esteem and autonomy might take were often very concretely posed. An article written in *El Cuarenta*, for example, made a detailed study of the issue of factory cells as a form of ensuring working-class independence and organisational efficiency.[16]

Formal ideology and practical consciousness

The specific forms of subjectivity produced by the process we have

been outlining found partial expression in some of the notions and principles which, we have suggested, were present in working-class
discourse in the post-1955 period. This rank-and-file culture, this
'common sense' of working-class Peronists evidently implies an ambivalent dimension in our understanding of the impact of formal Peronist ideology on workers in the period immediately following the fall of
Perón. We should be careful, however, not to rigidly oppose and
separate the two. We are dealing here with an ideological and historical
process. The more formal, traditionally validated tenets of Peronism
were clearly, as we have shown, an important presence in working-
class culture, powerfully shaping working-class perceptions. Rather
than a separation and rigid opposition we are dealing with a tension,
both explicit and implicit, between the two. This tension was itself related to an ever-present tension between experienced reality, and the
'practical consciousness' that it generated, and the particular tenets of
formal ideology.

Raymond Williams, referring to this tension, has commented:
'Where this tension can be made direct and explicit, or where some
alternative interpretation is available, we are still within a dimension of
relatively fixed forms. But the tension is as often an unease, a stress, a
latency: the moment of conscious comparison not yet come, often not
even coming.'[17] The mechanisms involved in handling such stress are
various. Thus, for example, in the post-1955 period one potential solution adopted by working-class Peronists was to insist on a literal interpretation of traditional ideological tenets. This was partly a yearning
for a past where reality and formal ideological notions coincided.
Partly, it also involved an insistence on the legitimacy of concepts
which experience now challenged. One thinks here of notions such as
'class harmony' and 'social justice' espoused by working-class Peronists not as a denial of reality but as a registering of a moral alternative, a
claim for a potentially superior society. Such literal insistence on the
value of traditional ideological maxims in radically altered social con-
texts evidently had potentially disturbing consequences for the internal
coherence of formal Peronist discourse.

Another mechanism for resolving this discrepancy is the posing of
alternative, or even opposing, notions which correspond more adequately to working-class experience. Elements of such alternative interpretations were clearly present in the rank-and-file discourse we
have been examining, with its emphasis on working-class autonomy
and the unique role of workers in society. The most explicit expression

of these alternative interpretations within Peronism can be found in the programme of the 62 Organisations adopted at La Falda in November 1957. This programme contained a demand for workers' control of production and the destruction of the oligarchy.

We must stress again the ambiguity, contradiction and unevenness of the process we have been describing. Traditional tenets were rarely simply abandoned. Instead they remained, sometimes in modified form, perhaps with altered implications and meanings, sometimes they were overlain with new, alternative elements; or sometimes they persisted in unaltered contradiction with other elements of working-class ideological discourse. Examples of the latter are numerous in the rank-and-file materials of the Resistance period. We have already seen the affirmation of working-class autonomy go hand in hand with the affirmation of Perón's mystique. The perception of a common interest between workers and bosses in the protection of national industry persisted even at times of heightened class conflict, as did the notion of humanised capital. The identification of a class enemy was often similarly ambiguous, even for workers suffering from both the employers' blacklist and state repression. At times the national bourgeoisie were included among the enemies of the working class which stood virtually alone in the social spectrum. A strong sense of corporate identity of the working class in this case implied a strong identification of a class enemy. At other times the national bourgeoisie were regarded as simply incapable of realising their common interests with workers.

Part of the reason for this ambiguity lay in the very nature of the general political context in which the working-class Peronist operated at this time. The division of the nation into Peronist and anti-Peronist implied that intense class conflict was absorbed into a political polarisation which was not, ultimately, class based. Peronist and anti-Peronist were not necessarily synonymous with class positions. The very thoroughness of the government's anti-Peronism compounded this. A decree such as 4161 issued in 1956, which forbade and punished with imprisonment the possession of a photo of Perón in a private house, the singing of a Peronist song, or the playing of a record, impressed the political dichotomy of Argentine society onto the most mundane level of daily existence. If a worker could be arrested for going to work on a bicycle with a picture of Evita stuck on it, then it was hardly surprising that the figure of Perón and his return to power should serve as a focus for his rebellion. A clear cutting across of class lines was implied. For all the bitterness and isolation of the working class, there was a strong strand of perception which considered the Resistance as a classless struggle :

> For the Peronism of the Resistance there was no doubt that the fundamental enemy was anti-Peronism whatever its different guises; and conversely the fundamental friend was another Peronist. Delegating in Perón the sum total of what was good and just, the Resistance saw no need for any internal differentiation. In this way, the neo-Nazi could fight shoulder to shoulder with the proto-communist.[18]

The fundamental enemy was the *gorila* and he could, theoretically, be just as easily a fellow worker as an oligarch.

Moreover, it is apparent that certain of the values and assumptions found in working-class culture at this time were more easily assimilated and reflected within the formal tenets of Peronist ideology than others. Assumptions concerning the full integration of Peronist workers as citizens into the wider polity, their political role within civil society, posed few problems in terms of their articulation within official Peronist ideology. These were elements Ernesto Laclau refers to as 'popular democratic' elements within an ideological discourse and which refer to a level of social and political antagonism which does not coincide with economic class conflict but refers to what he calls the 'people/power bloc antagonism'.[19] Notions which affirmed the role of the working class in economic development and defence of the national popular state also fall within this category.

On the other hand, assumptions and principles drawn from the experience of class conflict were less easily expressed. This was particularly the case with conflicts emerging in the labour process. One of Peronism's most important legacies had been a shop-floor culture permeated with notions concerning workers' rights within the labour process. These notions were rarely articulated explicitly in more concrete ideological terms. To the extent that they were formally expressed and justified it was in terms of traditional Peronist maxims of social justice and social welfare. More often than not they remained implicit, present in practical consciousness within the workplace, explicit in concrete shop-floor struggles. Official Peronism had little to say about these areas of working-class experience and the tension produced by this void between formal Peronist concepts of social harmony, humanised, non-exploitative capital and lived experience on the shop floor was largely expressed as – to use Williams's phrase again – 'an unease, a stress, a latency'. Yet the presence of these latent, half-submerged class elements should not be ignored. They would represent a persistent stumbling block that would confront both employers and the state in Argentina in the course of the next decade.

Nostalgia and *obrerismo* in working-class consciousness

Raymond Williams has developed the concept of 'structures of feeling' to refer to these stresses and displacements which escape formal ideological expression yet 'define a particular quality of social experience and relationship'. They are distinct from formal ideology and are 'concerned with meanings and values as they are actively lived and felt'.[20] In the Peronist Resistance we encounter a period of working-class history whose 'structures of feeling' were profoundly penetrated by class resonances, and whose characteristic elements helped set the tone of political and social relationships not only for the immediate post-1955 period but also for a whole generation of working-class Peronists.

One of the characteristic elements defining this 'structure of feeling' was undoubtedly a deeply ingrained *obrerismo*, an exaltation of what one could call 'workerist populism'. It is easily missed in formal analysis but its resonances can nevertheless be discerned. It can be seen in the language used. Working-class Peronism exalted in its identification with *la chusma, las grasas, los descamisados, las cabecitas negras*. Conversely there was a bitterness and contempt for the non-worker. I think that it is in terms of this particular resonance that we must consider the many crude, single-page *barrio* broadsheets of the period. One which circulated in Rosario in 1957 with the title *Juancito* contains a story which might be relegated to the purely trivial if it did not speak precisely to this issue of 'values as they are actively lived and felt'. Entitled 'Everyone should have one' it urges Peronists to choose their own *gorila*:

Choose him in his club or wherever, look after him, but be a little perverse, make his life amusing. Anything will do; break his windows, piss on his garden path, send him anonymous notes, ring his bell at three in the morning. When the time comes the bastard will know that he is a marked man.[21]

The tone of this and many other similar pieces in this type of press is redolent with bitterness, frustration and a visceral contempt for the social and political enemy.

At the same time this latent, implicit *obrerismo* included an affirmation of working-class existence. Not always, however, in terms of a politically articulate call for autonomous organisation, or a conceptualisation of the function of the working class as producers of social wealth. Instead we often find an affirmation of class feeling almost in terms of sentimental folklore which celebrated the harshness and grief of working-class life, together with the affective values associated with home and family, *barrio* and workmates. We find, for example, in another issue of *Juancito* a piece calling on mothers with sons in the army to awaken them to their solidarity with their fellow workers:

Make him feel your love and miss his home; remind him of the bitter sweat of his father and the tender tears of his mother, all the grief and the love of your humble home. The feeling of his own room, the gang on the corner, the boys in the workshop. Nothing more will be necessary. If you do this, your soldier son will never fire on his own.[22]

Another, more problematic, element of this distinctive 'structure of feeling' characteristic of this period was nostalgia for the Peronist era. Running through personal testimony and clandestine pamphlets was an insistent contrast between the chaos and conflict of life under the military regime and the harmony and social unity of pre-1955 Argentina. Clearly present in such nostalgia were elements of regressive fantasy for 'the good old days' of a 'golden era' – a plaintive reflection on a glorified, utopian past. But this was not all. If the vision of the Peronist past was idealised, this was not simply a wishful construct arbitrarily created. Elements of this recently passed 'utopia' were appropriated selectively from the past to meet present needs and to point the way for future hopes. In particular, the past was appropriated not simply as a longing for the recreation of a comfortable idyll of fat wallets and union vacation resorts in Mar del Plata, but also as a basis for a claim for a future society based on social justice and non-exploitation.

The ultimate basis for such hopes was a notion of the state – drawn from the experience of the Perón era – as the engine of national development and, more crucially, the arena where the working class should look for satisfaction of its desire for social justice. This did not imply that workers were unaware of the partisan class nature of the existing state. Rather, it represented a statement of what *ought* to be in the future, based on a selective interpretation of what *had* been in the past. The state as a sovereign public sphere *ought* to be the guarantor of justice and it might again achieve this status if it could be protected from the power of the rich, the oligarchy. It was this vision of an idealised *potential* state which was to form the basis of working-class support for Frondizi in 1958.

Similarly, the personal position of Perón in this nostalgia involved more than a search for a comforting, paternalistic leader. Perón's figure and his attributes attained almost mythical proportions in the

1955–8 period, but once again we must insist that the elements of such a myth were not arbitrarily imagined. Faced with a recognition of the power of the oppressors and their ability to pervert the use of public power from its ideal course, Perón himself became the ultimate guarantor and precondition in the minds of many workers against such a future recurrence. This involved, as with their vision of the Peronist state, a certain selective amnesia in order to create a mythical Perón who would serve their needs. Part of this was certainly conscious myth making. Memories of Perón's fallibilities – both personal and political – were still present and discussed by militants in this era; jokes about his personal life were also common. Yet, a recognition of the 'reality' behind the myth hardly diminished the symbolic importance of the figure created by working-class Peronists. The 'return of Perón' was not evidence of a mindless political and emotional loyalty. Instead, as the activist whose statement appears at the beginning of this chapter indicated, the return of Perón came to symbolise and synthesise a range of aspirations which workers held concerning dignity, social justice and an end to bitterness.

The picture which emerges from this analysis of ideology and consciousness in the 1955–8 period is, therefore, a complex, nuanced one. Certainly, many of the traditional tenets of Peronist ideology continued to maintain their hold. Traditional notions continued to have the capacity to express certain needs and antagonisms emerging from workers' everyday experience and activity. The intense class conflict of the period was ultimately absorbed into an overriding political dichotomy which was not class based. Yet, it is also clear that there was no simple conflation of the traditional maxims of Peronist ideology and working-class perceptions and actions. In certain spheres, particularly those relating to class-specific issues emerging from the production process, there was an evident discord between lived reality and formal philosophy. This discrepancy formed the basis for the potential emergence of elements of a counter-discourse. There was a complex interrelationship between these two areas which, I have suggested, was sometimes resolved explicitly in favour of new alternative interpretations, or, more often, resolved through the coexistence of contradictory elements.

Thus the sorrow, resentment and nostalgia felt at the passing of an idealised, harmonious society and its appropriate discourse went hand in hand with the unveiling of the coercive social and political relationships of the present. While this clearly led to radicalisation and

increased strains within Peronism and Peronist discourse this radicalisation took place within the context and terms provided by the existing
rhetoric of Peronism and there was to be an ambivalent balance between formal Peronist ideology and elements of an emerging, though
often latent, counter-discourse. The ambiguity inherent in this situation was to lie at the root of the social and political instability of the
following years. The notion of the recreation of a genuine, national
popular state where social justice could finally be located would clearly
underlie support for Frondizi and help lend legitimacy to the union
hierarchy's political activity in the 1960s. However, the experience of
the Resistance and its specific structure of feeling, made up of pride,
bitterness and a sense of class solidarity and strength, would also form
the basis of a protracted working-class opposition to Frondizi and
union bureaucrats by providing social and moral criteria for public
policies which were directly at variance with the rationale of the developmentalist state.

PART THREE

Frondizi and integration: temptation and disenchantment, 1958–62

5

Resistance and defeat: the impact on leaders, activists and rank and file

The union leadership don't give way because they are traitors, nor because they have sold out to Frigerio; they give way because they have accepted in their minds the argument that the workers share responsibility for the nation's problems and because of the tremendous pressure of government and employer propaganda with all its emphasis on the 'national popular' alliance. All that is starting to carry far more weight with them than the feelings of the workers in the factories, from which the leaderships have become more and more alienated since Frondizi's victory.

Anonymous delegate to 62 Organisations meeting, November 1958

Desarrollismo: attraction and rejection in Frondizi's first nine months

At the end of October 1958, five months after Arturo Frondizi had assumed the presidency, a strike broke out among workers in the Mendoza oil field. The strike was led by a coalition of communist and radical militants and was in protest at the contracts signed by Frondizi with the foreign oil companies. The union with jurisdiction over the state-controlled oil fields was the Sindicato Unido de Petroleros del Estado (SUPE). The Peronist grouping in the union, while claiming the support of the majority of the workers, had not been able to effectively demonstrate this because new elections, although scheduled, had not yet taken place. The reaction of the Peronist union grouping, Junta de Petroleros, 13 de diciembre, and indeed of the official movement as a whole, was overtly hostile to the strike. When the issue of the new oil contracts had first emerged in June and July the leadership of the 62 Organisations had denounced the opposition of 'certain elements using supposedly nationalistic banners'.[1] In language very similar to the government's official explanation of the contracts it had justified them as necessary to ensure future energy self-sufficiency and thus break the bond of colonial dependency. Recourse to foreign capital for this purpose was legitimate. The same line was adopted toward the strike in October. The Junta de Petroleros called on Peronist workers to ignore the strike call. The Consejo Coordinador y Supervisor del Peronismo, the body newly created by Perón to oversee the movement inside Argentina, followed this lead as did *Línea Dura*, the semi-official organ of Peronism. In the sectors of SUPE controlled by the Peronists such as Comodoro Rivadavia, Salta and the refineries at Ensenada the strike did not spread. On the 4 November Frondizi declared the strike illegal.

The desire of the Peronist union leadership to avoid a direct conflict with the government over the oil contracts was not unprecedented. Indeed, on several occasions in the first months of Frondizi's presidency they had backed out of conflict with the government.[2] The reason for the leeway given to Frondizi was, in part at least, pragmatic. Initially, in the period between the elections and the inauguration in May, nothing was done which might delay the transfer of power to Frondizi. After he had entered the Casa Rosada they wished to give him the chance to make good on his campaign promises to the working class and the Peronist movement. In addition, the Peronist vote for Frondizi in the elections had been won in return for explicit, if secret, commitments on his part. These commitments included: a revision of all economic measures since 1955 harmful to the national sovereignty, the annulment of all measures of political persecution, the lifting of all union and political proscriptions, the return of the CGT and the holding of union elections within 120 days and the legal recognition of the Peronist Party. They did not wish to provoke an institutional crisis which would prevent the fulfilment of these compromises.

This position was to change drastically with the arrival in early November of orders from Perón to denounce the contracts. On 6 November the Consejo Coordinador changed course and counselled Peronist unionists to adopt 'a decided and energetic action of repudiation of the contracts'.[3] On 9 November, Frondizi, in a speech to the nation, said that the strike formed part of an insurrectional movement which had first been led by communists and then by 'those who believe in the restoration of the deposed dictatorship'. On the following day a state of siege was declared and troops moved into the oil fields; arrests of communist and Peronist union leaders began. Rogelio Frigerio, considered the chief architect of conciliation with the Peronist unions, resigned from the government. At the same time at a stormy plenary session of the 62 Organisations the delegates forced a reluctant coordinating committee to denounce the contracts and call a general strike for 20 and 21 November. The strength of rank-and-file feeling was evident; forty-eight delegates voted for the 48-hour general strike and seven for one of unlimited duration. The leadership of the 62 Organisations was strictly forbidden to initiate any negotiations towards a compromise on its own initiative.[4]

Despite this vote, however, the leadership of the 62 Organisations immediately began to seek avenues of compromise. In the days following the plenary session rumours circulated concerning the involvement of the vice president, Alejandro Gómez, who was known to oppose the contracts, in plots with extreme anti-Peronist sections of the armed forces. On 14 November the 62 leadership had a long meeting with Frondizi. Agreement was reached on most issues. The state of siege was to be lifted, measures taken to control prices, the new Law of Professional Associations was to be implemented as soon as possible and discussions begun on new collective contracts. Frondizi assured the union leaders that the contracts would not damage YPF's, the state oil company's, control of refining and marketing. On this basis the 48-hour general strike was abandoned. Augusto Vandor, the leader of the metal workers, was given the task of convincing Perón of the wisdom of this turn-around by phone.[5] The next day the strike in the oil fields was called off.

In itself this episode was not of great importance. The definitive clash between Peronist workers and the Frondizi government was postponed some six weeks. Yet it was, nevertheless, a symptomatic event. Most of the variables which would determine the relationship between the Peronist unions and Frondizi were present: a recognition of the concrete benefits from the union point of view of constitutional rule and an unwillingness to push agitation to a point where it might have provoked a military move against Frondizi; an ideological sympathy with some fundamental *desarrollista* tenets which helped prevent initial support for the strike; the divergence between union leaders and rank-and-file activists over the relationship with the state; finally the role of Perón in determining the strategy of the movement and the potential clash with the union leadership.

The attraction from the union leaderships' point of view of not contributing to Frondizi's ouster was evident. Already by November they had achieved concrete gains from Frondizi. The most important of these was the Law of Professional Associations, law 14,455. This was modelled on the Peronist labour code and allowed for the recognition of only one bargaining unit in any one industry. This effectively did away with attempts by the Aramburu regime to implement multi-union bargaining. The new law also abolished minority representation in union leadership; the Peronist system of the winning list taking control of the entire union was reestablished. New elections had already been held in many unions in accordance with the new law and others were scheduled in unions where Peronists were confident they could win now that military interference had been eliminated. There were also issues such as the reconstitution of union pension funds and social services which were of immediate concern to the unions. The salvaging of union finances depended crucially on the continued application of the new Law of Professional Associations which authorised the retention of union dues on behalf of the unions by employers. The law itself was to be a constant theme of military discontent. In the longer term Frondizi had also promised the return of the CGT once new elections were completed; since the Peronists were confident that they would win most of these elections they could look forward to a dominant role in the new confederation.

All this was to give Frondizi a card of considerable power to play in his dealings with the Peronist unions. In the first months of his government the clandestine sectors of the Peronist movement, and Perón himself, considered this a bogus card. They either discounted the possibility of a coup, or considered that it would make little real difference to the policies being implemented and the situation facing the movement. The union leadership could not, however, afford to be so sanguine. The declaration of the state of siege, the resignation of Frigerio and the rumours of a military coup in the Gómez incident, were all forcible reminders of the delicate nature of the institutional balance and of how much they stood to lose in any shift of that balance. While they had many specific areas of complaint against Frondizi, such as price rises and the slowness in implementing the new labour law, the union leadership in general recognised him as their best option. *Línea Dura* in the middle of the November crisis had recognised as much when it had warned its readers that: 'If we let ourselves be pushed too far we will inexorably serve the interests of reaction with all the consequences that implies: a *gorila* government, anti-Peronist terrorism and the end to any solution to our present problems.'[6]

The credit extended to Frondizi by the Peronist unions was not simply the result of pragmatic considerations. As the November crisis indicated there was also a fundamental *ideological* sympathy with certain of the basic tenets of *desarrollista* policy. Since the declaration of his presidential candidacy in November 1956 which had split the Rad-

ical Party and led to the formation of the Unión Cívica Radical Intransigente (UCRI), Frondizi had developed a coherent and distinct
economic and social programme which had become the focal point of
his election campaign.

Frondizi and the group of intellectuals which had gathered around
him – above all Rogelio Frigerio, the owner of the journal *Qué* – maintained that Argentina must break out of its old economic model which
was dependent for growth on a declining capacity to import generated
by its traditional agricultural export sector. It had to produce for itself
the raw materials and finished goods it now imported from the developed world. Only in this way could it overcome the externally imposed
international division of labour which condemned Argentina to a role
as supplier of certain raw materials to the developed world at increasingly unfavourable prices.[7] While they recognised the rapid industrialisation which had taken place since the 1930s they claimed that this had
been confined to light industry at the expense of raw materials, fuels,
machinery and industrial equipment, all of which still had to be
imported in large quantities. In the *desarrollista* schema development
was synonymous with industrialisation, and the creation of this
'genuine' industrialisation was the cornerstone of Frondizi's economic
strategy.

Within Frondizi's industrialising developmentalist rhetoric certain
key areas were given preference. By the election campaign of late 1957
and early 1958 petroleum production occupied pride of place in his list
of priorities, followed by the development of heavy industry and the
development of high technology consumer goods in the petro-chemical
and electro-metallurgical field. Much stress was also layed on the creation of an integrated road transport system which would form the
basis of a domestic automobile industry.

In general Frondizi and the *desarrollistas* framed their economic programme within a longstanding tradition of Argentine economic
nationalism. Certainly, for example, they had vigorously attacked
foreign capital and advocated the protection of national industry from
unfair competition and the development of a strong national market
based on the maintenance of high levels of internal consumption.
Agrarian reform likewise had a place in their programme. Frondizi had
himself been a leading critic of the contracts signed by Perón with Standard Oil in 1955.[8] Similarly the programme of the UCRI had adopted a
clear position of support for the nationalising of the oil industry and the
exclusive monopoly position of the state-owned oil company, YPF.
However, by 1958 Frondizi had come increasingly to accept the pos-

ition which Frigerio had argued since 1956, that foreign investment both public and private would be necessary for industrialisation on the scale envisaged. By the elections of 1958 foreign capital was considered to be not evil per se, but capable, under the proper control from the state, of providing capital accumulation in vital areas of industrialisation.[9]

Developmentalism also involved certain fundamental social notions. Once more working within a well-worn furrow of nationalist thought they started from a conception of the nation as an overriding category which subordinated and harmonised within it various social classes, economic interests and political forces. The working class as a dominant part of the nation had to pursue its goals within the framework of the common good. Class conflict was recognised but had to be resolved within the context of the common national good. If the working class attempted to prolong its sectional ideas beyond the limits imposed by the national good it was condemning itself to a sterile confrontation with other 'factors of power'. This had been exactly what had happened, they maintained, under Perón. The working class's sectionalism had ruptured the 'national popular' alliance with employers, the military and the church, to the immediate detriment of the workers who had had to endure the anti-worker and anti-national government of Aramburu.

Desarrollistas paid great attention to the relationship between employers and workers. While the historical antagonism between the two classes was to be submerged within the overall national synthesis, the role of a strong union organisation was to be assured: 'So that workers can participate with their own organisation and with an independent point of view in the course of national development it is necessary to strengthen and widen union action. This will ensure that economic expansion does not exclusively benefit national or foreign capital.'[10] This attitude to the working class and its organisations was part of a wider social rhetoric which drew together various economic and social strands of developmentalist ideology and which was usually referred to as 'integrationism'. Summarising this philosophy Juan José Real, a leading *desarrollista* propagandist, argued that: 'The Argentine employer has left behind the murky social horizon of Don Luis Colombo. The presence and representativity of the workers has already been recognised and actively promoted ... Machinery, raw materials and energy, to which are added the appropriate technology and a new employer-worker relationship, constitute the economic and social bases of development.'[11]

Within this context it becomes possible to appreciate the nature and depth of the attraction of *desarrollismo* for Peronist unionists. Clearly this attraction went beyond the immediate benefits promised by Frondizi. On a most general level developmentalist theory, as it was articulated by Frondizi and Frigerio, drew on a deep-running ideological well within Argentine nationalism and society which had its roots in the 1930s. This tradition, as we have seen, had been appropriated by Peronism. *Desarrollismo* was, therefore, in a general sense, scarcely innovative and this was one of its strengths. It drew on a strongly imbedded ideological tradition. More specifically, Frondizi's economic nationalism had parallels in the pre-1955 Peronist experience. The Peronist regime's second five-year plan, launched in 1953, foreshadowed very closely the economic programme advocated by Frondizi in 1957. Pride of place had gone to petroleum production, followed by steel, chemicals and motor vehicles. Similarly, the role of foreign capital in the industrialisation process had been first mooted by Perón. A new, more liberal law of foreign investment had been passed in 1953, and the targets for increased industrial and petroleum production contained in the second five-year plan were premised on large inputs of foreign capital.[12] Perón, himself, had continued to defend the Standard contracts.[13]

In the social sphere, too, *desarrollismo* and Peronism had much in common. The emphasis placed by Frigerio and his associates on the need for the workers, through strong independent unions, to cooperate with other 'factors of power' such as the church and employers corresponded with fundamental notions found in Peronist ideology and practice. The assertion found in Peronist rhetoric that the classic conflictual relationship between capital and labour was outworn and needed to be replaced by a recognition of the common contribution of both to the production process was echoed in developmentalist discourse. The language of the managerial revolution and modern labour relations philosophy, which had increasingly dominated the Peronist state's efforts to increase productivity in its last years, was also a commonplace of Frondizi's rhetoric.

There was, therefore, an underlying affinity between key tenets of *desarrollismo* and certain notions of formal Peronist ideology and the attraction this implied for Peronist unionists was to provide a consistent underpinning of union activity under the Frondizi government and its successors. The search for one version or another of this developmentalist strategy was to act as a consistent rationale behind the political and social activity of Peronist unions in the following decade. Yet, formal ideological affinities could not prevent a profound rupture between Peronist unions and Frondizi. This rupture was centred on the economic stabilisation plan Frondizi introduced in late December 1958.

In general terms Frondizi's economic policy followed closely the logic of the analysis propagated by developmentalist analysis in the preceding years: the deepening of industrialisation and the rationalisation of production. In practice, the most striking of his policies in the first nine months involved the effort to increase industrial investment and in particular foreign investment.[14] These measures and those introduced by the stabilisation plan of December were to have striking results. The proportion of domestic capital goods production to total supply of capital goods increased from 37% in 1950 to 63.7% in 1961. In the economy as a whole total fixed investment rose from 17% of the GDP in 1955 to 25% in 1961. Between 1960 and 1962 the new machinery and equipment purchased equalled in constant prices that of the entire 1953–8 period.[15] By 1962 also, Argentina had the basis of a motor vehicle industry and was self-sufficient in oil production.

By late 1958, however, Frondizi was facing a chronic balance of payments crisis. In return for an IMF standby loan he agreed to a crisis stabilisation plan which was introduced at the end of December. The plan included a drastic reduction in duties and surcharges on imported capital goods, a devaluation of the peso, the lifting of most price controls and the lifting of quantitative trade restrictions. The government also made clear its determination to operate what virtually amounted to a wage freeze. The plan broke the fragile alliance between the unions and Frondizi. The immediate impact of the plan on the working class was evident. Between 1958 and 1959 real wages fell some 20% and although there was some pick up in the following two years by 1961 they were still some 5% below 1958 levels. The plan also implied a notable redistribution of income; the wage share of national income declined from 48.7% in 1958 to 42.1% in 1961. It also affected employment by provoking a brief, sharp recession in 1959 when prices reached 113%.[16]

The economic policy of Frondizi, together with the union and political repression which accompanied it, was regarded by the Peronist union movement as a 'betrayal'. They condemned, of course, the immediate impact of the economic stabilisation plan on employment and wages. Most commonly their hostility to Frondizi's economic policy was framed in the language of economic nationalism and focused on his concessions to foreign capital. More fundamentally though, the unions condemned the betrayal of the notion that economic development could be achieved on the basis of a class consensus, that industrial modernisation could be achieved within a framework of a state-guided redistribution policy. They condemned Frondizi for not applying the social dimension of his pre-election ideology, with its insistence on a strong union movement working hand in hand with employers and government to ensure a 'genuine' national development from which the workers would equally benefit. This sense of betrayal was to remain strong throughout the Frondizi era and was to be a continuing obstacle to Frondizi's attempts to rebuild the shattered alliance with the unions.

Yet opposition to Frondizi was not homogeneous. Indeed the very notion of 'betrayal' indicated certain limitations to this opposition. It implied a continued belief in the efficacy of the 'betrayed' ideas – the burden was placed on the good or bad faith of the implementor rather than the validity of the 'betrayed' concepts themselves. Frondizi was to spend much of the remaining years of his government trying to persuade the Peronist union leaders of his good faith and continued commitment to the notions of 'national popular' development. He argued that the stabilisation plan had been an unfortunate, temporary necessity and that concessions to foreign capital were necessary to break the bonds of underdevelopment. As time went on, as we shall see, pragmatic considerations were to lead union leaders to increasingly extend the benefit of the doubt to Frondizi on this issue.

There was, however, another type of opposition to Frondizi, an opposition which was rooted in the legacy of the Resistance period. This working-class opposition drew its sustenance from the experience of rank-and-file resistance to the post-1955 military regime and the distinct set of values and 'structure of feeing' which this struggle had engendered. Whatever the weight of the identity between many of the fundamental formal notions of Peronism and developmentalist ideology in attracting the Peronist working class to an alliance with Frondizi, the experience and culture of the Resistance were to weigh more heavily for a sizeable militant minority throughout the Frondizi government. The bitterness of the struggle begun against Frondizi in 1959 would further confirm this. This opposition had already manifested itself in the 800,000 who had ignored Perón's order to vote for Frondizi in February 1958, it would find expression again in the rank-and-file demand for a strike on 17 October of that year, and again in the sympathy of the rank-and-file delegates for the oil strike and the call of these delegates for a general strike in sympathy with the oil field workers.

This opposition to Frondizi would draw on the elements of a counter-discourse which we have analysed in the previous chapter. This evidently involved certain notions which challenged formal Peronist ideology. More importantly though, the opposition to Frondizi and any compromise with him was based on a literal interpretation of traditional elements of Peronist ideology – those same elements which could also lead to alliance with the developmentalist state. A literal insistence on such elements would now form the basis of opposition to government policy. This implied a selective interpretation of the Peronist experience. As they insisted on taking the rhetoric of economic nationalism seriously, for example, they did not refer back to the Perón of the Standard Oil contracts, of the Kaiser deal or the visit of Milton Eisenhower but rather to the Perón of the nationalisation of the railroads and denunciations of foreign capital. Also present would be an implicit notion of the importance of Perón's own presence. Perón would be the guarantee that the power of the state would not be used to the detriment of the workers or the nation.

This would mean, as we shall see, that this opposition to Frondizi would not develop a fundamental formal critique of the basis of a developmentalist strategy, but would rather persist as a moral rejection of its impact, a deep suspicion of those who sought to implement it and an insistence on the relevance of social and moral criteria in carrying out state policy. To Frondizi and, indeed, increasing sectors of Peronism, this opposition seemed to acquire a self-destructive, almost luddite quality. It condemned as betrayal what were in fact logical solutions to capitalist development problems; problems and solutions which had been recognised by both Peronist practice and theory prior to 1955. Technically the *desarrollista* case seemed irrefutable, framed as it was in an overwhelming technical rhetoric which took full advantage of the intimidating power of what one author has called 'the discourse of competence' beloved of intellectual and technical elites. Within the framework of a capitalist economic system – which most sectors of Peronism remained formally committed to – there seemed few feasible alternatives to this programme. Nevertheless, this opposition, centred on a powerful militant minority within the working class, stubbornly maintained its rejection of this logic and ignored the rationale of formal ideological tenets, relying instead on notions of social justice, equity, class solidarity and a literal economic nationalism drawn from their experience of the Peronist era and the post-1955 resistance.

Mobilisation and defeat: 1959–60

1959: the crucial year of conflicts

At the beginning of January 1959 Frondizi faced a situation of uneasy stalemate on the labour front. While outright confrontation with the unions, particularly the Peronist unions, had been avoided, their response to the announced stabilisation plan was clearly to be feared. The Peronist rank and file had emerged from the period of the military regime with a greatly enhanced self-confidence; a confidence based on their proven ability to withstand military repression and to regain their unions. This self-confidence had already manifested itself in the early months of Frondizi's government. The rank and file had been far less reluctant than their leaders to show their disapproval of Frondizi's shortcomings. In the last two months of the year major confrontations with the government had only been avoided by the leadership of the 62 Organisations specifically ignoring the militant lead given by rank-and-file delegates to the plenary sessions. This feeling of confidence and militancy was reflected in the strike figures for 1958; some 6,245,286 days were lost to strikes in the Federal Capital alone.[17]

Another important indicator of self-confidence was to be found in the results of the union elections taking place in late 1958 to bring unions into line with the new Law of Professional Associations. In most cases new leaderships grouped in the 62 Organisations emerged victorious.[18] Both the confidence of the rank and file in the mainly new Peronist leaderships and their enthusiasm for union activity can be seen from the voting figures. In the textile union, for example, some 91% of the union membership voted and the winning list headed by Andrés Framini received some 60,000 votes. In Luz y Fuerza, the light and power union, there was an 80% vote with the Peronist list winning by some 8,000 votes. In the Frigorífico Nacional Sebastian Borro received some 80% of the votes cast. In the meatpacking federation 70% of the members voted and the two rival Peronist lists received 505 of the votes cast.[19]

The mood of confidence reflected in these figures was to lead the Argentine working class into a series of conflicts in 1959 of unprecedented scope and bitterness. In the course of 1959 10,078,138 days were lost in strikes in the Federal Capital, with the involvement of more than 1,400,000 workers – some six times the number involved the previous year.[20] The event which precipitated this upheaval and broke the deceptive calm of 1958 was the occupation of the Frigorífico Nacional Lisandro de la Torre by its workers and the subsequent general strike

called in support of this action. The *frigorífico* was owned by the mu-
nicipality of Buenos Aires, having been nationalised during Perón's
first government. Its return to private enterprise had been first mooted
under the Aramburu government and had been talked about after Frondizi's inauguration. In December rumours abounded that the IMF
would regard the privatisation of the plant as a sign of Frondizi's good
intentions. This was confirmed in early January when he presented a
project to congress concerning the meatpacking industry whose first
article called for the privatisation of the *frigorífico*.[21] Immediately following the passing of this law on 14 January an assembly of 9,000
workers decided to occupy the plant. The *frigorífico* was situated in the
barrio of Mataderos in the north west of the Federal Capital; it was a
barrio with a long working-class tradition of combativity centred
around the freezing plants. As news of the occupation spread throughout the zone, factories began to stop spontaneously in solidarity with
the packing workers. Shops in the zone and neighbouring areas like
Villa Luro, Villa Lugano and Liniers also started to close in sympathy.
On Friday 16th, the 62 Organisations called for a 48-hour general solidarity strike.[22] In many areas of the country the working class had
already struck in a largely spontaneous fashion as nation-wide industry
was grinding to a halt.

When on the morning of Saturday 17th 1,500 armed police accompanied by tanks burst into the plant the response throughout the
country was immediate. The growing strike wave escalated into a total
national stoppage. The non-Peronist groupings, the 32 Democratic
unions and the communists, were swept along by their rank and file and
gave their blessing to a solidarity strike. The coordinating committee of
the 62 Organisations was also taken by surprise by the speed of events.
In what was a dramatic improvisation they changed the planned 48-
hour strike into one of unlimited duration. It would seem to have been
an attempt on the part of the Peronist leadership to regain control of a
mobilisation which had clearly surprised and outpaced them. It certainly bore all the hallmarks of a spur-of-the-moment decision since no
precautions were taken against the repression that was bound to follow.
Effectively within twelve hours the strike was leaderless at a national
level. Many union centrals were occupied by the police. Leaders like
Vandor of the metal workers, Mena and Aosta of textiles, Eleuterio
Cardoso of the meatpackers and Alonso of the garment workers had
been arrested. Others like Framini and Sebastian Borro were in hiding.

By Tuesday 20th, those members of the 62 Organisations who were
still at liberty decreed the lifting of the strike. The decision caused con-

siderable internal debate. Representatives of smaller unions – glass workers, naval construction, rubber workers – called for the continuation of the strike.[23] Those from the larger unions like textiles and metal working, demoralised and disoriented by their leaders' imprisonment, were in favour of lifting the strike. No attempt was made by the 62 leadership to make the lifting of the strike conditional on the release of union prisoners and a promise of no victimisation. Having spent the previous nine months acting and being treated like 'responsible' union leaders they now seemed totally unprepared for the severity of the repression. Four days before they had visited the presidential residence in Olivos to discuss the issue with Frondizi, now they were being hunted and arrested.

In the rank and file of the unions the strike was not so easy to end. The response of workers in working-class centres like Berisso, Ensenada and Dock Sud, for example, was such that the military had to occupy these areas.[24] In the Federal Capital itself an enormous area of the city lying between Avenidas Olivera and General Paz and taking in the *barrios* of Mataderos, Villa Lugano, Bajo Flores, Villa Luro and part of Floresta was occupied by the workers for five consecutive days. One account of this occupation spoke of what took place in the zone:

> The public lighting of the area was totally out, trees were cut down to block the streets, and taking advantage of the cobblestones in the streets barricades were erected on all the access roads. In this way under cover of darkness combat groups moved around relatively easily at night time and impeded the movement of the police and army in their attempts to enter the zone.[25]

In Avellaneda the strike was run by a committee of local unions; preparations had been made here to counter the government's response and act in clandestinity. Some public transport began to appear in Avellaneda for the first time on Monday 19th, after the national transport union had called for a return to work. The local strike committee ordered the cessation of all such services. To enforce this, groups were sent out armed with molotoffs and a number of trams were set on fire. The strike lasted another two days in Avellaneda though in some factories in the zone it lasted even longer.[26] In Rosario, too, the strike lasted a further three days after it had officially been lifted by the 62 Organisations at the national level.[27]

The Lisandro de la Torre strike was to become a potent symbol for the Peronist movement. While it was fundamentally a defensive action and at no time presented a coherent political plan to overthrow Frondizi, it was nevertheless testimony to the extraordinary combativity of the Peronist rank and file and the range of spontaneous initiatives of which it was capable. It was also testimony to the depth of the impact of the experience of the Resistance period and the relatively superficial impact of Frondizi's integrationist blandishments in the pre-1959 period. It was also a clear demonstration of the depth of the working class's nationalism and the way in which this fundamental underpinning of Peronist ideology could be appropriated by the working class, not as the basis of class collaboration but rather as a rationale for class conflict.

In the short term the severity of the government's reaction to the occupation and strike was a stark indication of how far it was prepared to go to push through its economic programme. It marked the end of any immediate possibility of implementing an integrationist development plan based on the idea that a 'multi-class' national alliance – with a strong union organisation within it – could form the stable social and political basis for developmentalist economic plans. The section of the government most closely committed to these notions – principally centred around Frigerio – was highly critical of the government's handling of the episode. In May Frigerio was forced to resign as personal adviser to the president; in June the *frigerista* Minister of Labour, David Blejer, also resigned. In June, too, Alvaro Alsogaray, one-time Minister of Economic Affairs under Aramburu, was reappointed to the post. In August General Toranzo Montero, a notorious anti-Peronist, was named commander in chief of the army. These moves reflected a realisation by Frondizi of the hardline approach that he would have to follow to implement his economic plans. They also reflected the growing suspicion of the majority of the armed forces of Frondizi and his *desarrollista* advisers. Alsogaray's appointment had been preceded by a direct military demand of Frondizi that he adopt such a policy. This *plantamiento* had also led to the resignation of the subsecretary to the Minister of War, Colonel Raimundez, known for his contacts with the Peronist union leadership.

The working class was not, however, cowed by these developments. In the course of 1959 there were three more conflicts of unprecedented scope aimed at protecting living standards. From the end of April through to the end of June there was a national strike of bank workers. At the end of August the metal workers embarked on a national strike for a new wage agreement. This lasted until mid October. On 23 September the textile workers' union declared a general strike of indefinite duration over the same issue which lasted until 9 November. In addition to these major conflicts there were numerous smaller-scale strikes.

Within the 62 Organisations the militancy of the rank and file was reflected in the make up of the new coordinating committee elected in late January, immediately following the general strike. The committee was made up largely of delegates from the interior and from smaller unions who had opposed the lifting of the strike. The make up of the committee was partly due to the fact that most of the larger unions had been intervened during the strike. More importantly though it reflected the resentment at their handling of the strike and the feeling that the old committee had been too closely compromised with the Frondizi government prior to January.[28] This rank-and-file criticism continued inside the unions. In early February a meeting of delegates from twenty-four sections of the metal workers' union, convened in Rosario, strongly criticised the national secretariat for its actions during the strike.[29] The Federation of Health Service workers, whose leader Amado Olmos had been a member of the previous coordinating committee, withdrew from the 62 Organisations temporarily because of the severity of the criticisms thrown at the leadership during an assembly called to discuss the strike. The rank and file at the meeting accused their leaders of tacitly accepting the stabilisation plan.[30] Even the new leadership of the 62 was not immune from rank-and-file attack. At a meeting of the 62 called in early March the coordinating committee was 'bombarded from the floor with shouts of "traitor", "sell outs"'.[31]

The militancy and sense of confrontation present in a year which saw four national conflicts of such scope, and three general solidarity strikes, culminated at the plenary meeting of the 62 Organisations held in Rosario in December 1959. The policy document presented by the coordinating committee emphatically rejected Frondizi's economic policy:

With our industry unprotected we are once more going to be turned into exporters of raw materials and importers of manufactured goods ... we resolve to energetically oppose this economic policy which represents a retreat in our nation's advance ... they are trying to take us back to a nation exporting raw materials and importing manufactures which until 1944 placed us in the position of a colony. We reject the economic system supported by the IMF ... since it signifies quite plainly the exploitation of man by man.[32]

The document, which was unanimously and enthusiastically acclaimed by the meeting, clearly reflected the feelings of the majority of Peronist union militants and a good part of the rank and file. It spoke to a continuing nationalist, anti-imperialist strain within Peronist ideology. More importantly it also expressed an explicit assumption that any development not based on class consensus and a non-exploitative, humanised capital implied a regression, an attempt to return to the pre-1944 domination of the landed interests. This notion of the inextricable connection between social justice and economic development was, as we have argued, crucial to Peronist discourse in the 1940s and continued to shape the working class's vision of Frondizi's 'betrayal' and their belief in the possibility of a 'genuine' national development. The document spoke of how 'the government vilely swindled the people in the application of the promised national, popular programme'.[33]

While the developmentalist propagandists argued that it was absurd to speak of a return to the pre-1943 economic and social regime and that such talk showed a misunderstanding of the economic changes taking place under Frondizi, the Peronist militants and rank and file were marching to a different, less abstract, logic. The deliberations at the Rosario meeting were imbued with a sense of bitterness and betrayal which was deeply and genuinely felt, as the resolutions adopted at the end of the meeting indicated. The final two called for a union-organised campaign to blank vote in all future elections in order to reject a fraudulent and illegitimate government. The working class was declared to be in a 'state of civil resistance confronting the powers of the state wherever its jurisdiction might be'.

The conflicts of 1959 were, in many ways, the culmination of the militancy and self-reliance the Peronist rank and file had acquired in the years of the Resistance. The Rosario meeting marked an important step in confirming the maturity of the union movement, and its domination within Peronism as the organiser of opposition to Frondizi. Yet for all the militant bravado of that meeting 1959 also came to symbolise a series of crucial defeats for the working class. In March when the Lisandro de la Torre plant reopened only some 4,500 out of a total workforce of 9,000 were taken back. The plant remained in private hands.[34] The bank workers after seventy days of demoralising strike were finally driven back to work under similar conditions. Both metal workers and textile workers also lost their battle for a comprehensive revision of their contracts. The failure of the two strongest unions to effectively win new contracts inevitably tended to dissuade other, weaker sections from trying. The majority of the contracts signed were inadequate emergency increases rather than genuine renegotiations.

The unions, both Peronist and non-Peronist, found themselves in a highly disadvantageous position when faced with a government backed by the armed forces which was prepared to use the power of the state to hold to its economic policy. In the course of 1959 many of the key unions were intervened by the government. Moreover, with the sharp recession provoked by the stabilisation plan their bargaining position was greatly weakened. The unions were quite clear as to the desperate nature of their plight and had few illusions about a victorious outcome. The official organ of the textile workers' union argued in the middle of the textile strike that: 'We are not simply struggling for an increase in salaries ... we are struggling for the very survival of the textile union, because this time the intransigence of the boss does not simply boil down to a refusal to recognise our just demands but is now an attack on the whole existence of the union.'[35]

Management intransigence was backed up by the government itself. The *desarrollista* press criticised the government's refusal to force management to make serious efforts to settle in these disputes. The labour correspondent of *Mayoría* complained of the treatment of the union side in the textile and metal workers' conflict:

Before the unions, back against the wall, declare the strike the employers refuse even to talk about possible counter offers, sticking instead to their first offers which were unacceptable. And when the strike starts they then say 'we will not negotiate while the union takes measures of force'. Can this be a serious way of conducting labour relations? ... To add to this the strikes usually have begun after several months of useless effort in which the unions have been sent from one office to another in various ministries achieving nothing.[36]

This is not to deny the enthusiasm with which the working class participated in these conflicts; the textile strike was launched by a meeting of over 20,000 workers unanimously demanding the *huelga indefinida*. Yet, the result of this massive mobilisation was to mark a crucial turning of the tide as far as working-class mobilisation and confidence were concerned.

The impact of defeat: demoralisation and isolation

The impact of defeat can be measured in part in the strike statistics for the following years. From the peak of over ten million days lost in 1959 the figures declined to just over one and a half million in 1960 and 1961, finally plummeting to 268,000 days lost in 1962.[37] In less easily quantifiable terms these figures reflect a process of defeat and demoralisation – the abandonment of active militancy and participation by thousands of lower- and middle-ranking activists who had been the core of the post-1955 resistance and renaissance of Peronist unionism.

In part this was the result of state and managerial repression. Thousands of Peronist militants were arrested by the state security provisions brought in by the Frondizi government. The *Plan Conintes (Conmoción Interna del Estado)* was implemented in March 1960, giving the army full jurisdiction in the battle against all forces creating 'internal disturbances'. The blacklist was rampant in industry. Sebastian Borro was never again to work in the meatpacking industry; his case was symbolic of many thousands of other militants. In an extraordinary speech made by the subsecretary for labour and social security, Dr Galileo Puente, in May 1960, we can gain some idea of the extent of this purging of activists. He boasted of how 'we have eliminated the troublemakers from the unions'. The doctor described how this was done in the case of an important textile company, Piccardo:

The personnel manager came to see me complaining of the thousands of problems caused by the internal commission ... According to my instructions the delegates were thrown out of the plant. They came to the Ministry and I threw them out of there too. Because we are not here to protect idlers like them. Very soon the good workers were banging at the factory gates. The management then began to select, 'this one can start, this one can't'; and so of 800 workers 500 were taken back and three hundred troublemakers were left outside.[38]

Puente went on to boast of how 'in Ducilo, Alpargatas and Good Year the personnel have been purified of the troublemakers and everyone lives happily'. If this was the concrete result of defeat in the textile strike, an identical process can be seen in metal working. Raimundo Villaflor, who had been a member of the delegate committee which had run the metal workers' strike in Avellaneda in 1956, has described the situation that he and many other militants found themselves in: 'I spent year after year moving about from one job to another. It was a never ending series of moves for many of us. They wouldn't give us work, they persecuted us.'[39]

The blacklist was, however, only part of the story. The dropping out from active militancy also reflected a gradual, if reluctant, acceptance by many of the middle-ranking activists of the fruitlessness of continued intransigent opposition to both government and employer. After the prolonged militancy of the 1956–9 period the defeats of 1959, coupled with the repression and economic crisis of the following years, did much to undermine the confidence and morale of a crucial stratum of activists. The tiredness and demoralisation of these activists was clearly seen at the plenary meeting of the 62 Organisations held in the Federal Capital in May 1960. In a speech given on behalf of the 62 leadership Eleuterio Cardoso, the leader of the meat workers' national federation, outlined the situation facing the Peronist unions. He emphasised that there were only two courses open to the working class, one revolutionary and the other evolutionary. Faced with this choice the working class had to opt for the only feasible strategy – the legal, evolutionary one. Cardoso pulled no punches in either his description of the bleak scenario facing the unions or in his advocacy of the necessary solution:

The present panorama is characterised by a retreat of the masses, the majority of the working class is proscribed, the working-class movement divided and with a hostile government. Faced with this situation an economic development is necessary which will break the old structures, without this there can be no social justice. It is necessary to form a national front in which the different 'factors of power' and the working class are united such as occurred in the decade from 1945 to 1955. The working class is not the only factor of power. Whether we like it or not the church, the army and the entrepreneurial forces are also such factors. We must talk to all these groups, and for this the leadership of the movement must have a vital flexibility.[40]

The speech provoked virtually no opposition in the meeting. Pedro Gomis, the petrol workers' leader, spoke in its support. A more drastic change from the Rosario meeting and its declaration of the 'civil resistance' could scarcely be imagined. The pro-Frondizi press greeted the meeting with great enthusiasm.

The only opposition to the speech voiced in the meeting came from two, relatively minor, delegates. One of them, Alberto Belloni, a delegate from the Asociación de Trabajadores del Estado, was quite clear as to what the lack of opposition from the other delegates implied:

Cardoso spoke for over two hours ... and for me it was the end of the Resistance. 'We have to reconstruct,' he said, 'the "national front" with employers, the armed forces and the church' ... and in the meeting there was an amazing silence, the only ones to get up and oppose this were myself and a Republican Spaniard from the print workers ... A plenary meeting of more than 200 delegates and there was a mortal silence and a tremendous hostility to me and the Spaniard. My comrade, Américo Quijena, a man formed in the hardest school of the Resistance, remained seated at my side throughout and never said a word. And Vandor who was in the chair interrupted my speech two or three times.[41]

The silence of the mass of delegates, who twelve months earlier at similar meetings had castigated the 62 leadership for what they regarded as the betrayal of the strike in solidarity with the meat workers, was testimony to the growing sense of confusion and erosion of confidence.

The human core of the Resistance was thus withering away; the human basis for the militancy and combativity of the 1956–9 period was being eroded. This was not only manifest in such public expression as meetings of the 62 Organisations. It was also, and perhaps most fundamentally, evident at a personal, private level. Jorge Di Pascuale, a militant leader of the 62 Organisations, recalled how:

the hard struggle was wearing out many people ... the repression was ever more intense, the *Plan Conintes* was introduced and conditions got ever more difficult. There were many comrades who didn't want to continue along the path of confrontation and gradually we were losing them ... the majority began to separate themselves from combative positions and dedicate themselves exclusively to their own affairs.[42]

The frenetic pace of the previous years' militancy, the intensity of activity and the abandonment of a normal private and social life that this entailed now began to have a telling impact on many activists. A perhaps extreme, though by no means atypical, testimony to this process comes from an activist who recalled many years later his own coming to awareness of the personal price that activism involved:

My brother and I entered the Resistance when we were really just kids. I suppose I was eighteen years old when Perón fell, my brother was a little younger. We devoted most of the following years to union activism – because we were both pretty good with words we got the job of writing most of the leaflets, all that sort of thing. Well really we missed out on many of the things kids of that age normally do. The struggle was everything – the social revolution, the return of Perón. One day, it must have been in about 1959, my brother and I were working in our room – it was a Sunday – writing a leaflet. We lived in a cheap pension which was full of younger workers who had no family in town. We shared a room with another fellow who worked in the same plant as us – in fact he was quite a militant himself. He came in from a party and found us banging away at the typewriter discussing politics. He was amazed and said, 'But aren't you two ever going to get to see the face of God?' He was right of course and it suddenly hit me all the things we had missed out on.[43]

It was not only the activists who were affected by this process, it was also present in a growing fatalism among the rank and file of the unions. The defeats of 1959, added to the effects of the government's economic policy, inevitably took their toll here too. At a meeting called by the meatpackers' union in Berisso to discuss how to fight lay offs Eleuterio Cardoso announced that it was 'the hour of the bosses' and that one had to be realistic and make unpleasant compromises. Cardoso was speaking not simply as the archetypical union leader making excuses for a bad deal but was also touching on a vein of shared experience in the entire working-class movement. A delegate from the Armour plant in Berisso echoed Cardoso's argument at the same meeting: 'A general strike is impossible because of the number of dismissals and the general recession provoked by the government's policies; a strike is exactly what

Table 1. *Voting figures for eleven major metal-working plants in the Federal Capital in the 1961 UOM elections*

	No. of workers	Absten-tions	L.Azul	L.Rosa	L.Verde
FAPESA	1,800	929	662	107	102
CAMEA	1,200	574	378	46	202
Centenera	1,200	762	315	94	102
TAMET	1,000	530	355	283	32
CAIGE	800	520	144	56	80
FERRINI	700	545	83	30	42
RCA Victor	500	339	52	16	93
Decker	500	233	136	51	80
Volcan	500	189	202	51	58
Lutz Ferando	500	438	16	2	44
SIAM Perdriel	300	223	14	26	37
Totals	9,000	5,282	2,342	762	612

Source: Leaflet issued by the Lista Verde opposition group.

the bosses are looking for so they don't have to pay wages.'[44] Both he and Cardoso were speaking with the resignation of men active in a union where there were over seven thousand lay offs at this time. The meatpacking industry had been exceptionally hard hit – suffering not only from the recession provoked by the stabilisation plan but also from a long-term structural crisis which was to see the end of the large foreign-owned freezer plants. But their experience was by no means atypical; in the absence of counter-examples of victorious, militant methods the rationale of institutional pragmatism, which was increasingly used by the union leaders, was bound to win at least a passive acceptance by the rank and file in most unions.

A clear example of this, albeit reluctant, acceptance in other unions can be found in the internal elections in the metal workers' union in February 1961. In the Federal Capital out of some 97,000 officially listed members only some 17,085 bothered to vote, a drop of some 8,000 from 1958. The Lista Azul, the Peronist grouping built around Augusto Vandor and Avelino Fernandez during the Resistance, lost over half of its votes. In 1958 it had claimed nearly all of the 25,000 votes cast; now it could manage only some 11,053.[45] If we look at the voting figures in table 1 for the eleven major plants in the Federal Capital this can be seen in an even starker light.

The figures show that 58% of the workers abstained from voting in these plants; yet all these factories had voted overwhelmingly for Vandor in the 1958 elections. In this election in only one of the eleven plants did the Lista Azul's vote exceed the number of workers abstaining. In the case of the metal workers defeats and compromises led to abstention rather than voting for rival, anti-leadership candidates. This was not always the case. Defeat and compromise could lead to more positive forms of reaction against existing leadership. Even in the metal workers, for example, in the Avellaneda section the combined vote of three opposition lists far exceeded that of the 'vandorist' leadership. In the textile union some of the major plants were lost by the leadership of Andrés Framini. In the elections for the internal commission in the Grafa plant in September 1960 the communist list was victorious, beating a dissident Peronist list which had itself broken from Framini.[46] In La Bernalesa and Sudamtex, two of the largest plants in Greater Buenos Aires, dissident Peronist lists also won over Framini's candidates.[47] Yet in general abstention rather than more constructive expressions of dissatisfaction was the norm in other unions.

The growing resignation and passivity on the part of the rank and file inevitably had a debilitating effect on the activists who tried to stem the tide of the retreat. It was not uncommon for local leaderships and middle-ranking activists to be radicalised under the pressure of management attack and economic crisis; but this radicalisation had less and less rank-and-file basis. A militant in Avellaneda, active in these years, recalled an example of this phenomenon:

I remember that José Vázquez became the leader of the Frigorífico La Negra. He was a *muchacho* who had made his name after 1955 and had a good following in Avellaneda, and was on the 62 and the local CGT. When the crisis hit the freezing plants in 1960 and they started laying off people he gave a very militant lead and called the plant out on strike. But the heart of the bases was not really in it. They felt that the *frigorífico* was doomed and they soon started to look for other work. At one stage toward the end it got so bad that Vázquez himself had to do practically everything, he couldn't even find workers to give out strike leaflets so he and a few friends had to borrow a car and go around distributing them.[48]

The growing isolation of the activists became more and more apparent as the base support for the militancy of the Resistance gradually withered. Those activists who did draw radical lessons were increasingly separated from the experience of the mass of their followers:

Those leaders who called for increasing confrontation for more strikes were increasingly regarded by their bases as some kind of supermen. You just couldn't expect to go to these men who had already been on strike, who could expect no strike pay and who knew how little work there was around and expect them to join you again on the streets.[49]

The discrepancy between the experience, commitment and life style of activists and rank and file in unions is a constant feature which underlies much of the ambivalence and dilemma of a militant's life. Part of the working class, dependent on it for many of his actions, he is nevertheless in an important sense set apart from it. In times of general upsurge and confidence the gap can be minimised as leaders and led converge; in times of defeat and crisis, however, the gap can lead to a profound isolation and alienation of the militants from the mass of the rank and file. Raimundo Villaflor and his comrades in Avellaneda tried to rescue something from the débâcle of the early 1960s. The guiding force of their group was a militant who was well known in the working-class zones of the southern part of Greater Buenos Aires, Domingo Blajaquis. Blajaquis had been in 'virtually every prison in the country' since 1955.[50] Rolando Villaflor, Raimundo's brother, was not part of their group and they, half-jokingly called him 'the beast' for his unsophisticated opinions and lack of commitment to a militant life. Many times he would return home to find them meeting, talking politics. He recalled years later for Rodolfo Walsh one such occasion when he replied to their jokes:

But tell me something Greek [Blajaquis], I said, how old are you? He told me 40 odd. And tell me, what have you done with your life up to now? Because I don't see that you've done very much. You've always been in prison ... And when he said to me that he didn't have anything I said, Of course, what would you have if you've always been in prison, soaking up a beating, half dead of hunger, and you a mature man and you've got no family, you don't have anything.[51]

Blajaquis, Raimundo Villaflor and other militants could retreat into the circumscribed activity of small groups of activists. These militants might also, in the short term, through their own personal prestige become a dominant voice at the level of the local union movement – in, for example, the local 62 Organisations – but this position had less and less basis in the working class in terms of its consciousness and willingness to be mobilised.

The changing relationship between leaders, activists and rank and file

Within the unions the growth of resignation and passivity formed the backdrop to a process of bureaucratisation which was manifested in a changing relationship between leader and rank and file and a changing attitude of union leaders and an increase in personal corruption. The rank-and-file activist and middle-ranking local militants found their unions to be increasingly inhospitable places. Raimundo Villaflor recalled this happening in the metal workers' union:

None of us who had led the strike in Avellaneda could return to the union. It was gradually converted into a sort of mafia. Even the independent numbers game operators disappeared and everyone had to bank with the union leadership. The leaders also began to deal in scrap metal with the bosses. They amassed fortunes, and surrounded themselves with paid bodyguards.[52]

By 1960 this change was reflected in a clear erosion of internal democracy. This was particularly noticeable in the growing use of fraud in union elections. The opposition lists in the 1961 election in the metal workers' union, the UOM, issued a leaflet after that election detailing the fraudulent practices used by the UOM leadership:

With only 48 hours to go to the elections the places where the voting boxes were to be placed were unknown, as was the day on which they would be placed in the workplaces; something which the official candidates were not ignorant of, given that the election committees were not composed of people from rival lists but only of those from the official list ... the electoral list of the Federal Capital branch, a section with realistically some 65,000 members showed 95,000 eligible to vote ... no list that did not possess the money of the official organisation, like Vandor's did, could hope to have so many activists available for electioneering with expenses paid ... The junta electoral prevented the election monitors of the non-official lists from checking the details of the factory at which a voter worked, nor would they allow them to inspect in detail the membership cards.[53]

These manoeuvres were in contrast to the elections of 1958. In that election no attempt had been made to impugn the credentials of opposition candidates. In 1961 several of the leading activists of the Lista Verde, the main opposition grouping, had their candidacies ruled illegal by the officially controlled electoral junta.

There were many other similar cases in other unions. This was part of the tightening control of the leaderships over the rank and file, and their diminishing toleration of focal points for the expression of internal dissent. This was most clearly evident in the growing control by the national leaderships over the local plant leaders. This control often went hand in hand at this time with the purging of rank-and-file activists. In the big factories of the metal-working industry, for example, a steady process of selective purging of known militants was taking place. The most militant were fired, many of the internal commissions in the big factories were dissolved. In the textile union the opposition groups were claiming in April 1961 that over half of the factories in the suburb of San Martín, in Greater Buenos Aires, the largest concentration of textile plants in the country, had been intervened by the central leadership and the plant commissions suspended for 'oppositional activity'.[54] Later in the year the Framini leadership began to invent general secretaries in many of these factories.[55] With the demoralisation and isolation of many of the activists this process of asserting central union control did not necessarily involve overt coercion. Many of the internal delegates, exhausted by the uphill struggle, were willing to be bought off, to accept the inevitable.

Many of the leaders who were behind this process had themselves recently emerged from the factory floor during the struggle against the military government. They were not separated from the rank-and-file activists by years of enjoyment of bureaucratic privileges. It was only five years since Augusto Vandor had left the shop floor at Philips and his subsequent role in the Resistance had given him considerable personal prestige with his members. At this time, too, Andrés Framini was considered to be a hardliner calling for the most intransigent opposition to Frondizi. Lifestyle and personal habits were changing, but the hard struggles and bitter conflicts of the past were too near, too shared an experience, for personal corruption to be a complete explanation of the bureaucratisation process.

A large part of the explanation needs to be sought in the attitudes of the activists themselves. The fact that they shared the common experience of resistance to the military government, and of the struggles against Frondizi, created a symbiotic relationship between the national leaders and themselves. In a certain sense they recognised in their leaders men such as themselves, usually with the same backgrounds, aspirations and fallibilities. Indeed on a local level many of the activists of the 1955–9 period now themselves became part of local union hierarchies. Their common allegiance to Perón and the Peronist movement acted as a further binding in this relationship. Moreover, despite the fact that the resistance to both the military and Frondizi had been based primarily on rank-and-file activists and the internal commissions, there had never been an explicit articulation of the importance of this, of the need to have democratically controlled unions. In the enforced absence of a bureaucratic structure available to be used, Peronist trade union practice had, as we have noted, become more democratic. There had been, in a practical sense, very little ground on which the separation between rank and file and leadership could have been based. The end result of this democratically-based struggle had been defined as the recuperation of the unions for Peronism through free elections. Little was said of how these unions were to be run after the Peronists had regained them and the opportunities for manipulation of a bureaucratic apparatus had reappeared. There was very little thought of how to guarantee the continuation of the *de facto* democratic practice which had flourished after 1955.

The change in democratic practice within the unions should not be exaggerated. Peronist trade union practice was by no means uniformly democratic prior to 1960 in the same way that the changing nature of internal government at this time was not uniform either. The relationship between rank and file and leader remained far more open and democratic in some unions than in others. Nevertheless, some such change did take place and was clearly perceived by the militants. Alberto Belloni, for example, stresses both the original democratic practice and its subsequent perversion:

When we began as union militants we didn't even know what a motion for order in a meeting was; we would ask ourselves, 'What is this order motion thing? This motion to close the debate?' But we had a great democratic feeling ... we had assemblies two or three times a month in Rosario; we filled the local, no meeting had less than 500 attending, sometimes we had 1,500 out of a union branch of 3,500 members. I used to say '*Compañeros*, this is the order of the day; if you want to add something do so. Let us elect a secretary for the minutes and a President for the meeting.' I would always refuse to be elected. The President had to come from the floor of the meeting. And this used to happen in other unions too ... But gradually this began to change – *caudillismo* and personalism began again. The secretary general was the *caudillo*, the *capo*, the big *macho*. But originally, starting from a total ignorance of bureaucratic procedures we arrived at an ultra-democratic practice.[56]

Most probably the case of Belloni's union in Rosario was extreme and represented the far end of a spectrum of democratic practice. It seems unlikely that a majority of other Peronist unions shared the same naiveté with respect to formal bureaucratic procedures. Most were probably situated closer to the middle of the spectrum. But Belloni's case is significant and worthy of attention. Not being a Peronist he had a particular sensitivity to changing attitudes with the unions, to changing margins of tolerance within a union's internal government. The very fact that he, a non-Peronist, was a leading figure in a Peronist union grouping was itself testimony to a relative openness within Peronist unionism in the immediate post-1955 period. However, he recalls the results of his open opposition to Cardoso in the May 1960 meeting of the 62 Organisations:

The national committee of the 62 pressured my union to withdraw my credentials as their representative on the 62. An agreement was made that I shouldn't go to the plenary meetings. They began to close the doors to me, a non-Peronist, and I began to lose ground within the union. When the Resistance exhausted itself there was a frustration, a tiredness in the bases, they went less and less frequently to the meetings.[57]

Nor was this change in attitude only noticeable at the national level. While Belloni notes that the fact that he was not formally a Peronist had not been held against him before, his isolation at a national level now had an effect on his Peronist comrades in Rosario. All militants who had emerged during the Resistance, all sharing the same original *orfandad burocrática*, they too 'now began to isolate me, to treat me with suspicion. These comrades were for me becoming bureaucrats, too, in a small way.'[58]

Personal corruption also formed part of this process. A common charge levied against individual union leaders at this time was that of having been suborned by Frondizi. The accuracy of such charges is impossible to ascertain. It seems probable, however, that corruption tended to be indirect in character. It was widely rumoured, for example, that the moderate attitude of the national meat workers' federation during the Lisandro de la Torre occupation and strike was largely due to the fact that under the new *ley de carnes* the federation was to be granted funds for its social services in ratio to the amount of meat exported. The federation received some eleven million pesos from this arrangement in 1959.[59] This sort of subornation – of the spirit rather than of the individual pocket – was common not only among national leaders but also among middle-ranking activists.

The opportunities for enrichment, or for simply a far more comfortable life within the union system increased greatly at this time and inevitably attracted even those militants who had most selflessly immersed themselves in union activity. The rewards for compromising, for accepting a quiet life were considerable. Belloni recalls that in 1960 the salary paid to workers' representatives in the pension fund institutes was 35,000 pesos. John William Cooke writing to Perón shortly after the January 1959 strike accurately foresaw what was to be the dual attraction of Frondizi's strategy toward the Peronist unions. He told Perón that 'from now on there will be more repression, more prison and more truncheons. But there will also be much more money *and* many more facilities for those who want to come to some arrangement with the government. In every sphere the aim will be to try and weaken Peronism by means of a practical integration.'[60] It was on the basis of this sort of 'corruption' that many activists took up positions within local union hierarchies as local representatives of national leaderships.

The dilemma of the militants: the logic of institutional pragmatism

The basic issue underlying the process we have been analysing was the acceptance at the level of rank and file, activists and national leaderships of the logic of institutional pragmatism. The logic was inherent in trade union involvement in the day-to-day dealings of an industrial economy; the need to take advantage of the opportunities the system was prepared to offer. This, in turn, was based on a recognition that the situation facing the unions under Frondizi was different from that under Aramburu. While being very far from the harmonious utopia envisaged by developmentalist propaganda there had, nevertheless, been significant changes. The unions were, for example, faced with the reality of an increasingly complex industrial relations system. Law 14.455 of Professional Associations, while assuring the state a role in overseeing the unions, did also guarantee legally the existence of a centralised, industrial union system with enforceable bargaining rights and provide the financial basis, through dues collection, for the rebuilding of a powerful union apparatus such as had existed under Perón. Frondizi had also installed a system of compulsory conciliation and voluntary arbitration which, again, assured the state a role in industrial relations but also reinforced the functioning of the unions' bargaining rights with a new set of rights and obligations. The restoration of the union pension funds and union representation in their administration was another example of this growing complexity and intertwining of unions and government.

The implications of this more complex situation for the Peronist union leadership were clearly evidenced in what became known as the 'Cardoso Case'. After his speech at the May 1960 meeting of the 62 Organisations Eleuterio Cardoso, the leader of the national federation of meat workers, was faced with signs of displeasure on the part of Perón with the sentiments he had expressed. Sebastian Borro, on behalf of the leadership of the 62 Organisations, had gone to Madrid, Perón's new place of exile, and brought back a letter denouncing the concepts expounded by Cardoso and Pedro Gomiz. At the fifth national congress of the meat workers' federation several weeks later, Cardoso in his opening speech restated the legalist, evolutionary concepts he had argued for in May:

The executive committee has struggled for respect of the rights acquired by the workers ... we were careful that the state organisms recognised and acted on whatever violations of these rights took place. This attitude of basing ourselves on legal resorts did not always bear fruit but it did allow us to keep intact the union structures which were constantly threatened ... no social class has shown greater effort in the defence of constitutional legality than the working class, because the rule of law is for workers' organisations the same as oxygen in life ... as a citizen I am absolutely loyal to the Peronist movement and its leader ... as a workers' leader, however, I cannot lead my union by ways and tactics which experience has taught me are impractical and counterproductive.[61]

Cardoso offered his resignation which was rejected by the delegates. In his closing speech to the conference he attacked those who would 'undermine the morale of the masses, turning them against everything and everyone'. He again stressed the need to be realistic and adapt tactics to the realities of the situation. This reality included, above all, a legal system which gave workers and unions rights which they must use and defend. Several weeks after the conference Cardoso was expelled from the Peronist movement and from the 62 Organisations for disloyalty to Perón and the movement.

Now, what is noteworthy about the sentiments expressed by Cardoso is their absolute reasonableness; they represent, as it were, typical, common sense statements from a union leader. Cardoso's reiterated emphasis on the need to be evolutionists, to work within the system was, in practice, a view which had to be shared by other Peronist union leaders. They could not afford, for example, to be unconcerned about the fate of Frondizi's government when it was confronted with military threats. However illegitimate they might consider his government, the fact remained that ultimately Frondizi's legality was a legality which included the Law of Professional Associations. Union leaders had to take into account the possible repercussions of their mobilisations on military unease. Between January 1959 and April 1961 there were seven major military 'incidents' involving challenges to Frondizi, all of which involved military dissatisfaction with law 14.455.

In a similar fashion, however much they might dislike Frondizi they could in practice see no viable strategy to replace him. The logic of being trade union leaders inevitably involved them in bargaining, compromising, taking advantage of and insisting on the rights granted them by the system. This was clearly shown in the negotiations concerning the handing back of the CGT to the unions. Cardoso and others had argued that the handing back of the CGT was a number one priority for Peronist unions, and that a moderate stance should be taken to induce Frondizi to proceed with the promised return. This position was rejected by the 62 Organisations in 1959 and 1960. To accept the return of the CGT on Frondizi's terms would, it was argued, merely involve the unions increasingly in compromise and negotiations and give credibility to an illegitimate government. When, however, in late 1960 Frondizi called for discussions to set up a joint committee of Peronist and non-Peronist unionists to arrange for a CGT congress it proved impossible, in practice, for any Peronist union leader to ignore the call. A regained CGT would be an obvious step forward in terms of organisation and working-class unity, even if it were also a step toward integrating Peronist unions in a status quo which excluded the direct return of Perón or Peronism to power.[62]

Yet, if the logic of integrationism was unanswerable, in practice it was, nevertheless, not readily accepted. This was primarily because of the very bitterness of the conflicts of 1959, the harshness of the defeats and the repression that followed. Frondizi's integrationist plans were implemented in the wake of a stabilisation plan which had drastically cut living standards and which had been backed up by managerial and state repression. Involvement in bargaining, compromising and defending what would ultimately be seen as stake in the system inevitably involved the shelving to some vague, long-term future the principal aspirations which had underlain the working class's struggle since 1955, above all the return of Perón. Indeed the openly stated aim of Frondizi's policy was precisely the divorce of Perón from the movement and in particular its union wing. The institutional interests of union leaders would prevail over the more general political interests of the Peronist movement. It was this conflict of interests that Cardoso had frankly expressed at the fifth congress of his union and which had also surfaced in the first months of Frondizi's government.

The resistance to the logic of integrationism turned to the one terrain where it felt confident – the morality and values which had formed part of the lived experience of the resistance to Aramburu and Frondizi and which were, as we have shown, a crucial ideological legacy of that experience. Cardoso's arguments were condemned because they were considered to be betrayals of the heroism and suffering of the whole working class, and of the activists in particular, as well as personal disloyalty to Perón. Integrationism's chief evil was seen to be the personal cowardice and betrayal it induced in certain leaders. At the May 1960 meeting of the 62 Organisations the coordinating committee had presented an information document analysing the general situation of the movement:

We have seen comrades who for hidden reasons or owing to a weakness of spirit have abandoned the struggle ... hiding themselves under the cover of their unions in simple administrative tasks which allow them to stay at the head of their unions without giving a real lead to workers. Not only is one a traitor when one commits an act of surrender to the enemy but also when for reasons of ambition and personal comfort one tries to defend a position of compromise without confessing the real truth which is cowardice in confronting the common enemy; the executive power.[63]

This document, written very much under the influence of the most militant sector of the Peronist union movement, pointed clearly to an important phenomenon – the demoralisation of a certain level of leaders and activists – but failed to situate the roots of this in the defeats of 1959 and the general problems facing the union movement. Instead it placed the onus firmly on personal moral qualities: 'When we see reactionary bosses united in a common campaign to destroy workers' organisations it is necessary to look within ourselves and understand that more than the advance of reaction what we are seeing is the retreat of the timid and the vacillating.' The nature of the intransigent line, what was to be called the *línea dura*, emerges clearly from this document. In particular what becomes clear is its fundamentally moral stance. Recognising a growing demoralisation and tendency to compromise, these militants saw the problem as essentially one of vices such as timidity, vacillation, cowardice and dishonesty. The solution they proposed was an emphasis on the, equally subjective, virtues of hardness, intransigence and loyalty; of keeping faith with 'those who had struggled' and suffered for it and keeping faith with Perón.

The potency of this stance should not be underestimated. It provided at the very least an emotionally satisfying standard of conduct in difficult times. The *línea dura* was formally in a majority within the 62 Organisations throughout the Frondizi government, led by Jorge Di Pascuale, Sebastian Borro, Juan Racchini and Juan Jonsch. A 'soft line' hardly existed in any real sense; few union leaders could bring themselves to publicly agree with Cardoso. But, ultimately, morality was not a sufficient shield, nor a feasible basis for a specific union strategy, though it could provide a meaningful basis for the actions of individual militants and workers. At one time the possibility had seemed to exist for the development of a radical ideology from within Peronism which might have adequately expressed in formal ideological terms the militancy and sense of class conflict which permeated this period. Certainly, the *potential* for this was present in the elements of a counter-discourse which emerged from the 1955–8 period. The general institutional conjuncture, the defeats and demobilisation of 1959 and after, all conspired against such a development. In the last resort the *línea dura* became a state of mind, an attitude, a 'structure of feeling' rather than an articulated, political, ideological position. For many militants this did not seem to be a disadvantage and, indeed, morality, hardness and 'keeping faith' gave a militant core of Peronist unionism the ability to survive the abandonment of hopes and the disillusionment of the following years. For others the growing power of the union hierarchy and the logic of compromise would lead them to either compromise with this hierarchy or to seek a coherent ideological and organisational alternative in the theories of *focismo* and guerrilla struggle.

6

The corollary of institutional pragmatism: activists, commandos and elections

All of us who were going to make the Peronist revolution at this time lacked a formal revolutionary politics; we, of course, had a profound Peronist fervour and an inborn feeling rather than conviction. We lacked a revolutionary formation. We did everything under the influence of something which came from our guts rather than from our heads.

Anonymous Peronist militant, 1973

Productivity, rationalisation and internal control under Frondizi

The modernisation of Argentine industry based on the creation of an adequate capital goods industry and the production of intermediate consumer goods proclaimed by developmentalist propaganda implied the effective introduction of rationalisation agreements which would enable the efficient use of much of the machinery being imported and the intensification of output from existing plant. This in turn was premised on the effective control of the power of the internal commissions. Galileo Puente, the subsecretary for labour, in his speech to the industrialists attending the seminar on industrial relations, had defined the problem in familiar terms: 'When I took over the problem of labour relations I found anarchy, abuses and outrages of all sorts from the workers. The employers had lost control of factories; the internal commission ran everything; those who should obey were in fact giving the orders ... the employers must therefore retake control of the factories.'[1] Puente was not shy in demonstrating the result of firm government and management policy in dealing with this problem. In one textile firm he had authorised the mass firing of delegates: 'After the firings production increased and today the factory is a paradise. A little while ago they inaugurated a new, modern line, the firm has now been reequipped.'[2] It was precisely in these areas of concern that major innovations were introduced in the contracts signed from 1960 on: the introduction of new clauses concerning rationalisation and incentives, the removal of many existing clauses 'hindering productivity' and the defining and limiting of the powers of the internal commissions. Indeed the long-drawn-out struggle for the new contracts in 1959 and 1960 was centred precisely on the determination by management to force through the acceptance of new stipulations in these areas. Only after the defeats of 1959 and 1960 were the employers prepared to consider the full renovation of the contracts.

The textile industry acted as the touchstone in this struggle. From the beginning of the negotiations for the new contract in July 1959 the employers had made their position clear. The principal employers' federation, the Federación de la Industria Textil Argentina (FITA), in its first reply to the union demand for a wage hike and a full updating of other clauses had stated that 'the furtherance of the discussions remains entirely dependent on the approval by the labour sector of clauses on the rationalisation of production'.[3] They stuck to this position throughout negotiations. The union complained in September that 'the position of the employers continues to be absolutely intransigent, since only if we accept rationalisation clauses will they consider a derisory increase'.[4]

After weeks of a demoralising strike, negotiations were renewed in November 1959, but again broken off over management refusal to modify its demands for the control of the functioning of the internal commissions. By the middle of January 1960 the union had been forced back to work. While a new contract had been signed with the smaller firms, the big plants which dominated the industry and which were grouped in FITA were still adamant. On 19 January in a last fling, the Asociación Obrera Textil ordered a go slow in the fifty-four biggest factories in the country. The employers' response was immediate. Alpargatas and Sudamtex, the pace-setters in the industry, with Puente's backing, carried out mass firings which included virtually all of the internal commissions in the plants. After seventy-two hours the union retreated and suspended the go-slow. In Alpargatas the workers, all of whom had by now been suspended, occupied the plant but were immediately ejected by the police. At the beginning of February both Alpargatas and Sudamtex began the selective rehiring of the workforce.[5] The back of the textile workers' resistance to rationalisation had been effectively broken.

While the union leadership still in theory denounced rationalisation schemes, in practice on the factory floor the battle had been lost and there was little chance of opposing them. As a textile militant explained:

It is true that the leadership and the national negotiating committee have repeatedly declared that they are not going to sign any contract on the basis of rationalisation. But in practice these good intentions remain simple declarations of intent since with the weakening of internal organisation the bosses apply their new systems when and where they like.[6]

Another militant explained that 'there are several ways for them to get what they want: either they pay off the delegates with a good indemnity or they simply close the factory as they did at Piccaluga and Marulana and when they reopen they start with the new work system'.[7]

What rationalisation effectively meant in the textile industry can be seen from the case of Alpargatas. Employing over 10,000 workers it was by far the biggest textile plant in the country and it dominated the working-class suburb of Barracas in the Federal Capital. What happened in Alpargatas was very much a testing ground for the rest of the textile industry. After the reopening of the plant in February 1960, time-and-motion studies were put into effect, 'the technicians of rationalisation', as the workers called them, began to appear on the factory floor. The rank-and-file newspaper, *El Alpargatero*, produced by militants in the plant, summarised the impact of the new management policy in the following months:

The bosses maintain that when a modification is made which diminishes the task of the worker it is necessary to increase his task load so as to maintain his rhythm of work at a constant level. This is what they are doing in Alpargatas in any section where they instal new machines. Let's give an example: in Section A5 where they perform the toeing and heeling operation on the sneakers. This year they have installed new machines which do not require the tremendous physical effort needed for the old ones ... the work is now much lighter but the bosses now demand that instead of 75, 91 or 98 dozen pairs which they made on the old machines they now have to complete 316 dozen as an average figure. There is, therefore, no alleviation of the physical stress but rather a greater exhaustion.[8]

Together with time-and-motion went other innovations. There was an attempt to improve personnel relations – copies of handbooks on the subject were given out to supervisors in the plant. These contained advice on the need to 'advise them before hand of the changes which will be introduced', and 'persuade them to accept the change'. Music was also now to be provided to improve the workplace ambience.[9] Not all of the increased production was due to rationalisation in the strict sense of the word. A considerable portion would seem to have resulted from greater output from existing machines, often with a reduced workforce.[10] In Alpargatas, for example, in the *cardas* section each worker had been in charge of twenty cards in 1948, thirty in 1958 and after January 1960 the number had increased to sixty. No new machinery had been introduced. In the *sisal* section time-and-motion studies had reached the conclusion that instead of fifteen workers on each turn only eleven were actually needed. Four workers were dropped from each shift. Again, no new machinery accompanied this change.[11]

Militants in the plant were not slow to point out the significance of such policies. Communist workers in the plant, for example, argued that: 'the increase in productivity is therefore the result of different factors: an increase in physical effort of the worker, rationalisation of the organisation of the workforce, transformation of the machinery, together with the start of "personal relations" schemes and the repression of the unions'.[12] Official recognition of this reality on a national level came in the contract eventually signed in early 1961. Article 3 of the new contract affirmed that: 'The norms contained in this article applicable to productivity plans with new work systems shall not be interpreted as hindering or limiting the employers in the exercise of their powers of leadership and organisation, which are entirely their own ... the employers will direct and organise the work in their establishments in the form which they consider best serves the necessary coordination of material elements and labour power with the goal of obtaining optimum levels of production.'[13] Alvaro Alsogaray, the Minister of Economy, congratulated the union on being 'so realistic and signing the contract'; the union itself claimed it had made the best of a bad situation. The opposition inside the union undoubtedly voiced the feelings of many textile workers: 'The contract authorises the changes of sections, the moving about of a worker from one job to another, the lowering of a worker's category and the increase of the machines tended by a worker without our getting a cent for this increase in production.'[14]

An identical process was also taking place at this time in the metal-working industry. The contract of 1959 had simply been an emergency increase. However, in this industry too, with the growing demoralisation and fatalism of the rank and file and militants faced with unemployment and the failure of mass actions there was a *de facto* introduction of rationalisation schemes. This was initially met by considerable opposition from the workers. Indeed, by early 1960 something approaching a mass abandonment of incentive schemes by the workforce had occurred in the industry. Workers rejected employers' attempts to unilaterally alter job rates and resolved instead to 'work normally'. The employers retaliated with mass dismissals and lockouts.

The union was in a bad position to bargain given the economic recession and by July 1960 they had signed a contract negotiated in a matter of days without a single strike.

The concessions contained in terms of rationalisation schemes were total, even exceeding those of the textile contract. Article 83 simply stated:

The systems of bonuses and other forms of incentive schemes do not constitute a proper matter for this contract ... the UOM and/or its delegates in the different establishments cannot oppose the revision of existing schemes when it becomes clear that failure to adapt wage systems, methods of work, the renovation of machinery will detract from the higher goal of giving incentives to optimum production.[15]

This clause represented what was a virtual *carte blanche* for management in the field of production relations; the union abdicated the right to help determine manning, speed, quality control or shift arrangements. Similar contracts were signed in virtually every industry in the following years.

The cumulative effect of these clauses was to considerably worsen working conditions in many industries. 'Hindrances to productivity' – one of the employers' chief complaints since the Perón era – were now removed on a wholesale basis. The most important gains for employers concerned labour mobility within the plants. Labour contracts had, since 1946/8, included fixed job classifications and wage rates appropriate to such job descriptions. Nearly all contracts also contained wage stability guarantees in case of changes in such classifications, and, in general, contained clauses limiting mobility within the production process. All this tended to dissuade employers from reducing manning levels – one of the principal aims of rationalisation. The job categories provided workers with the legal basis for costly demarcation disputes as they used the existing job descriptions to oppose new production arrangements. The new flexibility management enjoyed after 1960 with regard to mobility of labour within their plants enabled them to effectively by-pass existing job categories and in practice create new ones on a plant-by-plant basis without any formal nationally-negotiated modification of job descriptions.

Underlying the concern of Argentine employers and the state with increased rationalisation and the removal of 'hindrances to productivity' there had been, since the last years of Perón, a fundamental concern with power on the shop floor as embodied in the internal commissions. From José Gelbard to Galileo Puente the refrain had remained the same: shop-floor power had to be curbed if management was to be able to reassert its control over production. It was in the wake of the defeats of 1959 that formal limitations on, and control of, shop-floor organisation were accepted by the unions and built into the collective agreements. This was often a formality since internal commissions were already in considerable disarray owing to management and state repression and the growth of unemployment. The metal-working industry led the way in imposing restrictions on the commissions. In the course of the 1959 strike the employers' organisation, the Federación Argentina de la Industria Metalúrgica, made public a project for the regulation of the commissions. The nature and extent of management concern are clearly apparent in these proposals. The main proposals were that: a delegate should not present any proposals to management if he had not first gone to his superior and waited five days; a delegate should be at least twenty-five years old, with two years experience in the plant and four in the union, together with a good conduct record; delegates were not to be allowed to oppose the orders of management concerning the arrangement of production; shop-floor meetings were not to take place within working hours, and delegates were not to be allowed out of their section without written permission from the head of their section.[16]

The emergency contract which ended the 1959 strike did not deal with the issue of the internal commissions but the July 1960 contract contained most of management's original proposals. Article 82 of the contract detailed the proportion of delegates to workers in a plant, the requirements a delegate needed to meet in terms of age and experience, the procedure the internal commission had to use in dealing with employers, the specific areas of appropriate concern for a shop-floor delegate. Finally strict limits on a delegate's ability to move around the factory were introduced.[17] Similar restrictions were to be found in most of the contracts signed in other industries in the following years.

The results of this process were soon apparent in economic terms. Whether it was in clearing the ground for the introduction of new technology or in enabling the increased exploitation of existing plant through new manning schedules and work intensity, the new contracts signed after 1959 had a marked effect on industrial productivity.[18] There were, however, other, less obvious results which speak to the process of militant decline and the growth of union leadership power and autocracy. The clauses introduced in the contracts of 1960 and after gave employers, as we have seen, a free hand concerning production arrangements and work systems. In doing this a whole series of issues around which rank-and-file interest in union activity could have been built were, *de iure*, precluded from the internal commissions' area of legitimate concern. Shop-floor organisation, to be viable, needs to base itself on those areas of immediate concern to a worker on the shop floor. The strength of the commissions during the Resistance had been precisely based on their perception by the rank and file as the only viable means of defending shop floor-conditions. This whole area of activity was now undercut. Issues on which delegates and commissions had previously bargained, and in so doing gained strength, were now removed from the legitimate constituency of the commissions. We may take a typical example: grievance procedures. The textile contract of 1961 specifically removed the issue of workers' dissatisfaction with the new work arrangements based on time-and-motion studies from the hands of the internal commission. The resolution of such grievances was placed first in the hands of a special section of the national bargaining committee and beyond that in the hands of the Ministry of Labour. This greatly limited the scope for potential activity of the internal commissions.

The possibilities, therefore, for the internal commissions to play a dominant role in organising and expressing working-class aspirations within the factories were becoming by the early 1960s very bleak. This was compounded by the fact that the dominant form of rationalisation scheme introduced involved one form or other of payment by results. Payment-by-result piecework schemes have in some instances, as for example in British engineering after the Second World War, become the basis for a strong rank-and-file organisation. In Argentina, however, the potentially positive side of these schemes was effectively precluded since the very context within which they were to be implemented was now deemed management's sole concern. Indeed in most cases even the setting of bonus rates and other rates for the job were now considered to be management prerogatives. In the metal-working industry, for example, Article 83 which started by affirming that 'systems of bonuses or any other forms of incentives do not constitute a proper concern of this contract' was usually taken to give employers the right to unilaterally set the rate for the job. The use by shop-floor representatives of the rate for the job as a bargaining tool with management over changes in production schedules such as speed up, shift arrangements and labour mobility, and the building up of a strong rank-and-file organisation around such bargaining power, were simply not possible. This left only the deleterious, divisive effects of payment-by-result schemes. Thus, while the introduction of the new work systems and the control of the internal commissions was based on the concrete defeats of 1959 and 1960, and the consequent demoralisation and demobilisation of rank-and-file organisation, the very nature of the rationalisation clauses in turn served to perpetuate and reinforce this, to confirm the decline of militant shop-floor organisation and the growth of rank-and-file apathy.

The union leaderships clearly benefited from this process. In many ways the implementation of the productivity offensive most clearly symbolised the attraction of 'integrationism' for the Peronist union hierarchy. In return for the control of the internal commissions and the acceptance of rationalisation, concrete benefits were gained from the leaderships' point of view. Not least was the formal recognition of the function of 'responsible' unionism. This was symbolised in the high-powered negotiations which now took place in the offices of the Ministry of Labour when an important contract came up. The provisions of the contracts did, moreover, confirm this. For the first time since the early 1950s the union leadership could be seen to have achieved the proper renovation of clauses in the contracts. The clauses in the agreements concerning areas such as maternity benefits, the bonus for the birth of a child, time off for marriages, additional bonuses for years of service, all of which had been effectively frozen since the early 1950s, were now brought up to date. There was, therefore, a *quid pro quo* involved in the acceptance of rationalisation. The contracts gave a considerable boost to the weakened financial state of the unions. The textile union, for example, obtained a retention of 150 pesos from the salary of each textile worker under the provision of the 1961 contract.[19]

The bargaining and administrative functions of the unions were not, therefore, weakened by the acceptance of rationalisation. The productivity offensive was aimed fundamentally at shop-floor power, not at the unions *per se*. Indeed the union leadership itself had a growing interest, as we have shown, in controlling this power. The imposition of managerial control and the weakening of delegate power also implied a greater facility for the union hierarchy in the control of its own membership. In fact, by writing the control of the internal commissions into the contracts the employers had succeeded in identifying their concern in the matter with that of the union leaders. The onus for the policing of the commissions was placed firmly on the shoulders of the union leadership as the executors of the responsibilities assumed by the union side in the contracts. To maintain their good faith with the employers, and their credibility as 'responsible' negotiators, they had to be seen to enforce the clauses of the agreement.

While the productivity offensive was premised on the control and elimination of autonomous rank-and-file action there was an intrinsic ambiguity to this process. The delegates themselves were granted a certain place in the emerging union apparatus by the new contracts. If they were willing to accept the crucial restrictions placed on their activity then there were certain rights and recognition accorded; they were formally recognised by management as union representatives. Moreover, we should bear in mind the logic of the situation facing the Peronist rank and file after the defeats of 1959 and the concomitant weight of pragmatic realism which was so powerful an element in the attraction and acceptance of 'integrationism'. There was, ultimately, an important element of acceptance of productivity clauses and the limiting of shop-floor power on the part of the union membership. They were, by 1960, generally prepared to accept rationalisation clauses in return for wage rises. The spectre of unemployment and the drastic fall in real wages in 1959, coupled with the failure of militant action to obtain decent wage rises meant that the offer of a money rise, and the renewal of clauses relating to fringe benefits, in return for rationalisation agreements seemed to most workers the only practical way left to try and recoup the decline in their living standards.

The clandestine groupings: the second stage

As the space available for independent militant activity in the unions became more and more restricted so, too, did the perspectives for effective action by the clandestine groups. The special formations had been ordered to cease operations during the opening months of Frondizi's government. They had, formally at least, become involved in the attempts undertaken in those months to reconstitute the political wing of the Peronist movement. They had been represented on the Consejo Coordinador y Supervisor del Peronismo after its foundation in October 1958. With the growing conflict between government and unions in 1959, and the dashing of any possibility of a legal political expression for Peronism, the special formations once again became active.

Throughout 1959 bombings steadily increased as the confrontation between the government and the working class intensified. There was a renewed flourishing of the commandos in Buenos Aires and the interior. There was an attempt to give this resurgence of activity a better organisational structure than had hitherto existed. A number of new co-ordinating bodies came into existence. A Central de Operaciones de la Resistencia (COR) was formed under the direction of retired General

Miguel Iñiguez. In charge of implementing the orders which came from COR was the Agrupación Peronista de la Resistencia Insurreccional (APRI). Under its command, in theory at least, were a number of local commandos operating mainly in Buenos Aires and to a lesser degree in the provinces. To facilitate communications between different organs and to ensure an effective chain of command there existed also a Comando Nacional de Comunicaciones headed by a retired lieutenant, Eloy Prieto.

It is difficult to assess how effective this new organisational structure was in achieving the desired coordination. As always when analysing clandestine activity we must tread warily between fact and fiction, subjective desire and objective fact. While the initial spontaneous chaos of 1955/6 was avoided, the effectiveness of the restructuring should not be exaggerated. Difficulty in assessing the effectiveness of this renewed clandestine activity comes largely from the sources available. On the side of the government and security forces there was an obvious tendency to exaggerate the extent of the overall planning of subversive activity. Every action was propagandised as part of a coherent, large-scale plot to overthrow the status quo. This was particularly true of the armed forces after they had taken overall charge of the security situation with the introduction of the *Plan Conintes* in March 1960. To justify their newly assumed powers they undoubtedly exaggerated the degree of efficiency and planning existing in the Peronist Resistance. They tended to see an unbroken line of responsibility for every terrorist action stretching from Perón personally, through the *Consejo Coordinador*, down to the local resistance commando.[20] On the other side, for equally evident reasons, the Peronists themselves were wont to exaggerate the efficiency of their organisation, and the formal titles of organisations such as COR seemed to bear witness to a military precision and centralisation of operations.

It is clear, however, that many actions resulted from the initiatives of very localised groupings. Even the security forces at times admitted as much: 'Even if there does exist an overall organising commando, coordinating the acts of sabotage and terrorism, many were actually carried out by cells of isolated individuals acting in parallel and independent fashion.'[21] It is significant, too, that Juan Carlos Brid, a leading participant in several of the chief actions of this period, in his memoirs of these years makes no mention of the guiding hand of the COR, or of any other overriding command.[22] Partly, independent, localised initiatives were the result of the relative autonomy granted to cells in any security-conscious clandestine organisation. But other factors were at work too.

Bodies such as COR and APRI were staffed by retired military officers who had been weeded out of the armed forces in the anti-Peronist purges of the post-1955 era. There was often a mutual suspicion between these and other militants of the Resistance. Thus, for example, in the province of Córdoba retired military personnel had an organisation restricted entirely to themselves.[23]

The extent to which this renewed clandestine activity corresponded to an overall plan originating with Perón is debatable. Instructions did circulate in 1960 purporting to come from Perón. They envisaged a series of escalating stages of the Resistance which would gradually make the country ungovernable and culminate in 'the carrying out of the great national insurrection, during which the clandestine groupings will constitute the nuclei around which the military forces will be grouped while the unions paralyse the country.'[24] Whether Perón himself really believed in the possibility of reaching this final stage is questionable. However, with the openly anti-Peronist repression taking place at this time, and the evident exclusion of any possibility of either Perón's personal return to Argentina or the legalisation of Peronism as a political movement, Perón had little to lose from adopting such an insurrectional stance. In the face of the virulently anti-Peronist military commanders in charge of the *Plan Conintes* the adoption of a legalist, moderate pose would have meant little. A militant stance, on the other hand, would enable him to underline his nuisance value and undermine the position of would-be compromisers in the movement.

The actions carried out during 1960 certainly represented the peak of activity of the special formations during the Resistance. A brief look at some of the major actions can demonstrate the scope of this activity. On 15 February a deposit of Shell Mex Argentina in the city of Córdoba was blown up, destroying over three million litres of petroleum. The damage was estimated at 70 million pesos, and there were thirteen deaths. A month later on 12 March the storage plant of the state gas company in Mar del Plata was also bombed, with a loss of 1,400 cylinders of gas and 10 million pesos of damage. The same day in Buenos Aires the house of Major Cabrera of the army intelligence service was completely destroyed in an explosion. In Mendoza on 26 May, the house of General Labayru, commander of the Andean region, was also destroyed. At the same time in this region a major road bridge in the Andes was blown up.[25] These actions were carried out against the background of more minor bombings and arson.

The scope of these actions undoubtedly argues a greater depth of professionalism than had existed prior to 1959. No actions of comparable scope had occurred under the Aramburu regime. The old improvised *caños* of 1956/7 were used less frequently. Charges of commercial dynamite were not used with far more sophisticated timing mechanisms. These in themselves required a highly organised back-up structure since most of the gelignite had to be stolen from mines and quarries outside of Buenos Aires, brought to the city and prepared in safe houses. The stealing of the explosives was in fact a major function of the provincial commandos. A commando in Mendoza, led by a retired officer, Ciro Ahumada, stole over 4,000 kilos of gelignite in a raid on the Huemel mine in early 1960. Much of this was later found to have been used in operations in Buenos Aires.[26] Despite the increased scope of the actions which took place there was still no attempt made to directly engage security forces in even limited armed actions. Documents found on one of the leading organisers in Buenos Aires, José Normando Castro, included detailed plans of the training barracks of the Federal Police and other police buildings. This may indicate that actions were contemplated against the police but no direct armed confrontation with security forces took place in the major urban areas.[27]

Yet, for all the increased professionalism of the clandestine organisations their activities never posed anything like a serious threat to the stability of the status quo. In fact by mid 1960 the repression of the *Plan Conintes* had effectively eroded much of the structure of the commandos. *Conintes* was effectively brought into effect in March 1960. Until this time terrorist activity had been investigated by the police and the militants involved had been subject to the normal legal procedures of the judiciary. Decree 2,628 changed this by making the police forces of the Federal Capital and the provinces subject to the authority of the armed forces, who were now to divide the country into a number of zones of defence against subversion. Decree 2,639 of 16 March placed under military jurisdiction all those engaged in terrorist activity, and set up special councils of war to try them according to military law. An estimated 2,000 people were arrested under these provisions and perhaps some 500 of them sentenced by the special commissions.[28] Many of these may not have been directly involved in clandestine operations, since *Conintes* was used indiscriminately against union activists too. By mid 1960, however, it had effectively done its job.

The last fling of the clandestine groups was an attempted military *golpe* of 30 November 1960. Under the overall direction of COR plans were made to seize certain key military installations. This would then serve as a signal for the more generalised rising to be accompanied by a general strike. The rising scarcely got started; Rosario was one of the few places where anything like an armed conflict took place. With the failure to take the initial key points the rest of the rising failed. In the aftermath many of the activists who had evaded the net cast by the *Plan Conintes* were now arrested. The attempted rising was the last in a line of traditional Peronist/military *golpes* with its antecedents in General Valle's rising of June 1956. The action was planned and controlled by the ex-military personnel centred around Iñiguez in the COR and it was premised on their successfully convincing enough active military officers to join them and throw in their lot with the rebels. There was no prior distribution of arms to the civilian commandos waiting to back up the surrender of these garrisons. The role of the non-military activists was to be a strictly secondary one and they were to receive arms when and where the ex-military officials deemed appropriate.

What was the relationship between these special formations and the Peronist trade union leadership and rank and file? The term resistance as it was used amongst Peronists in the 1950s and 1960s tended to be an all-embracing, diffuse one covering a wide range of differing activities, while at the same time blurring the distinctions between these different activities into a single vague image which was to become ensconced in Peronist popular culture. In fact, however, the growing differentiation which we observed in the pre-1958 period between union activists and the clandestine groups was to become even more accentuated in this period. In part this was due to the security demands of the more stringently organised clandestine groups. The risks of having activists who were also open union militants were too great, and the demands of clandestine activity generally required the full-time attention of the activists. Partly, too, it was due to the changing perceptions of rank-and-file Peronist unionists of the relevance of clandestine activities to them as unionists. With Peronism banned from the unions, and with outright repression the order of the day, the relevance in both emotional and practical terms had been easier to perceive. Now the rather more subtle approach of 'integrationism' blurred this perception. Then again, the special formations could not remain unaffected by the general demobilisation and growing apathy arising from the defeats of 1959 and 1960. Their ability to recruit in the working class was bound to be affected. To adapt Mao's, by now hackneyed, metaphor, the working-class sea in which they might hope to swim was by 1960 drying up.

Naturally, there were ties between the two areas. The largest strikes of 1959 and 1960 were all accompanied by a sustained campaign of bombings and sabotage. During the two-day general strike called to support the metal workers in September 1959 there were some 106 acts of terrorism in Buenos Aires alone, according to official calculations.[29] Brid mentions, too, that the blowing up of the gas storage plant in Mar del Plata was partially at least in response to an appeal for help from the workers of the state gas company who were on strike.[30] The failed *golpe* of November 1960 had been widely canvassed in the Peronist union movement, and a promise of a general strike if it showed signs of success was proffered by some union leaders. On the night of the *golpe* union locals were used as gathering points for activists waiting for the signal to move. In Mendoza, for example, both the UOM building and the local CGT headquarters were used in this way.[31]

However, the growing divergence between the two areas of action was evidenced by the increasing weight within the commandos of the youth and student sections of Peronism. The commandos tended to look to these groups for recruitment, rather than to the younger union militants who had been prominent in the previous period. Those Peronist unionists who were still most actively involved in the clandestine actions were those attached to the old CGT Auténtica. Many of these men were, by now, more like professional revolutionaries than trade unionists. Often blacklisted for their activism of the early post-1955 days, or for their positions in the Perón regime, they had become, more often through necessity than choice, full-time clandestine activists with little or no direct contact with everyday trade unionism. In the metal workers' union, the UOM, there were, for example, men such as Benito Moya and Armando Cabo, who, while playing a full-time role in the commandos, were at the same time on the payroll of the union and were close friends of Augusto Vandor, the leader of the UOM. Others like Avelino Fernandez still took an active role in the union, but also acted as intermediaries between Vandor and the special formations when necessary. The union leaderships increasingly adopted a pragmatic attitude toward involvement with clandestine activities. While usually allowing the use of union funds or buildings they avoided direct links or closer commitments.

There was a price to pay for the immersion of these unionists for such a long time in clandestine activities, as the Resistance was ground down by repression, demoralisation and desertion. It was not uncommon for some of them to drift into the role of paid bodyguards and enforcers of the decisions of their comrades in the union leaderships. As the opportunities for corruption increased, as the union finances improved and, particularly in unions like the UOM, the dividing line between the underworld and union financial operations became blurred, their familiarity with weapons and their readiness to use them together with a certain charisma deriving from their past actions, could be put to good use by the union leaderships. Effectively declassed by their years of clandestine activity and then left high and dry as the tide of the Resistance retreated, they found a role as part of the newly emerging Peronist union hierarchy preferable to an attempt to go back to the shop floor. Armando Cabo, a prominent member of the metal workers' leadership prior to 1955, closely involved in the projected union milita apparently mooted by Evita, and by all accounts a man of considerable personal courage during the years of resistance to Aramburu, was to become from the early 1960s on one of Vandor's chief enforcers within the UOM. There were many other cases like his. The lower echelons of the *burocracia sindical* were largely staffed by ex-militants of the clandestine groups.

The political and ideological context within which the second phase of clandestine activity unfolded was both ambiguous and limited. The influence of the Cuban revolution was becoming more apparent. The first guerilla formations, the Uturuncu in Tucuman and the Unión de Guerrilleros Andinos in Mendoza, were founded in these years. Both were soon crushed by the military before they could begin effective operations.[32] As the Cuban revolution became radicalised in these years it had a growing impact on activists, both Peronist and non-Peronist, in Argentina. Guevara's 'guerrilla manual' was amongst the documents captured by the army when they rounded up both guerrilla *focos*.[33] At the same time there was a move away from a reliance on military uprisings, the search for military leaders who would be faithful to their 'true' calling. Some clandestine groups had also rejected the idea that sections of the armed forces could be persuaded to lead a popular insurrection.

The Comando Nacional Peronista had, for example, in 1959 maintained that the real problem Peronism had to resolve was 'the lack of a revolutionary political leadership of the movement'.[34] John William Cooke came to embody these tendencies. As his correspondence with Perón clearly shows he had long been contemptuous of would-be military saviours. By 1960 he was in Cuba where he would fight with the militia at the Bay of Pigs and become an ardent champion of guerrilla warfare. It is possible that he was involved in the setting up of the UGA and the Uturuncu guerrilla.[35] Cooke attempted to place his advocacy of guerrilla warfare within the larger perspective of identifying Peronism with Third World national liberation struggles. As a part of this he increasingly came to stress the need to turn Peronism into a revolutionary party with an appropriately defined ideology in place of the generalised loyalty to a leader which substituted for such an ideology in the Peronist movement.

These developments must, however, be placed in perspective. While the growing attraction of the guerrilla strategy was significant it had only a minor impact on most of the militants of the Peronist Resistance at this time. There was a general admiration for the *muchachos* in the sierra, and there is also evidence of collections taking place in factories in Buenos Aires.[36] But the guerrilla was fundamentally supported by, and composed of, the youth sectors of Peronism and the non-Peronist left. Most of those who were recruited came from the university ambience of the Federal Capital and other major university centres. Much of the logistic support for the attempted *focos* in the Andes and Tucuman came from this area too.[37] The security forces found that most of the guerrilla fighters captured or killed were between the ages of sixteen and twenty.[38] Most of the activists in the clandestine groups still tended to look, with perhaps less and less real conviction, to retired military figures to lead a *golpe* rather than identify themselves with a strategy of guerrilla warfare inspired by Cuba. Indeed, there was at this time a widespread suspicion of Castro among Peronist militants. When Castro had visited Buenos Aires in 1959 he had been feted by the *señoras gordas* of the *barrio norte* and lauded in the press of the traditional Argentine left.

Similarly, the growing identification of Peronism with Third World liberation movements was very much a minority trend. While there was undoubtedly some discussion among activists about the Mau-Mau in Kenya and the Algerian struggle against the French, this was rarely followed through and developed into a clearly worked out ideological position. We have already commented on the difficulty Peronist militants had in developing a formal ideological critique of developmentalism, of sustaining an alternative ideology adequate to the experience of class conflict; this was equally applicable to the activists of the commandos, for all their involvement in clandestine activities. Ultimately the political ideology of many seems to have boiled down to a personal loyalty to Perón. For these activists the inadequacy of a developed formal philosophy was not compensated by the strength drawn from the continuing validation of values and experience of shared struggle and solidarity, separated as they were from even the reduced union struggle of the last years of Frondizi.

Cooke was, therefore, very much an exception, a lone voice speaking to a very restricted audience within Peronism. His letters to Perón mirror his increasing isolation; they become a monologue, a litany of wishful thinking as he urges Perón to set up his exiled home in Cuba and commit Peronism to the Cuban brand of Third World liberation. As his championing of the Cuban experience increased so did the coldness and formality of Perón's replies. The Comando Nacional Peronista was, too, by 1961 of minimal influence within Peronism. With the failure of the November 1960 rising and the success of the *Plan Conintes*, many activists in the commandos dropped out of activity or came to terms with the formal apparatus of Peronism. The ideas of people like Cooke were kept alive in very small groups mostly connected with the youth and student sectors of the movement.

The lure of politics: the election of March 1962

The success of the *Plan Conintes* in erasing any 'insurrectional' perspective for Peronism and the demobilisation of the union struggle after the highpoints of 1959 increased the attraction of the 'pragmatic' option for the Peronist unions and strengthened Frondizi's chances of successfully 'integrating' them within a new status quo. Certainly, there appeared to be a greater air of pragmatism about. The 62 Organisations had, for example, agreed to share power with non-Peronists on the provisional organising committee set up by Frondizi as a first step in calling a reorganising conference of the CGT. The committee, known as the committee of twenty, consisted of ten Peronist union leaders and ten independents. Frondizi promised to allow the reconvening of the CGT congress by December 1961. There was, clearly, some risk to Frondizi in allowing the creation of a new union central, and indeed the committee of twenty organised a general strike against a proposed rationalisation of the railroad service, and against a presidential veto of a new law which would have improved redundancy indemnity. However, these union activities now conformed more closely to what the government considered to be a 'legal' opposition, and with the working-class resistance broken they lacked the explosive potential of the struggles of 1959. The government began, too, to relax some of the worst strictures of the stabilisation plan, and allowed something more closely approaching free collective bargaining. Strikes were not now automatically declared illegal and unions were able to make up some, though not all, of the ground lost in 1959 and 1960. Government propagandists, including the most forthright *desarrollista* press, began speaking confidently of a new 'legal stage' the country was entering.

Other factors seemed to bolster this new confidence. In April Frondizi felt strong enough to fire the army commander in chief, Toranzo

Montero; in May Alvaro Alsogaray was dismissed from the Ministry of Economy. Politically, too, the fortunes of the Unión Cívica Radical Intransigente were improving. In April 1961 they had won elections in Catamarca and Santa Fé, while the conservatives had taken Mendoza. In all these cases there had been a marked decline in the Peronist *voto en blanco*. In elections for the senate in the Federal Capital in February 1961 Alfredo Palacios running for a splinter socialist party won with 308,000 votes to the 232,000 votes *en blanco*. This seemed to indicate that the cohesion of the Peronist electoral force was being undermined.

A concomitant of this was the rise of the neo-Peronist parties. Based primarily on figures from the pre-1955 political apparatus of Peronism these parties had been allowed to operate by Frondizi. In many provinces they were centred around the figure of a local caudillo who had controlled the provincial apparatus of the Peronist Party prior to September 1955. While claiming a general allegiance to justicialist principles they, in general, did not feel bound to follow the formal dictates of Perón concerning strategy and tactics in Argentina. They attempted to fill the vacuum created by the political proscription of Peronism. As such they were encouraged by the government as an 'acceptable' Peronism. By 1961 a not inconsiderable number of Peronist votes were going to these parties.

The touchstone for the effectiveness of this hoped for 'legal stage' would be the elections of March 1962 when many of the major provincial governorships would be contested. There was an intense debate within the circle of presidential advisers and the UCRI in general as to the wisdom of allowing direct Peronist participation in these elections. Frondizi's decision to allow the Peronists to present their own candidates was a tempting, though risky, option for the government. If Peronism could be shown to do worse than expected then it would be concrete proof of the efficacy of 'integrationism' as a strategy for dealing with Peronism. It would relieve much of the military pressure on Frondizi by showing that the political sting of Peronism could be drawn much more effectively by his policy of controlled concessions and toleration of a strong union organisation, than by a return to a policy of outright repression favoured by most sectors of the military. From Frondizi's point of view the ideal position for Peronism to take would be to continue the blank vote or, failing this, to divide their votes among a wide range of neo-Peronist candidates. If, however, Peronism contested the elections in its own right then Frondizi's calculation was that he could still win by presenting himself as the only viable anti-Peronist force. The gubernatorial elections in Santa Fe in December

1961 seemed to confirm this calculation. The UCRI won, defeating an amalgam of neo-Peronist forces which had enjoyed official Peronist backing. One national newspaper was moved to say after this election that 'Peronism at present has ceased to occupy first place and is no longer the enemy that many believe it to be.'[39]

The situation within Peronism was itself complex. There was a common recognition that the blank vote was no longer a creditable tactic. Iturbe, the head of the Consejo Coordinador y Supervisor del Peronismo, announced in a press conference in June 1961 that 'Peronism was now in a line of legality' and called for a positive vote in future elections.[40] The abandonment of the *voto en blanco* as a form of repudiation of what they considered an illegitimate government, and as an affirmation of intransigent opposition to that government, was not an easy step to take for many sectors of Peronism. In the course of 1961, however, most came to share the view expressed by an anonymous union leader that 'in the past most sectors of the movement have not gone beyond the classic formula of the blank vote as a repudiation, a sanction against the government – motives which may make sense on the plain of morality but which do not signify anything from the political point of view'.[41]

In September 1961 Américo Barrios, a close political associate of Perón's, took over the newspaper *Recuperación*, and under the headline, 'The tremendous power of legality', began advocating active Peronist participation in the forthcoming elections. At this time Perón's own attitude seems to have been to favour abstention with a positive vote – that is to leave Peronists free to vote for other non-Peronist parties rather than putting up Peronist candidates.[42] When Perón let it be known in mid January 1962 that he wished to share the ticket for the governor of Buenos Aires province with Andrés Framini it was commonly assumed that this was a manoeuvre to scupper the growing movement within Peronism to run Peronist candidates, since he was well aware of the unacceptability of his candidacy for the military. This impression seemed to be confirmed in early February when a letter was brought back from Madrid in which Perón affirmed that: 'The present situation in which they want to place us is a dead end; the only solution is abstention ... the government is not going to give Peronism an electoral opening and we mustn't waste time waiting for them.'[43]

Paradoxically the political wing of Peronism was generally in favour of this position, since it was increasingly fearful of losing out to the union wing in a fight for places on any lists of Peronist candidates. They were in addition worried that a union-dominated Peronist electoral success would provoke a military intervention. They preferred to gradually penetrate electoral positions in the provinces under the guise of neo-Peronism. Perón's own opposition to the movement running its own candidates was very probably based on similar calculations. A good showing by a union-backed electoral campaign would give the unions a negotiating power within Argentine politics which would be, to a degree, independent of his control. The 62 Organisations had, from the beginning, been whole-heartedly in favour of participating in the elections with Peronist candidates. They had also made it clear that they were not prepared to accept lists of candidates dominated by figures from the political wing. On 10 January a meeting called by the CGT Auténtica and the 62 Organisations was attended by 230 delegates from fifty-seven zones of Buenos Aires province. They unanimously called for a Peronist unionist to be the gubernatorial candidate of the Peronist movement. Buenos Aires was divided into seven zones, each of which would hold meetings under the direction of the 62 to select candidates for the elections. At the same time the meeting issued a statement opposing the proposed candidacy of Attilio Bramuglia, Perón's former chancellor, who was being spoken of as a candidate by neo-Peronist forces.[44]

With the only effective apparatus in Peronism, and with the finances to back this up, the unions were able to impose their will. In Buenos Aires province the formula for candidates was established as six unionists and one candidate each for the feminine wing, the Partido Laborista, the Unión Popular and the Partido Justicialista, and two to be nominated by Perón himself. In the Federal Capital itself the 62 Organisations announced their list of candidates before any formal agreement with other sectors. The list was comprised of Sebastian Borro, Jorge Di Pascuale, Rolando García of the rubber workers, Eustaquio Tolosa of the port workers and Paulino Niembro of the UOM. As a concession a representative of the political groups was included at the last minute.[45] Even after the publication of Perón's letter in February, Andrés Framini, the 62's candidate for governor of Buenos Aires, continued campaigning. A delegation of Vandor, José Alonso of the garment workers, Roberto García and Amado Olmos immediately flew to Madrid and on 17 February returned to say that Perón had now agreed to ratify the *concurrencista* position.

The reasons for the union leaderships' determination to take part in the election campaign were various. Partly, it was a reflection of the groundswell of feeling among rank-and-file Peronists in favour of voting for Peronist candidates as a means of protesting against the Frondizi government; this feeling increased with the deepening economic crisis that had been evident since the end of 1961. The depth of this feeling was illustrated by the fervour with which the campaign was surrounded. Beyond this we have Miguel Gazzera's assertion that the initial idea to run separate candidates had come from Amado Olmos and had been taken up by Vandor with the specific aim of forcing Frondizi from office.[46] This would seem to be an oversimplification. The *línea dura*, which was still dominant in the councils of the 62, undoubtedly viewed the elections as a potential means of deposing Frondizi; a Peronist victory would, in Jorge Di Pascuale's words be 'un hecho más' for Frondizi to contend with. Whether it provoked his overthrow was not something they should worry about. Indeed some of the hardliners may well have welcomed this possibility as a way of countering the debilitating temptations of integrationism.[47]

A more general feeling, articulated by Olmos and shared by most union leaders in the 62, including many 'hardliners', was that the elections offered an opportunity to establish union weight both within Peronism and within the Argentine political system. Certainly the dangers of such a tactic were evident. They must have realised that with a strong union organisation as the basis of the Peronist campaign there was a good possibility of victory in several provinces, and that this could well have serious institutional consequences. It was precisely this fear which Frondizi had counted on to sway the Peronist unions against direct participation. Most union leaders felt that this was a risk worth running on the grounds that even if the military did intervene the weight gained by the unions because of the elections would mean that any new government would have to take them into account. At the very least Peronism and its unions would have demonstrated that they were the dominant force in Argentine society, and the onus for denying them their rightful rewards would be seen to rest firmly on the shoulders of the military.

The effectiveness of the union campaign was borne out by the results. Peronism was victorious in eight out of fourteen provincial gubernatorial contests, including the province of Buenos Aires. Frondizi immediately annulled the elections in these provinces and intervened them. The armed forces had, however, lost all confidence in him and on 29 March, after fruitless negotiations with Frondizi, José Maria Guido, the vice president was sworn in with an eminently *gorila* cabinet. The Peronist unions, after a protest strike at the annulment of the elections on 23 March, adopted a cautious attitude.

The March elections demonstrated the change of emphasis taking place within Peronist unionism. The transition from the high points of the Resistance – the bitter rear-guard struggles of 1959, and the terrorist campaign of 1959/60 – to the organisation of an election campaign and the haggling over candidates and offices implied a profound change. Within Peronism the unions had clearly imposed their own terms on the other sectors of the movement. The political expression of the Peronist working class would now be very much bound up with the union movement. The roots of this can be traced to the original formation of Peronism as a movement and the foundation of the Partido Laborista in the 1940s. While Perón had created a political apparatus to replace the laboristas the relevance of this as a vehicle for political mobilisation and expression had remained secondary to the union movement. The working class's impact and influence on the state had been assured primarily by unions and their intimate relationship with Perón and Evita. The Partido Peronista had little immediate relevance for most Peronist workers. The formal proscription of Peronism as a political movement after 1955 and the intensity of the resistance within the factories and unions had simply confirmed this. Even with the possibility of the legal recreation of a Peronist party during the halcyon first months of Frondizi's presidency the unions and the working class had shown little real interest in establishing a political apparatus. Now, with other militant options eliminated by defeat, demoralisation and rationalisation, the emerging union hierarchy could turn its attention to politics and develop its peculiarly syndicalist brand of politicking and power seeking.

Much of this was not immediately apparent, however. The military coup, the swearing in of a hardline anti-Peronist cabinet, the by now familiar anti-union and anti-Peronist rhetoric, seemed to herald a return to the pre-1959 situation. There was, moreover, the fact that formally the hardliners like Di Pascuale and Borro were still a majority within the leadership of the 62 Organisations. As the list of candidates for deputy in the Federal Capital elections showed they could still impose their candidates at this level. This was, however, misleading since it reflected by now their personal prestige in the movement rather than any real weight within the organisms of Peronism. The figure who emerged from the election campaign as the really dominant figure was Augusto Vandor. As head of the Unión Obrera Metalúrgica, the most powerful industrial union in the country, he had been the one who had basically organised the election campaign. The term *vandorismo* was being used by friend and foe alike more frequently. The fact that he had

had to accept in the Federal Capital the candidacies of the *duros*, many of whom were becoming increasingly suspicious of his power and intentions, should not obscure his growing influence. Miguel Gazzera, a close confidant of Vandor's, aptly summarised the elections and their results:

Vandor prepared a whole apparatus destined for the elections in the province of Buenos Aires and other places, which later became the structure of *vandorismo*. This apparatus brought together the legions of aspirants to posts which arose with the elections, provided the money and all the profuse publicity ... the fall of Frondizi placed Vandor at the very highest level of political power in the country.[48]

The implications of this for Peronist unions and the working class were to become apparent in the following years.

PART FOUR

The Vandor era, 1962–6

7

The *burocracia sindical*:
power and politics in Peronist unions

> Within the Justicialist score I wanted to call upon the different melodies
> ... I assigned to Vandor the leadership of the conservative, evolution-
> ary currents which were the only ones the regime would tolerate; Fra-
> mini, on the other hand, assumed the leadership of the revolutionary,
> aggressive wing, that of permanent rupture with the system ... both
> came to correspond to the different aspects and currents which go to
> make up the national, Christian content of our labouring masses.
>
> Juan D. Perón

Vandorism: elements of an image

In late November 1963 management in the TAMET metal-working factory in Avellaneda dismissed some twenty militants belonging to both
the communist union grouping and the dissident Peronist list. The prel-
ude to management's action had been the expulsion of these activists
from the Unión Obrera Metalúrgica for supposed infractions of union
rules. Once shorne of union protection the field was open for management to act. The assumption by all concerned was that union and management had acted in collusion. Perhaps more significant was the
acquiescence of the internal commission in this process. One of the
activists expelled was in fact a leading member of the *cuerpo de dele-
gados*, the delegate commission, of the plant. He was expelled from the
union for distributing a leaflet against the original dismissals without
official approval from union headquarters. Of the thirty-eight delegates in TAMET only fourteen attended the meeting which expelled
him, and of these only seven actually voted for it.[1] The incident, scarcely unique in itself, was eloquent testimony to the extent
of the demobilisation and demoralisation which we have charted in
the previous section of this work. It also exemplified an important
element in the process of integration of the union apparatus into
the Argentine political, institutional system and its corollary of

bureaucratisation and the growing use of autocratic methods to regulate the internal life of the unions which reached its apogee in the 1962–6 period.

The figure who came to symbolise this process in the minds of both militants and the Argentine public was Augusto Vandor, the leader of the metal workers. Vandor came to personify – especially for his opponents within the Peronist movement – the transformation of the movement and its unions from a position of outright antagonism to the post-1955 status quo to one of acceptance of the need to compromise with it and find a space within its boundaries. *Vandorismo* came to be synonymous, on both a political and union level, with negotiation, pragmatism, the acceptance of the realities of the *realpolitik* which governed Argentina after 1955. On the political plane *vandorismo* implied the use of the political power and representativeness which the unions derived from their position as the dominant force within Peronism and from being the only fully legal part of the movement in order to negotiate and bargain with other 'factors of power'.

The image of power and influence within the system was symbolised on the formal level by the frequent talks between government and trade union leaders on economic and social issues, and on the informal level by the equally frequent consultations between Vandor and other union leaders and politicians, employers' leaders, prelates and army commanders. The sight of the shirt-sleeved and tie-less union leader, Vandor, entering the Casa Rosada or the Ministry of Labour, or visiting the Ministry of Defence to consult with the chiefs of the armed forces, became a dominant element in the social and political imagery of Argentina at this time and, being constantly emphasised by the media, reinforced the perception of the Peronist unions as a fundamental, if conflictual, part of the social and political system. This was an image which the union leaders readily embraced. The CGT in particular attempted to bolster this image at both a national and international level. These years saw a welter of CGT publications and analysis and a number of conferences on a variety of themes of national import. A statistical department was created as was a juridical assistance commission. Ties were also reestablished with foreign union bodies.

Peronist control of the CGT had been assured in the negotiations which took place in November and December 1962 preceding the January 1963 congress which finally marked the formal reconstitution of the confederation. The 62 Organisations were in a clear majority position in the labour movement vis-à-vis the non-Peronist unions. They controlled all the industrial unions and all but one of the local regional committees of the CGT.[2] The militant anti-Peronist grouping – the 32 Democratic Unions – had by 1962 virtually disappeared, and the communist grouping, the MUCS, was restricted to a few small unions. Most of the large, mainly white-collar, anti-Peronist unions which had formed the 32 Democratic Unions in 1957, had by this time declared themselves to be independents. Though not as coherent a unit as the 62 Organisations they shared a common basis in recognising the reality of the Peronist presence in the unions and the need to find some sort of working arrangement with them.[3] The negotiations which paved the way for the January congress represented an agreement between the Vandorist sector of Peronism and the independents. While agreement was reached in general terms on the equal representation of both sectors on the central committee Vandor successfully insisted that a Peronist should be secretary-general. In addition the independent unions also gave up the vital posts of secretary and pro-secretary of the interior, and also of union affairs, in return for the lesser posts of assistant secretary-general and the posts of finance and social welfare. The secretary-general, elected at the congress in January with Vandor's blessing, was José Alonso, the leader of the garment workers. The new body claimed to represent some 2,567,000 members.[4]

More fundamentally still, Vandor's power base outside the metal workers' union was his control of the 62 Organisations. From the March 1962 elections on he was increasingly the dominant figure within the 62 and by 1963 the most intransigent leaders of the *línea dura* – Di Pascuale, Borro and Jonsch – had all resigned, or been pushed out of the coordinating committee. Within the individual member unions the domination of the emerging Peronist union hierarchy was confirmed as the process of demobilisation of the rank and file and victimisation of the activists continued. The economic crisis of 1962–3 saw the culmination of this process. By June 1962 over 40,000 metal workers were either suspended or permanently without jobs – 20,000 of these were in the Federal Capital and Avellaneda – as the Argentine economy entered one of its severest cyclical crises. The situation in the textile industry was even more desperate. Employers and union leaders often took advantage of this situation, as in the TAMET case, to rid themselves of many well-known activists who had survived earlier battles. The ruthless control of any internal dissent by what was increasingly referred to as the *burocracia sindical* was, too, synonymous with Vandorism, as was the employment of *matones* (enforcers) to intimidate any such opposition. The plenary sessions of the 62 Organisations, a few short years before the scene of innumerable rank-and-file demonstrations and expressions of disagreement, were no longer in any real sense a forum for expressing rank-and-file views. They had simply become part of the apparatus of power at the disposal of the union leadership. Indeed, the *barra* (gallery) was now an instrument of leadership control, intimidating any attempt at expression of dissident opinion within the meetings.[5]

With their base in the 62 Organisations secure, and their dominant position within the CGT confirmed, the Peronist union leadership was ready to make its weight felt in both the social and political fields. In terms of the social and economic conditions of its members, decisive action was clearly necessary. By 1962 the Argentine economy had entered a profound crisis. The industrial leap to the production of consumer durables and capital equipment which was at the heart of developmentalist policy from Perón to Frondizi had made great strides; Argentine steel production increased sevenfold between 1954 and 1965; auto production rose from 6,000 vehicles in 1955 to over 200,000 in 1965. By 1962 it was becoming clear, however, that there were limits to the whole process of import substitution. The Argentine market was too small to provide a steady stimulus to the new dynamic branches of industry. In addition, the production of more sophisticated durables in petro-chemicals, autos, and electrical appliances required large capital inputs in terms of investments, largely from foreign sources, and the importation of more technologically advanced industrial equipment.[6] The attempt to push through expanded industrialisation in this context led to a deepening balance of payments deficit which could be met in the short term by foreign loans while awaiting a hoped for expansion of exports of the new industrial products. This foreign exchange bottleneck had inevitable inflationary results. As the deficit worsened Argentine governments were forced to turn to traditional agricultural exports in order to pay interest on the foreign debt and maintain industrial inputs. To increase the value of these exports at a time when world market prices for them were generally declining Argentina resorted to successive devaluations. These devaluations helped fuel an inflationary spiral, especially after Frondizi in January 1959 abandoned exchange controls. After reaching a high of 113% in 1959 inflation would run at between 25% and 30% throughout the governments of Guido and Illia.

The Guido government in 1962 responded to the growing balance of payments crisis and inflationary spiral by adopting an emergency, IMF-sponsored stabilisation plan very similar to that adopted by Frondizi in 1959. The aim was to restrict industrial production by limiting credit and squeezing the home market by salary limits and increases in public tariffs. At the same time a further devaluation attempted to encourage new exports. The result for the working class was immediate and drastic: an industrial recession which saw unemployment rise dramatically in areas such as textiles and metal working and continuing high levels of inflation which inevitably adversely affected real wages.[7]

The union leadership's initial response to the crisis was muted, largely because of the institutional instability of the second half of 1962 as different factions of the armed forces struggled for domination and influence on the state. With the resolution of the conflict in favour of the more moderate faction favourable to a continuation of the civilian government and the return of the CGT, the union leadership felt confident to initiate a campaign for solutions to the economic and social grievances of its members. The first stage of this campaign culminated in May 1963 with a *Semana de Protesta* against the Guido government's economic policies. The climax of the campaign was a 24-hour general strike. As the economic situation gradually improved in the latter part of 1963 and into 1964 the CGT increased its campaign to recover lost ground. Its attempts to pressure the Radical Party government of Arturo Illia led to the implementation of the second stage of the *Plan de Lucha*, in June and July of 1964. The plan consisted of a series of escalated factory occupations which extended to virtually the whole of Argentine industry. The chief advocate of this tactic in the councils of the CGT was Vandor and the metal-working industry led the way in the occupations. Carefully planned, and carried out under the firm control of the union apparatus the occupations were an impressive display of organisation and discipline. Spread over a five-week period the CGT claimed that more than 11,000 plants were occupied with more than 3,900,000 workers participating.[8]

In the political field, too, the union leaders increasingly exploited their role as the direct brokers of the Peronist electoral following. In the July 1963 presidential elections the 62 Organisations were the chief organising force behind the campaign of Vicente Solano Lima who ran for a Frente Nacional y Popular of Peronists, Frondizi supporters and popular conservatives. The front was eventually proscribed because of military pressure and Illia, the Radical Party candidate, was elected with scarcely 20% of the popular vote. The March 1965 congressional elections saw the election of a powerful block of Peronist deputies on the Unión Popular ticket. The campaign was predominantly run and financed by the 62 Organisations. It also saw the election of many union candidates. The head of the Peronist block in congress was Paulino Niembro, an intimate associate of Vandor's from the UOM.

The picture which emerges is, therefore, one of a union leadership seemingly at the height of its power. The image was a curious amalgam of factors – ranging from semi-organised gangsterism, which as one author put it could 'conjure up the gangsters of American trade unionism like Jimmy Hoffa',[9] right up to the highest level political manoeuvring and bargaining. If to many militants this union hierarchy was symbolised by incidents such as the TAMET victimisations, to the Argentine public, and indeed to rival social and political forces, Vandor and his union comrades were also associated with the massive mobilisation embodied in the factory occupations. To understand the ambivalence of this image, the complexity of the phenomenon, we must examine in closer detail the elements contributing to the power of this union leadership.

Important factors contributing to the power of the union leadership

The structural base of the institutional power of the unions lay in the Law of Professional Associations, law 14,455, passed by Frondizi in 1958. Fundamentally the law reinstituted the system, first created by Perón, of the *sindicato único*, that is the legal recognition of only one union with bargaining rights in any one industry, whether on the local or national level. Within this overall context the law distinguished three levels of union organisation and structure. There were unions of the first degree which in each province and the Federal Capital organised workers of the same trade or area of industry; a second category was also recognised which included federations grouping together first-degree unions from various provinces; and finally there was a third level of organisation, the confederation bringing together the federations. The important point to note concerning union leadership power was that although Argentine labour law allowed for either a federative structure or the more centralised and concentrated union structure of the first-degree unions, among the largest and most important unions in the country the non-federative structure predominated. Unions in metal working, railroads, textile and construction, as well as the major white-collar unions, all have highly centralised structures which concentrate power in a central leadership elected at a national level. In these unions of the first degree the control by the central leadership over the activities of the branches and sections was, in formal terms, nearly total. In the Asociación Obrera Textil, for example, the central leadership was empowered by article 53 of its statutes to intervene any section 'which practises acts of indiscipline or commits irregularities'. The internal commissions which led these sections were, moreover, as article 55 reminded them, 'merely acting in the character of direct representatives of the central leadership' and their powers were limited accordingly.[10]

It should be borne in mind, too, that although there were also many federations representing local unions in any one industry, this was in no way synonymous with real freedom from centralised control. Most federations have their offices in Buenos Aires and are inevitably dominated by the Federal Capital union. The government's own census of professional associations conducted in 1965 found, for example, that 38.4% of all unions had their central offices in Buenos Aires. The concentration of unions of the first degree in the Federal Capital was 42.9% and of federations, 86.6%.[11] In addition many federations had in their statutes the power to severely discipline member unions and to strongly limit their independent activity. Thus, for example, article 59 of the federation of petrol workers' unions laid down that the affiliated unions were 'obliged to respect the resolutions adopted by the national secretariat and central directive committee of the federation'. Article 60 stated that in no case could the local unions 'pursue, at a local level, problems of a general character, nor take up positions which might compromise the opinion of the federation'.[12] Thus the Law of Professional Associations not only guaranteed the union leaderships' bargaining rights, without fear of competition from rival unions, but it also laid the basis for a union structure which did much to ensure centralised control *within* a union. The central union leadership also derived important elements of control from the use of the disciplinary clauses contained in all statutes. Most unions have statutes so elastic that anyone could be found guilty of breaching them at one time or another. Clauses abound which prohibit the 'provocation of disorders', 'notorious misconduct', or the even vaguer 'undecorous behaviour'. The central committee of a union was usually empowered to judge on infringements of these clauses, and although there might be an appeal procedure this, too, was generally controlled by the central leadership. Article 9 of the metal workers' statutes, for example, empowered the leadership to expel an affiliate by simple resolution of the central committee, without the necessity to take the decision to any assembly of the union.

This prevalent type of structure had important implications in terms of the financial powers accruing to the union leaderships. Union funds

Table 2. *Union income derived from workers, classified by branch of economic activity, 1964*

Economic activity	Total	Cuota sindical	Cuota asistencial
Food products	145,693	90,288	55,405
Manufacture textiles	145,513	126,969	18,544
Basic metals	410,178	295,300	114,878
Manufacturing ind.	984,795	687,311	297,484
Total all unions	2,080,072	1,384,461	695,611

Source: *Censo de Asociaciones Profesionales, Ministerio de Trabajo,* Buenos Aires, 1965, Cuadro 7.

came from a variety of sources. The two most basic sources were the *cuota sindical,* basic union dues, and the *cuota asistencial,* also paid by the membership and designated for the maintenance of the various social services offered by the unions. In general these dues were either set as a percentage of the monthly wage, usually 1%, or at a fixed monthly rate, usually between 50 and 100 pesos in the mid 1960s.[13] In addition, the employers also paid a certain contribution towards union social welfare funds, the amount varying from contract to contract. This *aporte empresarial,* as it was known, accounted for 40.9% of total union social welfare funds in 1964.[14] Finally there were the extraordinary quotas, chief of which was the percentage of every new wage increase that the union was entitled to retain in the first month following the signing of a new contract. This retention applied to both union and non-union members.[15] The Law of Professional Associations instituted a system of automatic retention of these different dues at source by the employer. Given the prevalent type of union structure discussed above this system endowed a union leadership with great financial power. In simple terms it meant, for example, that in the major industrial and white-collar unions the membership dues of the metal worker in Córdoba, the textile worker from Rosario or the railroad worker from Tucumán, were deducted by their employers and deposited directly into the respective bank accounts of the central union in Buenos Aires.

The sums thus placed at the disposal of the union leaderships were considerable. Table 2 gives an idea in general terms of the quantities involved in major manufacturing unions.

To these sums originating from the union membership should be added those arising from the employers' contributions to the union social welfare funds. This was worth 234 million pesos in 1963 and 464

Table 3. *Social services offered by unions, 1964*

Libraries	194	Pension offices	235
Canteens	38	Hospitals	13
Holiday camps	64	Wholesale stores	69
Sports fields	28	Sanatoria	122
Cooperatives	6	Insurance offices	75
Union technical	274	Workshops	15
Schools	–	Others	127
Pharmacies	67		

Source: Censo de Asociaciones Profesionales, Ministerio de Trabajo, Buenos Aires, 1965, p. 7.

million in 1964.[16] A proportion of this income was, of course, invested in various ways and became part of a union's permanent assets. Thus, we find that the total value of assets held by the unions in the industrial manufacturing sector calculated in 1965 at 592,245 million pesos and total assets for all unions valued at 4,201,041 millions.[17]

Such huge sums were in themselves an important explanatory factor behind the gangsterism and violence that was becoming increasingly associated with Peronist unionism, and also of the personal corruption which frequently went hand in hand with this. Stories, many of them well documented, abounded concerning the diversion of these funds to the private benefit of individual union leaders.[18] However, more significantly, these sums provided the basis for a whole range of social services offered by the unions to their members and also, given the concentrated centralism of most union structures, put an immense source of patronage and pressure at the disposal of the central leaders. Evidently these two aspects were closely interrelated. An idea of the extent of these social services on a national level can be gained from Table 3.

We can better appreciate what these figures meant if we take the case of a major industrial union such as the Asociación Obrera Textil. By no means the wealthiest of the large unions the AOT was in the year from May 1965 to May 1966 receiving 198 million pesos from the basic union dues and over 2 million pesos from the special levy granted them by the labour contract on the new wage increase. To this had to be added over 250 million pesos from the *cuota asistencial* and the employers' contributions to the social services. The union boasted at this time of investments of a net value of 154 million pesos.[19] The social services deriving from these funds were considerable. In the Federal Capital the medical services were centred on the Sanatorio Primera Junta, which had a capacity to deal with up to a 100,000 families a year, and a central dental clinic. In the various districts of Gran Buenos Aires there were seventy clinics of one sort or another; in the twenty-four districts of the union in the interior of the country there were some sixty-four medical and dental services. Tourism, too, was catered for. The union in 1966 owned two hotels and holiday camp complexes in Córdoba, and two in Mar del Plata.[20]

These sums of money and the services they underwrote had a profound effect on the image of union functions propagated by union leaders and the perceptions of their unions' role held by rank-and-file members which we will return to later in this section. From the point of view of the immediate discussion it is also important to emphasise that they were the bedrock on which negotiations between different factions of the bureaucracy could take place. They were important not simply for what they represented in monetary terms, but for what they represented in terms of jobs, influence and prestige. The patronage system in the unions was built upon a complex pyramid of interlocking interests both within individual unions and within the movement as a whole, with the most powerful unions at the apex of the pyramid. Miguel Gazzera has given a picture of what this could imply for a man of Vandor's stature:

They used to buzz around him ceaselessly, waiting for his favours to convert them into leaders. They were at his disposal because they needed inspectors from the Ministry who would be partial in their decisions, or they wanted the UOM printing press to print propaganda for their union elections. Or they wanted Vandor 'to persuade' some rival leader of theirs to give way.[21]

The methods of persuasion could vary. It could imply the physical intimidation of individuals or, for a particularly recalcitrant union sector, a delay in the building of a union health clinic or the withdrawal of a branch's quota for the union holiday resort in Mar del Plata or Córdoba.

Even more important as a factor in maintaining union leadership power was the ability an already ensconced leadership had to control the election procedure, to head off challenges from an internal opposition. Again the legal basis for this ability was to be found in law 14,455. Reversing the attempts made by the Aramburu government to implement proportional representation in the leadership of the unions, the Law of Professional Associations reintroduced the system found under Perón of the winning list taking all. The list that had a majority took complete control of the union, even if it had a minority of votes cast overall. There was no provision – except in exceptional circumstances in some unions – for minority representation.

Moreover, there was no such thing as electoral competition by individuals for specific posts. Each list consisted of a complete list of candidates for all posts, and the members voted for the list in its entirety, not for individual candidates. This in itself was also conducive to violence surrounding elections since the list of candidates elected not only took over the posts contested in the election, but once installed, with no opposition vigilance to worry about, it almost always proceeded to install its own supporters throughout the administrative apparatus of the union. This was obviously an example of the patronage powers mentioned above, but it also added another dimension to the electoral process, since in addition to the posts contested in the election, a whole network of employment opportunities was also at stake.

This system meant that once elected it was extremely difficult to dislodge a leadership group, since they were in sole charge of organising the subsequent elections. Effectively, it was a system ideally suited to the self-perpetuation of an ensconced union leadership. A number of ways of ensuring this were available to such a leadership. Most basically, considerable obstacles could be placed in the path of any group attempting to present their list of candidates. Individual unions had specific requirements which a list had to fulfil in order to present a list. A certain number of union members had to formally give their signed support for a list to be eligible; the exact number of signatures required varied but was usually in the range of 10–35% of a union's total membership. This was in itself a considerable obstacle, not merely because of the numbers involved but more importantly because, in a growing atmosphere of leadership intolerance of internal dissent, to put oneself forward as a sponsor of an opposition list was to run the risk of victimisation. Moreover, even if an opposition group did obtain the required number of signatures these could be questioned by the scrutinising committee which was dominated by the leadership. They could eliminate many of the signatures by simply claiming that they were not members in good standing with the union. Since being in good standing was determined by criteria entirely dependent on the existing leadership this was a procedure which was very difficult to challenge. There were, in addition, a number of requirements that a list of candidates had to fulfil; a certain number of years membership of the union, the prior exercise of some union function. As the TAMET example demonstrated, candidates of opposition lists were more exposed to victimisation than simple supporters. A simple device practised in the TAMET

Table 4. *Contested elections as a proportion of total elections*

Elections	1964	1965	1966	1967	1968
With single list	55.6	59.7	68.9	76.1	71.4
With opposition	44.4	40.3	31.1	23.9	28.6
No. of elections	111	124	132	176	175

Source: *El proceso político interno de los sindicatos en Argentina*, Juan Carlos Torre, Documento de Trabajo, Instituto Torcuato Di Tella, CIS, 1974, no. 89.

case was for the management to dismiss opposition leaders before they had fulfilled the requisite number of years of working in their plant.

The result of this capacity of an entrenched leadership to make the presentation of opposition lists difficult was the predominance of non-contested elections in Argentine trade unions. Figures taken from an official government survey in the mid 1960s indicate this fact very clearly (see Table 4).

Another vital weapon in the armoury of an existing leadership was their control of the *junta electoral* (election commission), since this controlled the actual running of the elections and the vote counting. The use of fraudulent procedures, which we noted was becoming more prevalent in the early 1960s, continued unabated in the following years. The exact extent is difficult to assess with accuracy but the opportunities were evidently numerous and there were enough proven cases of disappearing ballot boxes and false voting lists for one to assume that fraud was common.[22] In 1965 the Ministry of Labour suspended the elections in the textile workers' union for irregularities committed during the election procedure. In its resolution putting this suspension into effect the Ministry detailed some of the practices uncovered by its inspectors:

... considering the adulteration of voting lists in numerous factories sufficiently proved ... one of the clearest examples being the Platex company in Quilmes where, out of some 930 on the electoral register some 139 were not dues-paying members ...; considering that the electoral register which had more than 100,000 members was only given to the opposition lists some 24 hours before for them to scrutinise and challenge; that with less than 10 hours to go before the start of the election procedure the leaders of the Lista Azul y Celeste and the Lista Blanca did not know the order in which each one of the different travelling ballot boxes would be taken around the plants ...; that the electoral commission did not impugn the candidacies of two of the official list despite the fact that one of them has not been a textile worker for the required time and the other although he appears as a worker for the San Marco factory has never in fact worked there.[23]

The result of such practices was to make it nearly impossible for an internal opposition, even if it cleared the hurdles surrounding the presentation of its list, to displace an existing leadership at elections. One authority has calculated that of twenty-five unions with more than 25,000 members between 1957 and 1972 there were only two cases where an official leadership was defeated in elections.[24]

All of these factors undoubtedly helped give a union leadership a considerable base of power. It is important, however, to also emphasise the *ambiguity* of this power. The source of this ambiguity lay in the role of the state in labour affairs in Argentina. Evidently, a close relationship between state and unions is a common enough phenomena in the majority of urbanised and industrialised nations. However, in Argentina labour law, particularly law 14,455, gave the state exceptional powers vis-à-vis the union movement. Argentine labour law gave a government potential control of most areas of a union's internal affairs. A union's very ability to bargain collectively with employers was dependent on its being granted *personería*, legal recognition that it was the sole labour body able to bargain for and represent a certain industrial activity. Without *personería* the union lost its *raison d'être*. Labour law, moreover, laid down stipulations covering every area, from internal democracy, the running of elections, to keeping adequate records of where union funds go. The secretary of labour had the power to oversee the entire election procedure, checking the list of those eligible to vote, appointing inspectors to check polling on election day. He also had great power to check all financial matters – where the funds went, how they were collected. The law also regulated the frequency of general assemblies, who was eligible to be a delegate, how much notice had to be given of the holding of such assemblies.

The precise use made of all this power by the government of the day varied and was itself the basis of negotiations and bargains between governments and unions. It could be a subtle, negative use – the turning of a blind eye, the tolerating of some abuses practised by a union leadership whose good favours it suited a government to cultivate at a given moment. Alternatively, it could be a more positive, direct use – the harassment of a recalcitrant union whose leaders' actions were perhaps a political obstacle for a government. Given the wide area that labour regulations covered, very few unions could claim to adhere to the letter of the law in all matters and a secretary of labour could usually find a lapse when pressure needed to be brought to bear on a particular union leadership. In August 1962, to give an example, a fairly minor breach of regulations by the textile union, then a leader of union opposition to the military-imposed Guido government, was used as a pretext for the government's withdrawing of the union's *personería*. This meant that for six months the union was unable to start negotiations for a new wage contract. It also meant that the union received no funds because the employers, in spite of still having by law to stop union dues from textile workers' wage packets, did not now have to pass the money on to the union – since without *personería* it was not the legally recognised representative for the textile industry. This hit both the union social services and basic administration since they were unable to pay professional staff. In addition, grievances which were normally dealt with by the Ministry of Labour's conciliation department now had to go to the labour section of the justice department, where they could take many months to be dealt with.[25] Ultimately, the Ministry of Labour had the power to appoint an 'interventor' – that is to hand over the running of a union to a government-appointed administrator.

The fact that so much of a union's normal functioning was subject to such tight potential supervision by the government of the day inevitably led to an increased 'politicisation' of union affairs in Argentina. This must be understood on two levels. First, it meant that a union leader had to be interested in the complexion of a national government – its potential hostility or friendliness to him. The institutional future of his organisation – the future satisfaction of its needs – were intricately bound up with his relations with the state. This in itself was an important factor behind the 'integration' process which we outlined in a prior chapter; a powerful inducement to the adoption of pragmatic, 'common sense' realism by a union leadership, over and above their own ideological convictions and personal views. Yet, we should be aware that this did not simply imply union leadership vulnerability. A government determined to extend its legal supervision of the unions could find itself confronted by union determination to participate in its removal from power. In March 1966 the Radical government of Arturo Illia passed decree 969 modifying the Law of Professional Associations. The decree represented a wholesale attack on union leadership powers, enforcing stringent guarantees for internal democracy, weakening central union financial power by ordering the depositing of union dues with local branches, and also restricting the use of union finances and facilities for overtly political purposes. Faced with such a strategic attack on the structure of central union power, rather than the *ad hoc* use of government power against an individual union which could be negotiated over as part of some tactical manoeuvring, the Peronist unions replied in kind. Much of their negotiations with the military in the latter part of Illia's government, and the intransigence toward that government, should be seen in that light.

On a more personal level, this also meant that the particular personnel involved in the running of government departments – particularly the Ministry of Labour – became of some importance for union leaders. The process of 'integration' as a national strategy was built upon an interlocking of personal relationships built up between union leaders and ministry officials in the post-1958 period. Clearly, this itself was part of the process of 'corruption' of previously militant union officials. More to the point, in a system where the state had such considerable potential powers over union life it became essential for the union leaderships to be able to feel that they could trust the ministry bureaucrats with whom they dealt, to be confident that they talked the same language and shared a common view of the limits of the pressures and counter-pressures unions and governments could exert on one another. Continuity of officials was evidently important in building this trust and, in fact, it was the breaking of the continuity built up in the 1958–63 period when the Radicals under Illia took office that undoubtedly played an important role in the Peronist union/Radical government confrontation of 1963–6. The union leaders who had built up personal relationships and influence with ministry officials, who they knew shared a common appreciation of the 'realities' of union life, of the need to manipulate, control and compromise suddenly found that this personal network was swept away, that their normal 'connections' and 'understandings' no longer worked with the same smoothness as before.

The political role of the Peronist unions, 1962–6

Peronist union leaders did not simply derive power from their ability to bargain with the collective labour power of their members; they also derived considerable power from the political role of the unions as the chief organising force of the Peronist movement as a whole – what one author has called the 'juego doble' of representing the working class in its struggle for economic demands and representing the Peronist movement in its conflicts and manoeuvrings with other political forces in Argentina.[26] The March 1962 elections had posted warning not only of the dominant role of the unions in the actual organisation of an electoral campaign but also of their increasingly important role in determining general Peronist strategy in relation to other social and political forces. The tensions and conflicts which this role engendered, both within the Peronist movement and with relation to Perón himself, were to become increasingly apparent. Indeed, the underlying leitmotif of the often byzantine political history of the Peronist movement in these years must be sought on the one hand in the attempt of the Peronist union leadership around Vandor to confirm their domination of the whole movement, and to institutionalise this domination in a political expression acceptable to the other forces in the socio-political set up, and on the other hand, the determination of Perón to counteract this implicit challenge to his own position as sole ultimate authority in the movement.

The lessons drawn by the union leadership centred around Vandor from the March 1962 elections were boldly stated soon after in an editorial of the newspaper *Descartes*, edited by Miguel Gazzera, and set up as a voice for the 62 Organisations. The editorial was quite explicit in affirming the dominant position of the union sector of Peronism:

In the events following the 18 March elections the 62 Organisations have played the most definitive leading role. Its ethical position and the struggle it had led for it have clearly shown the role which it plays in the major events of the country ... it is also public knowledge that it was the coordinating committee of the 62 which decided on going to the polls with candidates of its own. The results proved without doubt the political vision and leadership capacity of the men who integrate the committee ... in the face of such evidence General Perón has decided that the integral leadership of the national movement should pass to the hands of the union leaders.... The facts had already been pointing in that direction. After September 1955 it was the workers' movement which adopted the initiatives of struggle against the government ... Augusto Vandor, helped by Miguel Gazzera, will have the enormous responsibility of assuming the maximum leadership of the movement. In him will be synthesised the domination gained by the union leadership in political matters.[27]

For the time being, however, this remained more a statement of intent than a reality, and in September 1962 Perón appointed Raul Matera as his chief representative in Argentina and head of the Consejo Coordinador y Supervisor del Peronismo. Matera had no previous history within the movement, and indeed it would seem that his complete lack of any organised personal following within Peronism, together with Matera's respectability and contacts with the military, were precisely the factors which appealed to Perón. Matera was primarily charged with negotiating Peronist participation in the presidential elections slated for July 1963. The formula which emerged of a popular conservative, Solano Lima, and a follower of Frondizi, Sylvestre Begnis, running on a Frente Nacional y Popular ticket, was supported by the 62 Organisations who prepared to run the campaign in very much the same way as they had the March 1962 elections. When the armed forces declared the formula to be unacceptable the 62, with Perón's approval, called for a blank vote.

In October 1963 Perón sent orders calling for the complete reorganisation of the movement. This reorganisation was to be led by a Junta Reorganizadora of four – Andrés Framini, Hilda Pineda, Ruben Sosa and Julio Antún. This was clearly a move against Vandor's growing power within the movement. Framini was at this time the most important rival to Vandor for leadership of the union sector, and Pineda and Sosa were associated with what was known as the *línea Villalón*, centred on the figure of Hector Villalón and identified with an insurrectional position.[28] This sector of the Peronist movement consistently criticised Vandor and the mainstream union leadership for their willingness to compromise, and for what was considered to be their overall plan of integrating Peronism within the status quo. Vandor's response was quick in coming; a statement by Sosa criticising Vandor led to the UOM's withdrawal from all the representative bodies of Peronism. Faced with what was effectively a boycott by the most powerful Peronist union Perón retreated and Sosa was removed from the Junta.[29] Vandor's position was further strengthened when a little later Alberto Iturbe, a close associate of Vandor's from the political wing of the movement, was appointed Perón's personal delegate. The Junta's effective demise was confirmed in January 1964 when Perón announced the creation of a new seven-member commission under Iturbe's leadership charged with the task of reorganising Peronism. This commission, known as the *heptúnvirato*, was clearly Vandorist in its composition; its members were Juana Matti, Andrés Framini, Carlos Gallo, Julio Antún, Jorge Alvarez, Miguel Gazzera and Delia Di Parodi. Of these seven only Framini and Antún were not committed to Vandor.

In the following six months the commission's task was to organise an inscription campaign which would culminate in the election of delegates to a founding congress of a new Justicialist Party, which Perón had determined would be the sole representative of Peronism. Vandor, through his control of the 62 Organisations and the UOM apparatus, effectively dominated this process. The inscription campaign was, numerically, not a success, some 33,000 members registering in the

Federal Capital, and some 170,000 in the province of Buenos Aires. This, however, made it all the easier for Vandor to control the election of convention delegates which took place in June 1964. The election was a contest between candidates loyal to Vandor and those following Framini's lead. Vandor's organisational superiority gave him a clear victory. The majority of delegates were from the 62 Organisations; in the metropolitan area of Buenos Aires some 60–65% of delegates were Vandorist, and in the province some 55%.[30] The party authorities elected from the convention duly reflected this balance of power.

The future strategy to be followed by the new union-dominated party was clear. The immediate objective was participation in the mid-term elections due in March 1965. Indeed, the internal election procedure had been carefully carried out in accordance with the existing statute of political parties, to show, as one union leader put it, 'that we follow the rules of the game'.[31] This electoral orientation was reinforced by the apparent failure of the CGT to follow up the factory occupations of June with other actions directed against the government. Similarly, the failure in December of the much heralded *Operación Retorno*, which had been built up as laying the groundwork for Perón's return to Argentina, confirmed the growing consensus feeling that the only viable strategy for Peronism lay along the road of electoral gains. The only open question was under which institutional banner Peronism would fight the elections.

The question of political strategy clearly involved the neo-Peronist parties. They had disobeyed Perón's order to blank vote in July 1963 and they had achieved some success, gaining two governorships and several national deputies. This led to considerable friction with the union sector, which regarded them as a threat to their attempt to act as the political arbiters of Peronism. The neo-Peronists offered the government an alternative channel with which to bargain politically with Peronism. The decision to reconstitute the Justicialist Party in early 1964 did much to weaken the position of the neo-Peronists which depended on their ability to present themselves to the authorities as the only legally constituted, moderate political body of Peronism. The union leadership hoped that with the legal recognition of the Justicialist Party they would be spared the need to bargain with the neo-Peronists for the use of their party labels. The latter in turn did not respond to Perón's instructions to integrate themselves into the new party structures, arguing instead that the movement should be organised into a federation of different groupings.

When in January 1965 the electoral judge refused to grant the Justicialist Party legal standing, some compromise became inevitable. It was agreed that Peronism would use the Unión Popular in the Federal Capital, Buenos Aires province, Chaco and San Juan, and a range of other neo-Peronist parties in the other provinces. There was no doubt, however, that the Justicialist Party would dominate selection of candidates, especially in Buenos Aires. Assemblies were held in the different sections of the party; each section was to put forward three candidates – one from the union wing, one from the women's sector and a third from the political. In Buenos Aires these were then to be scrutinised by a commission, controlled by Vandor's union people, where the order of the candidates was to be decided. In this process opponents were weeded out and the prime positions on the lists given to the women supporters of Delia Di Parodi, and the political and union allies of Vandor. The first position on the list of candidates for deputy in the Federal Capital and Buenos Aires went to Paulino Niembro and Geronimo Izzetta, both union confidants of Vandor.

The election of 14 March 1965 represented a considerable victory for Peronism, and above all for the union sector centred on Vandor. In the national Chamber of Deputies there now existed a Peronist block of fifty-two deputies, compared with the Radical Party's seventy. In the provincial assemblies there were more than 150 Peronists elected. In total the official Peronist lists received 3,032,186 votes, compared with some 318,197 for the neo-Peronists.[32] Paulino Niembro became the head of the Peronist block in congress, symbolising union power and domination of the movement. This was confirmed in April with the creation of a new body to lead Peronism. It was known as the Mesa Analítica and consisted of the five *grandes* – Framini, Vandor, Iturbe, Di Parodi and Lascano – three representatives of the 62 and two from the CGT.[33] The task of the new body was to determine the priority projects to be presented to congress by the Peronist block and to act as a general coordinator of the block's activity. The political task of the movement under its leadership was to consolidate the voting base gained in March and prepare for the 1967 elections, and beyond that for the 1969 presidential elections.

Perón's response to what was clearly intended to be the institutional confirmation of the union leadership's domination of the movement was not slow in coming. While he had consented to the electoral strategy, he could not remain indifferent to the implications of the post-election situation in terms of the balance of forces within Peronism and his own position of authority. In July 1965, he sent instructions calling for the creation of a broad based body of nineteen, which was to include the existing leadership together with delegates from the neo-Peronists and the youth sectors. The aim of this move was to dilute the power of the five *grandes* and their allies who effectively controlled the Mesa Analítica. The Vandorists tried to convince Perón of the folly of such a move but he remained adamant. At the beginning of September they therefore wound up the Mesa and announced the formation of a new, and broader, body called the Junta Coordinadora Nacional. This opening up was, however, more apparent than real. The new body consisted of representatives from the neo-Peronists, the congressional block, the 62 and the Justicialist Party, in addition to the five *grandes*. Thus although the leadership group had been formally expanded it still remained very much tied to, and dominated by, the Vandorist leadership.[34]

The implicit refusal of the union leaders around Vandor to dilute their power within a broadened national body inaugurated a six-month period of overt struggle between this leadership and Perón and his more loyal followers in Argentina. Whilst the language of the dispute remained the typically opaque idiom of internal Peronist discourse – with both sides at various times swearing ultimate allegiance to Perón – the issues in contention were clear enough beneath the rhetorical surface.

Perón's response to the challenge of the union leadership was to send his wife, Isabel, to Argentina with instructions to reorganise the movement. On her arrival she initiated discussions with various political and military figures and began to draw together the anti-Vandorist forces within Peronism. Her presence enabled the Vandorists to phrase their disagreements with Perón in terms of criticisms of his representatives in Argentina – they were, thus, ostensibly criticising the king's advisers rather than the king. Yet the real challenge to Perón himself was apparent. Nor was it merely a question of Perón's personal position. Intricately bound up with this was the question of the legal institutionalisation of the movement. The fundamental concern of the Vandorist leadership on these issues was made clear at a special conference of the 62 Organisations held in Avellaneda on 22 October 1965. At this conference of 100 representatives loyal to Vandor a motion was carried repudiating 'the pacts between those who invoke a non-existent representativity in the movement, and the spokesman of the government'.[35] While this was, on the surface, an attack on Isabel's representatives who were busy speaking with various official government and military spokesmen, it was more fundamentally questioning the authority of Perón himself to carry on negotiations in the name of the movement, over and above the locally elected authorities. The Avellaneda conference reaffirmed 'its will to promote the immediate institutionalisation of the movement', which would take the form of a legal political party organised 'from the bottom upward in a clean, internally democratic process'.[36] Clearly, Perón's role in a party whose leaders were elected at national conventions would be limited, since crucial political decisions, such as negotiating the terms of Peronist participation in the 1967 elections, would inevitably pass out of his hands.

The dispute split Peronism from top to bottom. In the union field José Alonso and a group of other union leaders challenged Vandor's right to speak in the name of the 62 Organisations, and after their expulsion for this dissent they formed a rival body the 62 Organisations *de pie junto a Perón*. In early 1966 they held the founding conference in Tucumán and gathered together a wide range of union figures, particularly from the interior of the country and from those hardliners who had been marginalised by Vandor since 1962.[37] Vandor kept his control of the base of the 62, and with communist and some independent support he displaced Alonso from the head of the CGT. He then reconvened a national congress of the CGT and elected a new secretariat headed by a Vandorist, Francisco Pérez, of the power workers' union.

In the political sphere Perón sent orders in late 1965 demanding the dissolution of the Junta Coordinadora Nacional and the submission of the Vandorists to a newly created Comando Delegado Nacional. While they could not refuse to disband the Junta, the Vandorists prevaricated when it came to joining a new body whose composition would be determined by Isabel Perón. They also managed to keep control of most of the official apparatus of the Justicialist Party. The crucial test of strength between the two sides came in a by-election for deputy in Mendoza, in April 1966. The Justicialist Party's candidate was Alberto Serú García; Perón countered by naming an alternative candidate, Enrique Corvalan Nanclares. The Vandorist leadership of the party argued that whoever had been democratically elected by the local party would by law have to be the candidate. The symbolism of this assertion was obvious; on the one hand Vandor was asserting the right of the local leadership to determine their own political decisions, and on the other Perón was insisting on his right to dictate such decisions. The result of the contested election between the two Peronists was a clear victory for Corvalan Nanclares, and ultimately Perón. From this time until the coup of June 1966 which overthrew Illia, Vandor largely concentrated on consolidating his union base and undermining the position of the rival 62 Organisations.

Advantages and disadvantages of playing politics

Their role as political leaders was a role which could turn union leaders into national figures, courted by other social and political forces and with powers beyond those of traditional union leaders. Yet, as the preceding account makes clear, we are, once more, faced with issues of ambiguity. The power the Peronist leadership derived from their political role was not an unqualified one.

There were several ways in which their political role could be advantageous. The very fact that they were the ones on the ground in Argentina charged with the day-to-day negotiation and running of the movement, the distribution of Perón's political patronage, and with a base of power in the unions relatively free from his direct control, helped to enhance the union leadership's authority. Moreover, their ability to mobilise the working class in the name of Perón was an important weapon to be used to pressure a government for concrete economic gains. Out of the sustained mobilisation of the *Semana de Protesta* of 1963, the *Plan de Lucha* of 1964, and the mobilisation during the state visit of General De Gaulle in 1965, concrete concessions such as the minimum wage law were obtained from the Radical government.[38] The entire operation mounted by the Peronist unions for the return of Perón at the end of 1964 can also be partly seen as a way of maintaining the pressure of the *Plan de Lucha*, with the more concrete political demand for Perón's return of relatively secondary importance.

Being the principal political representatives of Perón vis-à-vis the Peronist rank and file gave union leaders a certain added authority, and a basic reservoir of support that failure in the economic field might otherwise have denied them. Every visit to Madrid or letter from Perón could be used to offset a strike lost or a bad contract signed. This could evidently be regarded as no more than a specific Argentine twist to a common practice of union leaderships – the 'selling' of collective agreements and leadership decisions. Their political role could be said to have helped the union leaders to maintain what one author has described as the 'illusion of achievement'.[39] This was not a simple, one-way process. If their political authority buttressed their union positions it could also be argued that their ability to mobilise their unions on ostensibly bread-and-butter issues was also used by union leaders as a weapon in their political manoeuvrings. Thus, it is clear that while the factory occupations of 1964 responded to a genuine demand for economic and social gains, they also had a political dimension. The *Plan de Lucha* was intended to be a demonstration to the military of both the weakness of Illia's government, and the corresponding power of the unions. The armed forces would thus be persuaded either to come to terms with the union leadership in the event of any coup they might be planning against the Radical government, or to modify objections they had concerning Peronist electoral participation, on the grounds that absorbtion in the election process would diffuse the militant social power displayed by the factory occupations.[40]

In general, though, political mobilisation could give an embattled working class hope and a realisable substitute for victories in the economic arena. In the generally uncomfortable economic climate in this period, union leaders often emphasised the difficulty of making gains in the purely collective bargaining field and directed their members' attention to the need to seek a solution to their problems in the wider field of political action. They spoke to them as both union and political leaders, and the latter undoubtedly helped to bolster the former. In the situation of general political proscription of Peronism after 1955, and the parallel recreation of a strong union movement, the political identity of the Peronist working class increasingly became incarnated in its trade unions, and this was a powerful factor in enabling union leaderships to maintain their strength in what were otherwise, on many occasions, highly unfavourable situations.

Yet, it is also evident that this union political power had its limits. First, because in an institutional framework dominated by the Perón/anti-Perón dichotomy, there was always a limit as to how far unions could push the bargaining threat of Peronist mobilisation, participation in elections and the like, before the armed forces stepped in, doing away, albeit temporarily, with the process of threat and counter-threat. The Frondizi experience illustrated very well the limits and dangers of the political game from the unions' point of view. For four years Frondizi used the threat that if the unions pressed too hard, struck too often, or participated in elections there would be a coup against his government, which would lead to a far tougher anti-union regime. The threat, naturally enough, worked both ways, and much of the *modus vivendi* between Frondizi and Peronist unions was premised on a recognition of this fact. The Peronist participation in the March 1962 elections had shown that Frondizi had been correct, since the Guido government was far less amenable to union pressure. Similarly, the Peronist gains at the 1965 elections, orchestrated by the union sector, and their likely success in 1967, were important calculations in the minds of those who carried out the June 1966 coup. It was, in short, a 'juego impossible,' which the Peronist unions could not win owing to the very fact that they were Perón's chief political expression.[41]

It is also important to realise that their power of bargaining politically came more from their position as Perón's political representatives before the masses than from the independent bargaining power they derived from the union field, and was, ultimately at least, dependent on the prestige of Perón's name. This was clearly a source of strength, but it was also a source of a fundamental weakness since their chief political bargaining weapon was, in the last resort, not theirs to control. The use of the *camiseta* did give them considerable room for manoeuvre and some independence in their relations with Perón and with governments, but it was not the equivalent of bargaining politically from a position of entirely autonomous union strength.

Perón did allow the union leadership very considerable freedom of action in their role as his political representatives, and very rarely interfered in their specifically union dealings. Partly, this reluctance to interfere was due to realism on his part. From his exile in Madrid he could not hope to control the daily details concerning the movement in Argentina. As he put it in an interview: 'I like to act a little like the eternal father, with the blessing "urbi et orbi", but letting providence do its work, without appearing too much. I think that the force of the Eternal Father is that he does not appear too much. If we saw God every day we would end up losing our respect for him, and moreover, we wouldn't be short of some fool who wanted to replace him.'[42]

Perón was, moreover, aware of the power of a union leadership, its capacity to control the union machinery, and the potential dangers of weakening what was from his point of view the 'vertebral column' of the movement. The prolonged clash with Vandor in late 1965 and early 1966 was evidence of the risks involved in challenging a firmly entrenched leader like Vandor, and the damage done to the movement in general by such a challenge. The problems implied in such a conflict were delicate. As Perón explained to a correspondent who had questioned his failure to curb Vandor's independence earlier:

If the UOM, as a Peronist organisation, names its secretary general we can do nothing else but accept it, especially when it is the case of Vandor who has always been a Peronist. To do otherwise would imply the expulsion of the union from the Peronist movement, which would be inconceivable because the metal workers are all Peronists. As you can see, the problem from the point of view of the leadership of the movement is not as simple as it seems.[43]

Perón was, moreover, generally very cautious about siding with one wing or another of the movement. This reflected both a pragmatic realism and also a recognition on his part of the contradictory amalgam of forces which went to make up Peronism and which he considered to be one of the movement's strengths. He preferred to act as a final arbiter of conflict, and direct intervention on one side or another was a last resort.

It remained true, however, that while possession of the *camiseta* did give the union hierarchy considerable room for manoeuvre, and a reasonable degree of independence in their relations with Perón and with governments, this was not the same as operating from a position of autonomous union strength. Vandor's reported remark that 'if I abandoned the *camiseta* I would lose the union in a week' is a realistic recognition of this fact.[44] When the union leaders' independence became too great and they started to use their powers in ways Perón disapproved of, he could remind them of the relative nature of that power. Perón and the union leaders were, thus, caught in something of a vicious circle. Perón was, given the nature of the post-1955 situation, bound to rely primarily on the unions as his principal means of bargaining and of asserting Peronist claims within the political system. However, the success which the unions achieved in this role, the confidence which they derived from it and the boost it gave to their organisational base, inevitably posed an implicit challenge to Perón's own capacity to determine the movement's ultimate fate.

One of the results of this situation was the frequent phenomenon of Perón being forced by circumstances to use and promote the union organisation of the movement and then, as this seemed about to reach some formalised expression, of his deliberately turning against it and provoking its demise. It often seemed as though the very success of the unions in developing their role as Perón's chief political representatives condemned them to ultimate failure in this sphere. Hence, too, we find the organisational chaos and eclecticism of Peronism. It was to remain, particularly after Vandor's failure to give it some coherent, union-based institutionalised form, essentially a loose federation of different groups loyal to Perón. This, indeed, seems to have been his intention. For all his reiterated statements concerning the need to organise the movement, organisation on the only terms really conceivable, that is based on and dominated by the unions, was precisely what he most feared. He seems, if one ignores his formal rhetoric, to have conceived of the movement ideally in terms of a semi-formalised, almost colloidal state, capable of constantly challenging the status quo, of preventing a peaceful institutionalisation which would have excluded Peronism, of evolving a concrete organisational expression for this or that tactical necessity, but never achieving anything permanent. This underlying notion seems to have been present since the immediate post-1955 era. For all the paraphernalia of organisational terms to be found in the documents of the time, Perón's own conception of the forms the political struggle of the movement would take comes across as curiously semi-anarchic in nature. In the correspondence with Cooke we constantly find Perón referring to the myriads of different actions by different groups, each indulging in the 'revolutionary gymnastics' which would in some almost metaphysical way undermine the will of the 'tyranny' to continue governing, and, unified only by a common loyalty to him, achieve the longed for 'national insurrection'. The organisational forms that this process might take were left imprecise. The implications for the union leadership of this attitude were made abundantly clear with the defeat of the Vandorist candidate in the Mendoza elections. Any plans Vandor might have had to create a union-based party with Perón as a simple figurehead had to be definitively abandoned after this débâcle.

8

Ideology and politics in Peronist unions: different currents within the movement

While Peronism does not structure itself on the lines of a revolutionary party, i.e. with a revolutionary politics understood as the unity of theory, action and organisational method, it will continue to be subject to spontaneism, to the juxtaposition of tactics that are not integrated into a strategy, into deadends that successive bureaucrats lead it into; leaders who can conceive of no other solution save electoral fronts or army coups. Yet, both *golpismo* and electoral fronts imply renouncing the seizure of power.

John William Cooke

The common basis

We have already analysed in a previous part of this work the process by which crucial notions of formal Peronist ideology had survived in the post-1955 period. We have stressed the potentially antagonistic coexistence of these tenets with notions and values which emerged from the class conflict and bitterness of the 1955–60 experience of the Peronist working class and, in particular, an important stratum of militants. As the tide turned against this militant experience something like an agreed-upon set of assumptions coalesced around the mainstream Peronist union movement. The notions which informed this ideological and programmatic agenda attenuated many of the ideological tensions and conflicts of the earlier period and went a considerable way to establishing a consensus between rival factions of the movement. Indeed, Vandorist hegemony within the Peronist union movement was based largely on its ability to articulate this consensus. The heirs to the more radical potentialities which had been present during the Resistance were to be increasingly restricted to marginal sectors of the workers' movement, and even they, as we shall see, would not deny many of the basic, formal notions of this Peronist orthodoxy.

A document issued by the 62 Organisations in August 1963 admirably summarised the main economic and social elements common to the variety of programmes and statements issuing from the Peronist union movement in the mid 1960s. The economic demands included: a policy of full employment and high consumption; control over costs, fixing of maximum prices and limits on profits; the stimulating of private activity of national capital; the nationalisation of bank deposits and the severing of ties with the IMF; the application of monetary and credit policies specifically aimed at stimulating production and reactivating the economy; rigorous exchange controls to eliminate the import of unnecessary goods, or ones which would compete with Argentine industry. In addition the document called for: a foreign commerce policy which would ensure the necessary state intervention to diversify exports; the cancellation of all petrol contracts with foreign companies; an agrarian reform which would eliminate the latifundios; the nationalisation of transport, all means of communication, basic industries and all others which 'might make possible the formation of monopolies'; the denouncing of all agreements which grant privileges to foreign capital and the instituting of controls on the repatriation of profits. In addition, economic priority was given to social investment in housing, education and the socialisation of medical treatment. These economic demands were conceived as forming part of 'an economic and social policy which will bring about the structural changes necessary to give the country back its economic independence, political sovereignty and social justice'.[1]

The ideological presuppositions informing these economic policy demands were clear. First, the underlying context in which these economic demands were to be met was not specifically anti-capitalist. There was, in fact, in the various programmes put forward by Peronist unionism in these years a consistent preoccupation with the encouragement of private industrial development; as witness the demands made in the programme of the 62 Organisations which we have quoted from above. There were, however, two important caveats. This industry was to be owned by national, Argentine capital. Point eleven of the 62's programme stated 'we must stimulate private national capital so as to achieve and consolidate a native capital which permits the development of all the internal possibilities which will enable us to free ourselves in the shortest possible time from the collaboration of foreign capital'.[2] Secondly, this industry must be subject to the limitations imposed by the national good. It must recognise its social responsibilities to other sectors of the national community. Thus, for example, the fixing of maximum prices and the control of profits was premised on the reasoning that 'in this way private activities will not become monopolies, nor will profits exceed the demands of the common good and the interest of the population and the country'.[3] Similarly, nationalisation was conceived as being 'a means to ensure that private capital takes into account the general interests of the nation and advances the welfare of the people'.[4] These twin ideological assumptions can clearly be traced back to the state-generated rhetoric of the Peronist era. They were present also in the post-1955 era and underlay, as we have shown, the search for, and belief in, a strategy of 'genuine' economic development overseen by the state.

The social philosophy implied in these economic demands was also clear. Fundamentally, the Peronist union movement clung to a formal commitment to a belief that the economic policies necessary to effect a change in structures within the Argentine economy could be implemented within a context of class consensus. They consistently emphasised their opposition to the notion of class conflict. On a general level this belief was reflected in a search for class allies with whom to form a multi-class alliance which would form the political basis for the implementation of the economic strategy we have outlined. One clear expression of this in the mid 1960s was the search for common ground with employers' organisations, in particular the Confederación General Económica.

The CGE grouped together the smaller industrialists – often based in the interior – largely based on national capital and dependent on the internal market. While there were frequent discussions between the CGE and the unions, it was primarily at particular crisis points in the economic cycle that contacts were closest. At the depth of the depression of 1962–3 the CGE found itself sharing the unions' preoccupation over the need to reactivate the economy. Serving the internal market, and having grown up largely under tariff protection, they were bound to be sympathetic to union calls for increased consuming power, extended credit facilities and discriminating tariffs, as well as sharing the general union concern with the effect of monopolies and foreign capital on Argentine industry.[5] In a similar vein the CGT went out of its way to involve other social sectors in the various stages of the *Plan de Lucha* against Illia's government. In the build up to the general strike of 31 May – the *Semana de Protesta* – there were scheduled discussions held with employers' organisations, other professional associations and a general meeting of political parties. Moreover, one of the principal slogans of the CGT called on the employers 'to accompany your workers in action against the parasites of the country'.[6] Only those parasitic sectors most closely tied to foreign capital and the native 'oligarchy' were considered to be beyond the scope of this sought-after consensus.

More specifically, the emphasis on class consensus was transferred to the realm of the capitalist enterprise itself. If the nation was conceived of as a community of interests which were, ultimately, non-antagonistic, so too was the individual company. While they remained formally committed to a belief in the benefits of private capital, these had to be limited by the common good both through the mediation of the state, and by means of a change in the nature and concept of the firm. In 1965 the CGT produced a document which explicitly spelt out what this implied: 'It was traditional, liberal capitalism which created the myth that the company is exclusively the property of capital ... it is necessary to recognise legally that the company is a unity of production, that is to say a community of people associated together for a common purpose, and whose fruits are the property of both capital and labour.'[7] This recognition of the social function of capital was to be expressed in practical terms in the introduction of worker participation – *cogestión*. In all the major policy statements of these years, from all the different tendencies within Peronist unionism, *cogestión* appeared as a prominent demand. The 1963 document of the 62 Organisations had given great emphasis to this demand. The union leadership emphasised, however, the non-conflictual nature of this coparticipation. Paulino Niembro, the leader of the Peronist block in congress and a prominent leader of the metal workers, replied when asked by a journalist how he reconciled the social function of property with free enterprise:

... it is necessary to erase the image of the owner of the factory as the boss. The owner is a leader in the same way that union men are leaders; the company is a common good which must be at the service of society. *Cogestión* is therefore necessary to avoid the excessive appropriation of profits. This does not signify, however, that the employers lose control of their company.[8]

This emphasis on the enterprise as a community of interests was continually reiterated as a rationale behind the actions of the Peronist unions. Even those actions which most directly challenged both the state and employers were justified on the basis of this essentially non-conflictual rationale. Thus in mid 1962 at the depth of the recession, when there was a wave of factory occupations in the metal-working industry to protest the factory closures and lay offs, and the UOM leadership had itself disposed that the occupied plants should continue to function with the layed-off workers operating their machines, it was nonetheless careful to emphasise that in doing this: 'The metal workers are not attempting extremist or collectivist solutions as some claim, but rather they are defending something which they consider their own: the enterprise as a community of interests.'[9] In a similar fashion the CGT went out of its way to reassure the public that the mass factory occupations of 1964 were not intended to initiate their expropriation from their rightful owners, but merely to demonstrate that 'while factories are the property of their owners they also belong to the country and, therefore, to the workers since they must fulfill a social function'.[10]

Another crucial element in formal Peronist union ideology was the assumption – common both to leaders and rank and file – that the role of the union went beyond the basic process of wage bargaining. This broadened notion of the function of trade unionism was an important feature which underlay much of the internal debate within Peronism and between Peronist unions and the state authorities. In the post-1955 era the Peronist union leaders deliberately fostered an image of the extensive functions of unions based on their previous experience under Perón, and it was an image which found a ready response among their members. What precisely did these 'extensive functions' imply? In general in the 1962–6 period we can see the development of two different trends of thought, two different emphases within Peronist unionism concerning this issue.

On the one hand, there was a clear tendency in these years to place increasing emphasis on the social function of unions, over and above their wage-bargaining role. With the growth of the financial resources of the unions after the upheaval of the 1955–60 period, and the subsequent expansion of social services which we outlined in the preceding chapter, union leaders frequently fostered an image of their unions as fundamentally service organisations providing a whole range of social services to their members. The year books and almanacs of the leading unions were more and more concerned with the details of their medical facilities with graphs displaying the wonders of the orthodontic services; fillings and extractions performed seemed to become a measure of union achievement. Nor, indeed, should the attraction of this be belittled; in the absence of anything resembling effective state social services the services provided by the unions – ranging from medical treatment to subsidised prescriptions to, in some cases, union-built housing estates – were an issue of no little importance to the union member.

Hand in hand with this there existed a tendency to use business criteria for measuring union effectiveness. Juan José Taccone, a leader of the light and power workers' union, in a speech of January 1966 celebrating the union's founding, contrasted its weakness in 1944 with its strength twenty-two years later: 'Today on the other hand we have an organisation with a real capital value of more than $1500 million, an annual economic turnover of more than $2000 million, a collective contract, participation with management ... sports grounds, hotels, apartments.'[11] A few years earlier Pedro Gomis, the leader of the state petroleum workers, had bluntly declared in an interview: 'We share the modern conception that an organisation's worth should be measured in terms of its economic capacity.'[12] Both the light and power union and the petrol workers' union operated in privileged state-run sectors of the economy, and the majority of unions could not hope to emulate their achievement in terms of the services provided, yet it is still true that the emphasis on such an image of a union's function was increasingly common among all unions at this time, both Peronist and non-Peronist.

The other principal trend of thought referred to above was specifically associated with the Peronist unions: namely the definition of the goals and functions of unions in the broadest political and social terms. Andrés Framini gave a clear definition of this fundamental ideological conviction in his speech to the eighth national congress of the textile workers' union in December 1961:

The union must also serve for other things of great importance which involve action far beyond the daily struggle that we carry on within trade unionism ... we have to convince ourselves once and for all that we will not be able to help ourselves even as textile workers if we don't aim much higher, because if we don't we won't even achieve our limited, immediate goals.[13]

It is true that in modern, industrial societies unions have as a matter of course tended to take an interest in a far wider range of issues than wage bargaining and working conditions; they have also routinely let their views be known on general economic and social issues, and have tried to influence the overall context within which wages and conditions are bargained over. This has especially been the case where the economic situation has been unfavourable for routine union bargaining. It is also true that, as we have seen, the specifically political role of Peronist unions could be used for non-political ends, namely to enable a union leadership to 'sell' agreements to their members. It could, therefore be argued that there was little specifically 'ideological' about the Peronist unions' insistence on a broadened union role. Statements concerning the need for unions to look beyond immediate economic demands were a natural development in a complex industrial society, and part and parcel of any union leader's rhetorical baggage. In this context, therefore, it could be argued that we should not attach too much ideological weight to what were essentially functional developments. Yet, it seems clear that what distinguishes the Peronist case was the insistence with which the political role of unions was emphasised; the conscious denial of the validity of a purely 'business unionism' conception.[14] When the weekly information bulletin of the CGT could claim in 1964 that 'it is incontrovertible that the *principal* objective of a union organisation is the changing of the political, economic and social structure', then it is clear that more was being claimed than a simple right to let their opinions be known concerning general questions of national policy.[15]

Certainly, both the non-Peronist unions and the anti-Peronist authorities were aware of the extensive nature of Peronist claims on this issue. The rock on which Peronist/non-Peronist union unity always foundered in these years was precisely the Independents' rejection of the Peronists' grander political and social claims. Thus, for example, the independents refused to continue with the *Plan de Lucha* after Illia had conceded many of the initial economic demands of the CGT. The Peronist claim that the *Plan's* fundamental aim was to pressure for a more profound social and political restructuring was not, in their eyes, legitimate. Similarly, there existed a constant polemic after 1955 between Peronist unions and the state on this issue. Every minister of labour or of the economy in the post-1955 governments had considered it necessary to argue that the unions must limit themselves to the non-political field. The Peronist press, on the other hand, frequently took up the theme to reject it. The culmination of the polemic, in legal terms at least, arrived with the Radical government's decree 969 regulating the Law of Professional Associations. Article 2 of the decree prohibited 'all acts of proselytism or ideological propaganda' on the part of the unions. The Peronist response to this was to argue that their interest in the wider political and ideological issues was not a narrow party-political one. They were, they claimed, reflecting the legitimate concern of Argentine workers for a more just society and a sovereign nation, a concern which found its ideological and political expression in their adherence to Peronism, and its chief institutional voice, the Peronist unions.

Despite the general ideological consensus which existed within mainstream, and even dissident, Peronist unionism the union movement was not a homogeneous body acting in unison in an agreed response to a commonly held set of ideological tenets. Within mainstream Peronist unions there was still a divergence of opinions concerning the different ways of achieving their general ideological aspirations. The issue of exactly which political tactics and forms were most appropriate remained hotly contested and resolved itself primarily into the question of how the unions should interpret the political function they claimed for themselves both vis-à-vis the state, other social forces and, indeed, within the Peronist movement itself.

The Vandorist project

Augusto Vandor, as leader of the metal workers' union and the dominant figure within the Peronist union apparatus, evoked extreme reactions within Peronism, ranging from hagiography at one pole to demonology at the other.[16] The images associated with these diverse approaches are correspondingly diverse, with the martyred leader of the one countered by the organiser of union corruption and gangsterism of the other. In these circumstances it is very difficult to find a way through the competing images and arrive at something approaching an objective judgement of the aims of Vandorism.

In part this difficulty is simply a reflection of the fact that Vandorism, as a current within Peronism, was not clearly definable as a coherent doctrinal and theoretical movement, easily distinguishable from other currents. Partly, too, it is a reflection of the essential pragmatism of most union leaders. Vandor was a master of the *realpolitik* of Argentine politics and of the methods necessary to control a union movement. He was, in this sense, the archetypal union boss, confident of his power to negotiate with politicians, army leaders and employers, and doctrinal principles were of secondary importance in the everyday turmoil of union affairs. Miguel Gazzera, an intimate collaborator, has given us an astute description of Vandor. He was not, says Gazzera, 'a leader of the barricades and even less a revolutionary leader ... all his acts had their roots in a solid pragmatism and intuition'.[17] Gazzera goes on to say that: 'Vandor was interested more in the details thrown up by a given opportunity than by the questions of overall strategy ... he never tried to talk about profundities of which he was ignorant, and if anyone tried to do this his firm and practical reply dissuaded them with his lack of interest.'[18]

This pragmatism and lack of interest in ideological discussions carried with it implicit problems for the researcher. The milieu Vandor operated in was that of the personal understanding, the deal sealed with a scotch in the ministry, or an arrangement worked out in a local *boliche*. By definition, this meant that there were very few neat summaries of ideological positions, nor even expressions of tactical reasoning behind specific actions. There are, certainly, no policy documents revealing Vandor's innermost thoughts which might form the convenient basis for some explanatory framework concerning his overall aims. In these circumstances it is tempting to agree with Amado Olmos, the hospital and sanitation workers' leader, a long-time intimate of Vandor's who was considered by many to be the *éminence grise* behind Vandorism in its heyday, when he said: 'Vandorism suffers from a breach which it is impossible to close up: its lack of ideology. Thus Vandor acts on the basis of adventurism, of political opportunism.'[19]

To accept such an evaluation at face value would, however, be excessive. First, because pragmatism and opportunism are themselves ideological; the conscious denial of ideology is itself part of the common-sense philosophy so beloved of pragmatists, whether union leaders or not. Second, because there *are* some statements of intent and principle by Vandor and certainly many more by his more loquacious followers. The little written evidence we do have suggests that his personal views were eminently unexceptionable; they precisely match the ideological presuppositions we have recently outlined.[20] From the point of view of the concrete political implications of this position for the Peronist unions we are dependent upon the evidence of actual trade union practice, and the rationalisations provided for this practice by some of the chief unions enrolled in the Vandorist current.

Viewing this evidence it is clear that there was a certain coherence, an underlying project behind Vandorist activity. This was the creation of a union-based political movement – the outlines of which we described in the preceding chapter. This was fundamentally no more than an elaboration of the *de facto* position in which the unions found themselves after 1955. It was the expression of the desire of the majority section of the union hierarchy to establish itself as the major political force representing Argentine workers, and as such to be negotiated with by other political and social forces. In this sense Vandorism represented the attempt of this leadership to consolidate and institutionalise the political power which had accrued to them both through their position as representatives of a majority of organised workers and through their role as the principal legalised expression of Peronism. While in 1958 they had delegated that power to an outsider, Arturo Frondizi, and then maintained a blank vote position in the face of his 'betrayal', from 1962 on they were determined to, wherever possible, construct their own political apparatus, based on their control of the union movement, and thus deal directly with other social and political forces.

This project was often described as the creation of a *partido obrero*, that is a working-class-based political party intimately connected with the unions, and modelled along the lines of classic social democratic labour parties. Evidently, such a project had certain historical roots within Peronism, in particular the emergence of the Partido Laborista in 1945. The conception as it appeared in the mid 1960s was most commonly associated with the names of Olmos and Gazzera. Yet, it is important to be clear as to what Vandorism meant by this conception. Olmos, in an interview shortly before his death in 1968, after he had broken with Vandor, was asked about his 'enthusiastic defence of *un partido obrero, un partido clasista*'. He felt called upon to correct his interviewer:

At a conference of the tobacco workers' union in 1959 I in fact expounded just the opposite; what I did demand was the domination for the unions in the tactical leadership of the Peronist movement and I pointed out the role of the political actions of the workers' movement. From this demonstration it was perfectly clear that the workers' movement was the great force, the basis and the sole factor which had sustained Peronism in its most desperate moments, and at that time I maintained that this hegemony must be exercised by the union leaders... This, I insist, does not mean excluding other forces because that would mean totally denying the essence of Peronism.[21]

From this two fundamental features emerge concerning the Vandorist project. First, the ideal political and social model of Vandor and the union leadership remained that which they derived from the Peronist experience of 1946–55. Olmos's insistence that union hegemony did not imply a *clasista* conception of the Peronist movement clearly indicated their commitment to a notion of Peronism as a multi-class alliance whose ultimate political goal should be the formation of a broad coalition with other 'factors of power' in national life: the church, socially conscious and nationally minded employers and the armed forces.[22] Notions of working-class autonomy and independent activity which had been part of the militant discourse of the Resistance era had, therefore, been largely erased from this concept of union hegemony within the Peronist movement. Olmos, in a lecture given to union cadres in 1966, spoke nostalgically of the pre-1955 era which had witnessed 'the great fraternal embrace between armed forces and the people' in the interests of the nation and social justice.[23] It was a unity which, Olmos affirmed, needed to be recreated.

Second, it becomes clear that the fundamental issue at stake for Vandorism was the internal balance of forces within Peronism. A constant theme of Peronist union propaganda in these years was to emphasise, as we have seen, the social and political weight of unions in a wider society. This implied, as Olmos's statement makes clear, a claim to hegemony within the Peronist movement against both the neo-Peronists and the official political wing. But what it also implied was a claim for relative independence from Perón himself. If they really were 'the vertebral column' of the movement, as Perón himself was fond of saying, then they must have the freedom to determine the tactics in Argentina, to negotiate their own destiny. At the height of the dispute with Perón and Isabel in 1965 and 1966 the influential Vandorist union of power workers published an editorial in its journal which summarised this aspiration:

The fundamental condition for Justicialism to make strides on the national political scene must be that the workers' movement, the vital mass of its structure, should not be relegated to being a mere appendage of the movement ... moreover it is not possible to keep management of the movement in the hands of one person, the key is the creation of a true leadership team made up of truly representative figures who work together with a team mentality; this organism must plan the activities and the internal developments of the movement.[24]

This had been precisely the message of the Avellaneda congress a few months previously, and was the root cause of the conflict with Perón at this time.

Within this general framework the question of the political tactics to be adopted was a flexible one. Vandorism was essentially agnostic and opportunistic concerning political methods and forms. It was at this level that Vandor's pragmatism came into its own. In general it is evident that his followers preferred to take advantage, when the opportunity was offered, of the legal party-political system to achieve their political goals. A leading spokesman of the Vandorist current emphasised in 1965 that while the unions must keep their options open as far as forms of struggle were concerned 'in general we must avoid both the *tremendismo guerrillerista* and abject collaboration, and triumph instead through successive electoral confrontations'.[25] Indeed at times the Vandorists were wont to wax lyrical about the fundamental representative role unions played within the political system, and how they would reinvigorate the institutions of an exhausted liberal system. This tone was particularly present after the 1965 elections. An editorial in the petrol workers' union paper immediately after the elections enthused over the election of union candidates. They had, it said, shown that 'the organic expression of the masses is the unions and these, confounding all forecasts, have revolutionised the electoral and representative system'.[26]

Their preference for electoral politics was logical. They fully appreciated that their ability to gain power and influence within the political system came from their capacity to mobilise their membership in political terms as Perón's delegates in Argentina and, in more purely union terms, as organisers of labour. It was the pressure which they could exert through this mobilising and representative capacity which was the crucial basis of their negotiating position. By definition a pluralistic electoral system gave them the most scope for the exercise of such pressure and negotiation. They were fond of telling journalists that they had the tactical option of either achieving power through elections or, if their electoral gains provoked a military reaction, of leading a popular resistance to military dictatorship.[27] They were, however, under no illusions about the difficulties military regimes posed for them in terms of political bargaining and pressuring. Negotiations with military regimes tended to be one-sided affairs, and from personal experience in the years after 1955 most of them knew what popular resistance to military regimes could entail in terms of their own comfort and prestige.

Nevertheless, this general preference should not blind us to two important qualifications. First, that as union leaders aware of the *realpolitik* of post-1955 Argentina they had to take account of the possibility – even probability – of military intervention. Vandor regularly received military visitors in the metal workers' headquarters, as did José Alonso in the CGT. As one union leader explained to a correspondent who questioned him about rumours of Peronist involvement in negotiations with the army concerning a coup against the radical government: 'We have a duty to speculate with these situations, they are facts of reality and we cannot ignore them, but this does not mean that we are supporting a coup d'état.'[28] Thus, while they might speculate with military dissatisfaction, they did not themselves initiate discussions about the overthrow of the democratic party system.

Moreover, the fact remained that while electoral politics and a pluralist system was an attractive option, it still remained exactly that – one option among several. By reason of the fact that they were union leaders with a base outside the political system, they did not have the commitment to, and stake in, electoral politics which traditional political groups had. It was this fact which partly underlay the suspicion of the neo-Peronists and the politicians of justicialism towards the Vandorists in the 1962–6 period. As politicians their future possibilities were entirely bound up with the continuing operation of a pluralistic electoral system, and the acceptance of Peronism as a legitimate contender within that system. The Peronist union leaders could, on the other hand, face the prospect of a military interruption of that system with far greater equanimity.

There was also the fact that, given the nature of the 'political game' in Argentina in these years, with its implicit limitations on the toleration of Peronist power and influence, the political gains to be made by the unions were peculiarly meagre. Participation in the party system while undoubtedly a source of power for union leaders, also equally certainly had its debilitating side and by early 1966 the feeling of disillusionment was gaining ground among the mainstream Vandorist leadership. This feeling was heightened by two factors. First, the passing of decree 969 by the Radical government, with its clauses specifically attacking the union leadership's political activity and their internal control of their unions through clauses enforcing internal democracy and granting local branches financial autonomy, seemed to symbolise the limitations to, and the debilitating effects of, political entanglement. Second, the victory of Perón's personal candidate in the Mendoza elections, which confounded the political schemes of Vandor and much of the local leadership, underlined in the most emphatic terms the limitations to their independent political activity. The high hopes they had entertained a mere twelve months before about their ability to use the system to their own advantage had now all but vanished. From the Mendoza election until the coup of June it is clear that the Vandorist leadership was looking with increasing favour toward a military intervention to put an end to this 'juego imposible'. The Peronist response to the coup was, indeed, uniformly warm. It was, said the petrol workers' journal, 'the end of a regime where empty words, inaction and the slow but sure collapse of the Republic were the definitive characteristics of a system which many years ago ceased to be effective'.[29] The contrast with the same journal's effusive praise some eighteen months earlier for the way union participation in the 1965 elections had revitalised the ailing liberal system was evidence of both their underlying agnosticism regarding political forms, and the genuine sense of disillusionment which they undoubtedly felt.

José Alonso and neo-corporatist illusions

From 1963 onward José Alonso, the secretary general of the CGT, and a group of ideologues and advisers, began to put forward a series of documents analysing the necessary 'change of structures' that Argentina required if she were to achieve real development and social justice.

The documents were chiefly intended to establish the image of a forward-looking, technically capable, workers' central which could discuss responsibly and scientifically the future of the nation. In economic terms there was little in them which distinguished them from general developmentalist and Peronist philosophy. Politically, however, they did address themselves consistently to the theme of the necessary political preconditions for the desired economic and social changes.

The clearest exposition of these ideas was to be found in a document entitled *La CGT en marcha hacia el cambio de estructuras*, published in January 1965. After analysing the economic and social situation it turned its attention to the political scene. The conclusion reached concerning the existing political parties was that 'there do not exist in Argentina, either qualitatively or quantitatively, political parties which can be said to have representativity ... It is therefore inadmissible that the political parties should be regarded as the only channel of expression of the political life of the Argentine citizen ... the great popular movements do not have, on the political plane, possibilities of real expression.'[30] In contrast to this limited form of representation the document counterposes the legitimate representation that social groups can acquire for themselves if the institutional organisms which should fulfil this function do not in fact do so adequately. Hence, given the rejection of political parties as inadequate representative bodies, bodies such as the CGT naturally came to assume this function themselves. The representativity of the CGT in comparison with political parties was then proved statistically by demonstrating the number of affiliates it spoke for. The crucial problem which the document then broached was how to institutionalise this representative function and to assure the social group proper recognition in the deliberations of the state. This issue was resolved by advocating 'the necessity of creating a specific organism, with union participation and power of decision at the highest level of the state'.[31] Only on the basis of this institutional formula could a genuine effort be made toward the necessary economic and social changes.

What this analysis implied in political terms, apart from a critique of the efficacy of liberal representative forms, was not clearly spelled out. In the document we are examining it is fairly clear that the new representative organisms are conceived of as supplementing existing political parties rather than replacing them altogether. However, at other times, a more thoroughly corporatist analysis was proffered. Thus, for example, in a union document of 1966 we find the following analysis:

The participation in the general solutions of the authentic and representative dynamic forces of national life is vital; in the labour sphere the employers' organisations and the forces of labour; in other spheres the institutions of culture and art, the sectors of technology and national science. All these must, by means of genuine representatives make up an *organism* which can act together with government and propose solutions to the extent that the country needs a great national solution. This organism will have to be made up of teams drawn from specific activities which will investigate and analyse the problems of each sector so that afterwards in a leading body, integrated by representatives of all the teams, partial solutions can be studied in the light of the overall context.[32]

A judicious mixture of neo-corporatism and technocratism was clearly apparent, as was its corollary of a denial of the legitimacy of traditional politics. This tone had, indeed, been implicit in much *desarrollista* ideology, with its consistent emphasis on the need to take into account factors of power such as the army, the church and employers' organisations. While the specific political form of organisation of these 'factors of power' had generally been described as a 'National and Popular Front' which would participate in the electoral process, the emphasis on crucial non-party-political forces – the *fuerzas dinámicas* – could evidently imply a more corporatist solution.

Despite the clear attraction of corporatist solutions and forms for many of the advisers who surrounded Alonso in the CGT, in general the contours of the desired new forms of participation remained very vague. At times, indeed, it seemed that the critique of the liberal party system led to a form of political quietism, the opting out of any form of political activity. Alonso himself, writing in 1964, stated that there were three ways of arriving at the sources of power which would allow the unions to either share power, or achieve sole power themselves. One was through political competition, another through violent revolutionary action, and a third was what he called 'multiple unionism'. Alonso rejected the first two alternatives and chose instead the path of peaceful transformation which would be achieved 'through the realisation of social works which we call "multiple unionism"'. This unionism was based on the premise that a union must be involved in every aspect of the life of its members, catering for a wide range of social needs. He went on to talk of 'the unions' own buildings capable of catering for a total union activity ... the building of recreation facilities ... a place in the open air, able to provide a happy and healthy day for the union member and his family ... the construction of workers' housing'. He ended with a question and an assertion: 'Is this not a good way of showing the good features of a union; is it not a good way of achieving the social transformation we desire? If all the workers' organisations carried out this sort of activity the sum total would inevitably give us the union government we want so much.'[33] This conception, which developed the notion of the social service function of the union to its logical extreme, also explicitly resolved the problem of the state and political power. For Alonso, it would seem, the creation of what was virtually a state within a state by the union movement would inexorably lead, by force of example, to a fundamental shift in political power relations. The unions needed to simply dedicate themselves to developing their social services.

However, more commonly, the critique of political liberalism led to a tendency to look, implicitly at least, toward the military as a means of concretely achieving 'adequate' forms of political participation. This was to be achieved either as equal partners in a reborn union–military alliance which would overthrow the decadent liberal regime, or as enthusiastic followers of a military coup. Alonso, who was well known for his good relations with the military, was one of the first to welcome Onganía's coup in June 1966

There was no fundamental ideological disagreement between Alonso and the dominant Vandorist sector of the movement. The differences that existed largely concerned issues of tactics and personal ambition. The Vandorists were quite capable, as we have noted, of lambasting the decadence and lack of representative credibility of liberal political organisms when the situation demanded. They, too, could be supporters of military neo-corporatist designs. Indeed, in this light it is tempting to see this strong corporatist undercurrent in Peronist unionism as a logical extension of some semi-fascist, corporatist element present in original Peronist philosophy, which was always liable to surface within Peronist unionism. Yet, while there was certainly a degree of influence from European corporatist and fascist thought in early Peronism it would seem unwarranted to seek the explanation for neo-corporatist undercurrents in some original sin of early Peronism.

In the first place, although anti-liberalism and indeed anti-politicism were a strong element in Peronist ideology we must be clear as to what this actually signified. While Perón himself and other Peronist ideologues sometimes tried to give this a profound theoretical content, in general within post-1955 Peronism it referred to the rejection of the anti-democratic political set up that existed rather than a rejection of pluralistic politics as such. Amado Olmos in the lecture to union cadres to which we have already referred, vehemently castigated those who appealed to the 'factors of power' formula as a justification for rejecting the democratic process as such: 'In Argentina the forms of representative democracy have served, provided that they were without fraud, to carry the representatives of the people to power. And only fraud and violence have been able to deny this reality.'[34]

A political set up which marginalised or at best restricted the open political expression of the majority party of the working class, inevitably had only a limited legitimacy. If we add to this the reality of a powerful union apparatus with both a political and economic function then we hardly need to look to a putative allegiance to some original fascistic ideas for an explanation of neo-corporatists tendencies. Even Alonso, who was exceptional in the consistency and depth of his espousal of neo-corporatism, took his ideas principally from social catholic, communitarian ideologues rather than from any pre-1955 fascistic theory.[35]

The Vandorists opposed Alonso's espousal of such views from his position in the CGT, not so much for reasons of ideological disagreement as for tactical considerations. At a time when they were engaged in the building of a political party independent of Perón's direct control which could conquer influence in stages through electoral contests, Alonso's jeremiads against the political system as a whole struck a discordant note. When the document *La CGT en marcha hacia el cambio de estructuras* was presented to the CGT national committee in January 1965 for approval, Alonso defended it by saying that with it the CGT was showing that it played a role that no political party could fulfil. Vandor's reply to this was to suggest that the secretary general must have forgotten that the Justicialist Party had presented a full programme. He successfully moved that the document be referred back.[36] Throughout the election campaign of 1965 Alonso continued to emphasise through CGT statements and documents the futility of the elections and how traditional politics could solve none of the nation's problems. Underlying this disagreement was also the issue of who was to negotiate and bargain with Peronist electoral weight. Alonso with his personal base in the weak garment workers' union found himself increasingly marginalised after the *Plan de Lucha* had petered out, as Vandor through his control of the 62 Organisations built up his political influence after the 1965 elections. Alonso's emphasis on the superior representative credentials of unions in general, and the CGT in particular, was in part an attempt to alter this internal balance of power.

The Peronist left: duros and guerrilleros

Beyond these sectors of mainstream Peronist unionism were those who had formed the nucleus of the *línea dura* in the pre-1962 period, and who were coming to be referred to with increasing frequency as forming part of a Peronist left. Weakened by repression, exhaustion and desertion, the *duros* were by 1963 increasingly marginalised both within their individual unions and within the 62 Organisations. In June 1963 they organised a national plenary meeting of the *línea dura* in Rosario, and in October of the same year they were still capable of drawing together some 300 activists from the Federal Capital for a meeting in the leather cutters' union.[37] The reality was, however, that they were a declining force organisationally. By 1963 most of their leaders had been forced out of the 62 Organisations. Sebastian Borro had, for example, been forced to resign on the grounds that since he had not worked in the meatpacking industry since 1959 he was not formally a trade unionist and thus inelligible to sit in the 62.[38] Borro's case was not atypical of many leading *duros*. By the mid 1960s many did not hold office in their unions. While they often maintained considerable personal prestige because of past actions, they had little organisational base from which to oppose Vandorist domination of the movement. The union influence they maintained was largely limited to a few small unions like the pharmacy workers, telephone workers, naval construction and leather cutting, as well as a number of smaller unions in the interior. Although the textile workers' union was generally considered to be within the *línea dura* the Framini leadership was increasingly reluctant to commit itself openly. There were also some attempts to draw together dissident groups both within the unions and beyond. In 1964 a Confederation of Orthodox Peronist Groupings was formed under Jorge Di Pascuale's leadership but its impact within the union movement was minimal.[39]

The extent to which this nucleus of *duros* could be distinguished in terms of formal ideology from the dominant currents within Peronist unionism was limited. As in the Frondizi era the *línea dura* continued to draw on the moral capital, the distinct 'structure of feeling' of the Resistance years – its small acts of everyday heroism, its arrests, its martyrs. It increasingly came to define itself in terms of defending the values of the Resistance and of opposing those it saw as the chief threat to those values – the union bureaucracy. Opposition to Vandor and Vandorism became a dominant tenet. The *duros* saw in Vandorism a betrayal of the sacrifices made in the pre-1962 Resistance era, of the possibilities that had existed then, and of the communal experience of the *pueblo peronista*. Vandorism was abandoning a position of principled intransigence; it had been corrupted by the lure of political and union power into accepting a *modus vivendi* with a fundamentally illegitimate and anti-popular regime. The epitome of this betrayal was the union leadership's project to turn Peronism into a union-based political party within the system. For them this implied acceptance of a system designed to exclude Peronism, and Perón himself, from political power. The price to be paid for union participation within the system could only be the abandonment of Peronism's authentic mission.

The *duros* counterposed to this participation within the political system the maintenance of the 'true' essence of the Peronist movement, its 'real' values as embodied in the Resistance to the post-1955 military regime. Marcelo Repezza, a member of the executive committee of Peronismo de Acción Revolucionaria, a Córdoba-based group, commenting on the July 1963 presidential elections argued that: 'there must be no participation in the elections because to do so would be to ignore the authentic revolutionary feeling of our movement ... you can't just throw away an experience of eight years of permanent and constant struggle to conquer power for the people'.[40] Indeed, it was precisely on the basis of a rejection of a reality which did seem 'to throw to one side' this experience of solidarity, heroism and suffering that the *duros* took their stand.

An intrinsic part of this stand was a continuing and basic loyalty to Perón. Indeed the existence of a clearly defined 'left' current in this period depended crucially on Perón himself and his tactical needs. The *duros* were able to organise most effectively in this period in the space provided for them by Perón's decision to move against a dominant current that was threatening his control of the movement, or by his need to give Peronism a radical stance to enhance his political bargaining position at a specific juncture. It was, therefore, very much his creature and was, in general, as strong and clearly defined as he wished it to be. Perón was for the *duros* the ultimate arbiter of the 'true' essence of Peronism and of its tactical and strategic needs. This was clearly manifested in their reaction to the attempt of the Vandorist leadership to give the movement as a whole an institutionalised, formally democratic structure. Most Peronist unionists had shown only mild interest at best in the attempt to reconstruct Peronism as a political movement in the early months of Frondizi's government. In the mid 1960s when any such formalisation could only be dominated by the union bureaucracy this lack of interest had turned, for the *duros*, into overt hostility to the whole idea. A speaker at the October 1963 meeting of activists in the Federal Capital made this clear when referring to the Junta Reorganizadora recently set up by Perón: 'If what they are trying to do here is to organise a democratic party with authorities elected democratically we are sure that this is not Perón's position.'[41]

For the *duros* the lack of a formalised party-political structure was a virtue since it made easier the maintenance of the essential link between the leader and his people. This in turn reflected a more profound lacuna at the centre of radical Peronist unionism. Its militant syndicalism – what we have defined as an ouvrierist commitment as it emerged in the Resistance era – left the issue of state power and the forms of political organisation of the working class essentially unaddressed. It could be argued that this could be traced back historically to the failure of the original *laborista* project in the early years of the Peronist regime. While, as we have seen, there were elements of working-class Peronism which began to raise notions of working-class autonomy and political organisation during the Resistance period these were largely still-born. Certainly, the *duros* as the inheritors of this tradition filled this vacuum by extolling the essential 'leader–masses' axis around which the working class should organise. This spoke to certain crucial notions in Peronist working-class culture. The symbolic meeting between the leader and his people on 17 October unaided by any political structures was certainly important here, as was the figure of Evita symbolising the unique dialogue between the workers and the state, personified in the figures of Perón and Evita. For the *duros* the recreation of this unique relationship became both a solution to the problem of state power and political forms and also a guarantee of defence against the corrupting pretensions of the union hierarchy.

That this also implied placing their organisational fate largely in Perón's hands also became clear in the 1962–6 period. Thus, for example, they responded to Perón's 'turn to the left' in mid 1962 when he was adopting a radical stance toward the Guido government, only to be left perplexed and uncertain by his orders to support the popular conservative Solano Lima in the elections nine months later.[42] In a similar fashion Perón momentarily resurrected the left in mid 1964 when he encouraged the formation of the Movimiento Revolucionario Peronista, MRP. The programme put forward at its founding conference was in some senses the most radical to be espoused within the movement. It maintained that 'the people must oppose the regime's army of occupation with its own armed forces and workers' militia which will allow it to conquer power'. The MRP set itself the task of 'building the structure and developing the centralised revolutionary leadership'.[43]

Yet, for all its programmatic radicalism, the MRP had little substance behind the revolutionary rhetoric. Encouraged initially by Perón, it was an unhappy amalgam of union *duros*, some youth sectors led by Gustavo Rearte, and those of the *línea Villalón* which had defined itself as Castrist and insurrectionist. The unifying factor behind this unlikely alliance was opposition to Vandor and loyalty to Perón. Framini accepted the leadership of the new organisation, though he seems to have played little part in its inception. Its rapid demise was due to Perón's lack of support for the venture. While the creation of an opposition grouping loyal to himself and with radical credentials was a useful tactical weapon at a time when the power and independence of the union leadership was becoming a threat to his position, he did not want this grouping to be anything other than a tactical pressure weapon. The creation of something approaching a dominant 'revolutionary' current would have been counter to his whole conception of the type of movement Peronism ought to be. He saw one of the movement's strengths as its all-embracing, umbrella-like nature and he was adept at using its different wings; in this context the resurgence of the 'left' at any given time could be no more than a convenient tactical ploy.

In late 1965 Perón again called up the 'left' current as part of his campaign against Vandor. They emerged from obscurity to join with the right of the union movement under Alonso to form the 62 Organisations *de pie junto a Perón*. The sole basis for this unity with a figure who they had regarded as a leading 'betrayer' of the true essence of Peronism was loyalty to Perón as the name of the new organisation made perfectly clear.

Many militants within this 'left' current were content to view themselves in this light, as a tactical option available to Perón. Sebastian Borro who took part in the founding conference of the MRP stated afterwards that 'we will offer Perón the revolutionary possibility if, as seems likely, negotiations with the government turn out badly'.[44] The meagre nature of the left's independent ambitions, its own limited estimation of its perspectives and possibilities is apparent, as is the personal tragedy of a generation of militants symbolised by Sebastian Borro's utterance. A personal trajectory which included the prisons of Aramburu's regime and the leadership of the Lisandro de la Torre occupation had ended in the farce of the MRP, and all in the name of loyalty to one man. Such a trajectory could, perhaps, be taken as an unfitting epitaph for a generation of militants.

In terms of formal ideology this left developed very little by which to distinguish itself. The Programme of Huerta Grande issued at the height of Perón's 'turn to the left' in 1962 contained little to distinguish it from the programme of other tendencies within the movement. Its political strategy, too, was in general ill-defined. The plenary meeting of the *línea dura* in Rosario called for 'revolutionary abstentionism' in the face of elections.[45] The *duros* rejected the union bureaucracy's strategy of electoral participation and offered what Borro termed the 'revolutionary possibility'. Yet what this 'possibility' meant concretely was not at all clear. In a sense, the entire dynamic of resistance and repression that had followed 1955 contributed toward this lack of formal ideological definition. We have already commented how the experience of the Resistance tended to be embodied in a distinct set of values and structures of feeling, rather than the development of a distinctive radical ideology. Peronism within the Perón/anti-Perón dichotomy that dominated the political and social context was *per se* leftist, anti-establishment and revolutionary, and loyalty to its exiled and vilified leader often seemed enough of a definition of a political strategy. Hence, too, the nature of the terminology in which the Peronist left defined its enemies and its own distinctiveness. Its political vocabulary was essentially a moral one. The union bureaucracy had 'betrayed' the hard struggles against anti-Peronist governments, the right were those who had been corrupted and betrayed the essence of Peronism; ultimately those who had betrayed Perón himself. Concepts like *leales, traidores, duros, blandos, fe, lealtad, intransigencia*, which were the traditional core of the *duros*' terminology, referred ultimately to moral qualities and ethical values rather than political programmes and ideological maxims. As such they were both a hindrance and a help to dissident sectors of Peronist unionism. On the one hand, the lack of a defined and distinctive ideology and politics left them unarmed when faced with the overwhelming practical logic of mainstream unionism, and very much subject to Perón's tactical whims. On the other hand, their assertion of the validity of these values, and the historical experience from which they derived, spoke to a clear feeling among both militants, and we may presume rank and file, that, whatever the necessity and inevitability of compromise and integration, Peronism as a social movement and working-class expression was about something else as well. In this sense, the 'left' within Peronist unionism came to represent the conscience of the movement, a voice which continued to be relevant for many militants and others in spite of the personal compromises and accommodations they had had to make. While in many ways they shared the same formal language of dissent and criticism with the mainstream bureaucracy – a rhetoric which targeted the 'oligarchy' and the 'parasitic classes' tied to 'imperialism' – the 'left's' insistence on defining itself in terms of the values and experience deriving from class struggle, suffering and solidarity, imbued that language with a radically different tone and implications.

There were, too, those who attempted to go beyond this moral intransigence and reassess in a more radical light the nature and needs of Peronism. John William Cooke, for example, in his writings in these years, criticised the unthinking nature of the personal loyalty to Perón that characterised much of the 'left's' position. In a letter to Perón, he very clearly denounced what he called the fetishism of *el lider*, the substituting of hard concrete analysis by what he described as 'tribal fanaticisms'.[46] In another letter to Perón he added: 'Instead of concrete positions in the face of an equally concrete reality, we are given general formulas, we all want to be free, sovereign and that there should be social justice, but this is pure rhetoric if it is not translated into concrete strategic proposals.'[47]

Cooke attempted to provide an analysis of the political, union bureaucracy that dominated Peronism. In his writings he moved away from the moralism of notions such as *traidores* and *leales* and suggested that the root of the bureaucracy lay in Peronism's nature as a polyclass alliance. To fight such a bureaucracy would only be possible for Cooke by changing a heterogeneous movement into a revolutionary party, not by retreating into a reassertion of the traditional values of Peronism. Cooke thus very directly confronted the problem of political power. Cooke defined the task of a left Peronism – a revolutionary Peronism in his terms – as the creation of a vanguard party that sought to reconcile the politics of Peronism with the role that objectively the confrontation of social forces in the everyday life of workers gave to it. 'Peronism as a mass movement is and always has been superior to Peronism as a structure for the masses; for this reason spontaneism has always dominated the planned action of the masses.'[48]

Cooke emphasised Peronism's role as an anti-imperialist movement. He defined Argentina as a semi-colony, exploited and dominated by foreign – principally North American – capital. As such her fundamental interests coincided with those of other nations struggling against imperialism. Peronism as the expression of Argentina's anti-imperialist struggle should seek her natural allies amongst other anti-imperialist movements. For Cooke, the end result of this anti-imperialist struggle in Argentina would be the introduction of a national form of socialism. Cooke specifically rejected Peronism's traditional ideological notion of a third position between Soviet communism and Western capitalism. While counselling vigilance towards the USSR and its satellite national parties, Cooke emphasised to Perón that in the final resort there were only two sides in the world struggle – the capitalist/ imperialist and the socialist/anti-imperialist – and that Perón should have no hesitation in committing Peronism to the latter.

The influence of Cooke's Cuban experience is apparent here. The notion of the vanguard political party which became increasingly debated in certain circles of the Peronist movement at this time had a largely Castrist origin. Intimately related to this was the growing attraction of ideas of guerrilla warfare derived largely from the Cuban experience. *Focismo* was by the mid 1960s almost a commonplace among certain sectors of Peronism. Cooke was in Cuba for most of the early and mid 1960s and in a certain sense his championing of *focismo* was the direct product of an isolated militant cut off from the mainstream of the workers' movement and its daily struggles. Nor should this isolation be viewed in either purely personal or geographic terms. The appeal of guerrilla strategy to militants inside Argentina at this time must be seen fundamentally as resulting from the process of demobilisation of the mass movement in the early 1960s, the consequent domination of an accommodationist union bureaucracy and the marginalising of the most militant activists and leaders which this process entailed.

The attraction of *focismo* for many of these militants was evident. First, the emphasis placed in guerrilla theory on the victory of subjective will over the objective conditions was bound to appeal to activists as a means of defying a reality of demobilisation and isolation. Second, the notion of a dedicated elite acting independently though in the name of the masses and galvanising them by their conflict with the oppressive authorities found a ready echo in militants increasingly cut off from any possibility of meaningful intervention in mass struggles – activists with no field of meaningful action. Third, guerrilla theory did provide a convincing solution to the problem of what had gone wrong with the movement, why the confrontation of the resistance and the militancy of the Peronist workers had been insufficient to achieve a real breakthrough. The answer was found in a lack of discipline and of an armed vanguard.

The number of union militants who followed Cooke's path was small in absolute terms. Some figures from the *línea dura* did move in this direction, and a separation tended to emerge between the more traditional *duros* and those who now defined themselves as 'revolutionary' Peronists. While some union figures like Jorge Di Pascuale and Gustavo Rearte, a leader of the cosmetic workers and the Revolutionary Peronist Youth, underwent training in Cuba, the majority of the traditional *duros* opted for waiting it out and, in Sebastian Borro's words, 'having faith in Perón'.[49] The impact of the guerrilla strategy was, on the other hand, especially strong among a younger generation of political militants. For them the guerrilla acted as a crucial explanatory variable, the absence of which had doomed earlier struggles. While Cooke made some attempt to place *focismo* within the context of a Peronism transformed into a mass revolutionary party, most of the younger militants who began to espouse the doctrine in these years, and in even greater numbers during the military regime of 1966–73, conceived of it as a means and end in itself. For this younger generation the reality of Peronism in the mid and late 1960s seemed plain enough: a movement which embodied the anti-imperialist, and anti-capitalist strivings of the Argentine masses, but a movement dominated by a union bureaucracy which had profoundly submerged and stifled these longings. Guerrilla warfare, armed struggle in all its many ideological variants, offered to these militants a solution to this dilemma. It implied an effective separation from union struggle since the power of the union bureaucracy was taken to be complete, and despite the constant evocation of the symbolic figure of the working class it meant, in the end, an elitist dismissal of the Peronist working class's history in all its complexity and contradictoriness. For this younger generation even Cooke's attempt to find a deeper political and ideological explanation for the failure of the Resistance was forgotten as they reduced the question to one of fire power and individual will power. The results of this legacy were to be tragically apparent in Argentina after 1973.

PART FIVE

Workers and the *Revolución Argentina*: from Onganía to the return of Perón, 1966–73

9

The Peronist union leaders under siege: new actors and new challenges

During the dictatorship there was certainly a relationship of forces favourable to struggle. Everyone, the political parties of the middle class and the Córdoba workers' movement were opposed to the government. Everything which came from the government was rejected. Therefore, you had to struggle to change it. There was a great struggle in which a majority of the population was involved, and so if we were hit hard we had the sympathy, the support of the whole population. We were all together against the dictatorship ... So anything we did to create a mood, a counterproposal against a government measure was correct and everyone supported us from all points of view and without political distinctions.

Militant in the Córdoba light and power union, 1973

The *Revolución Argentina* and the crisis of the union hierarchy

Despite a publicly expressed caution and reserve, the Peronist union leadership could scarcely conceal their satisfaction with the course of events which had led to the ouster of Arturo Illia. Leaders of a labour movement which claimed over 2 million members they had, under Vandor's leadership, developed a strategy which had led to their re-emergence within the Argentine status quo as a social and political force of undeniable weight; a force with which any aspirant to political power in Argentina would have to bargain. Events of the first month of the new regime of General Juan Carlos Onganía seemed to bear witness to the success of that strategy and to bear out the optimism of union leaders' calculations. An apparently sympathetic figure was appointed to the Ministry of Labour and many of the Radical government's measures designed to weaken the power of the union leadership were suspended. To symbolise a new era in state/union relations Augusto Vandor signed the new contract with metal-working employers in the presidential palace surrounded by dignitaries of the new military regime.

Within the union movement and within Peronism the position of the union hierarchy remained largely unchallenged. While their recent disagreements with Perón had demonstrated the lack of wisdom of directly challenging the political power of the exiled *caudillo*, the opposition which had emerged around this issue in the year prior to the June coup had made little headway in challenging their control of the union apparatus. The Peronist left was a marginal force and the militants of the Resistance generation remained isolated and scattered. Vandor and his followers held uncontested sway over a highly organised working class which had shown its capacity for massive and disciplined mobilisations but whose actions had been increasingly tightly controlled by the union hierarchy, with little of the active mass participation of an earlier era.

The tacit support of the union leadership for the June coup was based on a profound antipathy toward the Illia government, which they regarded as both lacking in legitimacy and hostile to their needs. In addition, they empathised with military figures who apparently shared their analysis of the solutions needed for Argentina's national problems. Their frequent contacts with the figures behind the coup in the months prior to June, together with the weight of union presence in Argentine society, seemed to assure them of privileged access to the new public authorities. Moreover, a military regime would, they reasoned, severely curb Perón's ability to manoeuvre politically and exert his authority within the movement at their expense. For all their plausibility these calculations were to be rapidly exposed as illusions.[1] Within a year the union movement was in disarray, faced with a strong authoritarian regime determined to force through the rationalisation of the Argentine economy and the modernisation of the Argentine state.

This confrontation with the Onganía regime was to plunge the Peronist union hierarchy into a growing crisis which would culminate in the years following 1969, even as the military authorities retreated from the policies which had triggered the crisis in the 1966–9 period. The crisis of the union leadership was characterised by a number of features: a growing problem of credibility vis-à-vis their rank and file at a time of radicalised social conflict; the emergence of a vigorous opposition movement within the unions which profoundly questioned the existing union structures; a growing problem of internal divisions amongst themselves; and finally an increasing danger of their isolation within a resurgent Peronism as their traditional domination within the movement was challenged by new actors.

The immediate cause of this crisis lay in the policies of the new military regime. On the one hand the new government suspended all political activity and organisation, hoping to thus abolish the complex system of political bargaining through which rival social groups attempted to press the claims of their constituencies on the state. In the minds of the ideologists of the *Revolución Argentina* this inevitably led, in a society such as Argentina in which social groups were so highly organised and mobilised, to a political system of great fragility which condemned political authorities to an endless round of horsetrading and vacillating economic policy. The *sine qua non* for the effective implementation of their economic policy was, therefore, to relieve the state of such obligations by suspending the operation of pluralistic party politics. Yet, one of the main elements of the Peronist union leadership's power, as it had emerged after 1958, had been precisely its ability to participate in a political system which obliged governments and political groups to bargain for their neutrality or support. One of the central premises of Vandor's strategy had been the effectiveness of applying Peronist union pressure within a political system characterised by weak governments and divided political adversaries. In this sense it is clear that the union leaders' ethusiasm for the overthrow of Illia was a fundamental miscalculation. By eliminating the ability of social groups to bargain politically Onganía laid the basis for the emergence of a state controlled by military and economic elites which was not beholden to other interest groups.[2]

The principal purpose of such an exercise was to push through the economic plan which was finally formulated in early 1967 and associated with the Minister of Economy, Adelbert Krieger Vasena. The main target of this newly immunised state authority was the working class and the union movement. Krieger Vasena's economic plan was not entirely novel. It represented a logical continuation of developmentalist strategies to modernise the Argentine economy. Modernisation and rationalisation would lead to the development of a dominant, dynamic sector of the economy based on those industries established by the first developmentalist wave of the late 1950s and early 1960s and dominated by foreign capital. On the basis of this modern manufacturing sector of durable consumer goods and modern capital goods Argentina would compete on the world market as an exporter of certain manufactured products.

The development of this dynamic sector was to be achieved by a significant income redistribution away from wage earners and the agrarian sector towards urban employers. This would be achieved through rigorous state control of wages and state redirection of the resources generated by agrarian exports. A tight monetarist stabilisation plan was introduced consisting of wage controls, fiscal restraint, credit restriction and a devaluation of the peso. In addition to helping achieve the desired changes in income distribution this would also reduce inflation and lead to general cost predictability so important for modern companies. Krieger Vasena's economic plan also proposed the eradication of what were considered to be irrational and unproductive areas of the economy. A principal target of rationalisation was to be the state sector – particularly transportation, but also in general the government bureaucracy – and subsidised regional economies. Another clear target was the small to medium-size national businesses which had previously used their access to the political resources of the state to gain economic protection. Access to tax exemptions, credit lines, state contracts, tariff protection and monopoly concessions were drastically reduced as their ability to pressure the state was reduced by Onganía's suspension of the 'political game'. The logical result of this policy was to be the intense concentration of economic resources in the dynamic pole of the Argentine economy.[3]

By imposing tight limits on wage increases and suspending normal collective bargaining, and at the same time suspending the operation of the political system, the military regime succeeded in undermining the two basic sources of union bargaining power in Argentine society. Wage control and the suspension of democratic politics were scarcely new; what was novel, at least most recent Argentine history, was the existence of an authoritarian regime which had greatly concentrated and centralised state power and was determined to make unambiguous use of the power of the state against the unions and the working class.

The new regime's determination to control, and if necessary repress, the labour movement was evident even before the formulation of Krieger Vasena's economic plan. In October 1966 the government announced a completely new labour regime in Argentina's ports, abolishing many labour gains dating back to 1946. When the port workers' union, Sindicato Unido Portuarios Argentinos (SUPA), declared a protest strike it was immediately intervened. At the same time the government began the unilateral application of rationalisation schemes in the railroads and the sugar industry of the north west. In response to this and Krieger Vasena's economic plan the CGT announced a Plan of Struggle which would culminate, if concessions were not forthcoming, in a general strike. The government retaliated by reinstating the Radical government's decree 969 which sought to strictly control union functioning; the authorities also broke off talks with the CGT and banned all public meetings. When the CGT reluctantly, in the face of government intransigence, declared a 24-hour general strike for 1 March 1967 Onganía's response was to suspend the juridical status of the textile workers, metal workers, telephone workers, pharmaceutical workers and the Tucuman sugar workers. On 15 March the principal railroad union, Unión Ferroviaria, was intervened and its leaders fired from their posts in the rail system. Nationally salaries were frozen for eighteen months and the collective bargaining law, 14,250, was suspended. Faced with this débâcle the CGT appointed a commission to seek to renew talks with the authorities. The response was silence. The dilemma the regime had placed the union leadership in was, thus, clear: on the one hand their institutional existence would be threatened if they resisted government policy and on the other they risked losing credibility with their members as they experienced the impact of that policy.

The first manifestation of the crisis this situation provoked within the Peronist union leadership came at the congress called to normalise the CGT in March 1968. The congress elected Raimundo Ongaro, the head of the Buenos Aires print workers, as its new secretary general. There was a clear majority of union leaders present who were critical of the inability of the previous authorities to resist the regime's policies and who advocated the adoption of a policy of outright resistance, in both political and union terms, to the government. Many of those unions which had borne the brunt of the economic policy and had been intervened were in the forefront of this move. Vandor and his allies withdrew from this body, which took the name CGT Paseo Colon or CGT de los Argentinos, and founded a rival central, the CGT Azopardo. While opposing government policy the Vandorists advocated a cautious strategy aimed at recuperating union strength and remaining open to dialogue with the government. The government refused to recognise either body and encouraged the emergence of a tendency amongst the union leaders which called for outright cooperation with the regime. Known as participationists, or more formally as the Nueva Corriente de Opinión, these leaders accepted the regime's corporatist rhetoric concerning the need for the unions to enter a close alliance with the state.

While the ideological choices of individual union leaders played a role in deciding in which grouping they aligned their unions, the existence of these different currents essentially reflected different logical responses to the new situation facing them after 1966. For those unions which had been hardest hit by government economic policy and who had been intervened by the state outright opposition held an initial attraction. The traditional union policy of mobilisation and negotiation had been proved untenable by the failure of the Plan of Struggle of 1967. With little left to lose in institutional terms outright opposition to the regime seemed a logical choice for some unions. This option could seek legitimation within Peronist political culture by posing as the embodiment of the traditional opposition to *gorila* military regimes. For many smaller unions with a traditionally vulnerable position in the labour market the option of seeking to carve a niche for themselves within the new regime and achieve through state protection and collaboration what they could not hope to do through bargaining seemed an equally logical alternative once the traditional Vandorist strategy on which they had relied became ineffective. This alliance with military figures could, too, seek precedents in Peronist ideology and history. As we saw in the last chapter an influential current of opinion had emerged in the preceding years within the CGT espousing a neo-corporatist strategy for the unions.

For the mainstream Peronist unions grouped around Vandor the need for such drastic choices as these seemed unclear. Recent history seemed to show that military regimes, sooner or later, had to come to terms with the union movement. For this sector, therefore, the best strategy seemed to be the traditional one of generally opposing government policy while keeping open lines of communication for eventual compromises. In the short term this implied laying low and not providing the regime with the pretext for further weakening union organisation. This pragmatic strategy was not inconsistent with the general tone of working-class demobilisation which followed the failure of attempts to resist the Onganía regime in its first nine months.

This weakened and divided labour movement was a vital precondition for the social peace achieved by the Onganía regime in the three years following the June coup. As a guarantee of this social tranquillity the regime streamlined and concentrated the repressive powers of the state. For the labour movement the results of this were apparent: strikes became struggles against the state and were, as such, to be dealt with by the armed forces. In these conditions coherent national opposition to the government's labour policy was, therefore, almost non-existent. Yet, Onganía's pretensions went much further as he attempted to control and suppress large areas of social and political life. Universities, for example, and all educational issues came to be directly controlled by the executive; universities were intervened and new courses of study dictated by the state. Police powers were greatly increased as the penal code was reformed to facilitate the struggle against 'subversion'. The police were also given judicial authority in some instances. The power of the central state was expanded through the creation of a number of conciliar bodies in charge of security and economic affairs which were directly answerable to the executive power.[4]

While the success of the military in achieving labour tranquillity and in suffocating social opposition was impressive in Onganía's first three years, beneath the surface a series of tensions had been generated. Many social sectors were harmed by Krieger Vasena's economic policy. Small and medium businesses, regional entrepreneurs, rural landowners and urban wage earners formed part of a wide spectrum who saw their positions deteriorate, if not always in absolute terms, at least in relation to the fortunes of the large industrial and financial interests in the modern sector of the economy.[5]

The dissatisfaction of these economic groups was by 1969 allied to a more generalised civil opposition to the authoritarianism of the Onganía regime. Broad segments of Argentine society had been alienated by the military's suspension of the normal channels and institutions of civil and political society. This democratic opposition was, like the labour opposition, controlled in the first years of the new regime. Indeed, the ideologists of the *Revolución Argentina* had foreseen the dissatisfaction and opposition which would be generated by the economic plan and the dislocation of traditional social and political institutions. Once the economy had been successfully, if painfully, reconstructed in what they called the 'economic time' they promised a greater participation to these social and political sectors in future 'social' and 'political' stages of the revolution. Such calm prognostications of social and political manipulation were to be rudely shattered in May 1969 as labour discontent and the tensions in civil society coalesced in a wave of generalised social disobedience.

The scenario for this eruption was the major cities of the interior, particularly Córdoba. In early May 1969 university students in Corrientes, La Plata, Rosario and Córdoba clashed violently with the police in a series of demonstrations. While the immediate issue was an increase in the cost of meals, the universities had since the beginning of the year been the centres of a growing opposition to Onganía's government. In the May clashes local regional delegations of the CGT and local unions declared their solidarity with the students. In Rosario the clashes were so intense that the army declared the city a 'war zone' and set up councils of war to try civilians. The impact of these events nationally was immediate. Both CGTs declared a 24-hour protest strike for 30 May to protest government repression and economic policy. This was the first sign of national organised labour mobilisation in more than two years.

In Córdoba these events provoked a particularly intense local echo. To the student unrest, of evident importance in such a major university centre, was added a peculiarly unpopular local governor imposed by the central government and a local labour movement already mobilised over specific grievances. The Córdoba labour movement had since early 1969 been campaigning for the abolition of the 'zonal discounts' which authorised Córdoba employers to pay 11% lower wages than their Buenos Aires counterparts. In May the national authorities also abolished 'English Saturday', a custom by which Córdoba workers were entitled to work a half-day on Saturday while being paid in full. This custom had in effect made the Córdoba work week forty-four hours in comparison with the national standard of forty-eight. On 14 May automobile workers in the IKA–Renault plants, the major employers in the city, resolved on a 48-hour protest strike. As they were leaving the assembly they were violently attacked by the police, provoking a 48-hour city-wide stoppage which expressed a wide spectrum of grievances: opposition to the government's wage policy, the 'zonal discounts', the abolition of 'English Saturday', and the intensification of production targets in the automobile plants. With a mobilised union rank and file, and with growing popular discontent against the local authorities the Córdoba unions called for a 48-hour general strike to begin on 29 May, the day before the planned national strike.

On the morning of the 29th students and police clashed in the principal student area, the *barrio* Clinicas. As local striking workers became involved, led by the transport workers and the Córdoba light and power union, clashes spread to the entire central area and barricades began to appear. At mid-day a column of more than 4,000 automobile workers from the Renault plants on the outskirts of the city reached the centre, cutting off the police forces there and forcing them to retreat. By 1 p.m. workers and students controlled a 150-block area of the centre of the city. In the afternoon the army began the operation to take back the centre and by nightfall demonstrators had retreated to the suburbs attacking local police stations and other symbols of authority. In the meantime, snipers slowed the army's movement through the city. When the *Cordobazo* was finally over on Saturday 31st some 300 people were in military detention, perhaps thirty had been killed and at least 500 had been wounded.[6]

In national terms the *Cordobazo* represented the beginning of the end of the 'Argentine Revolution'. First, and most immediately, it shattered the illusion of the regime's invincibility and broke the demoralising calm and sense of civic impotence inculcated by three years of military-imposed 'peace'. The army's reestablishment of order had been achieved through the spectacle of directly confronting its own citizens in the streets of the nation's third largest city. The social cost of implementing Onganía's policies was to be seen, increasingly, by the armed forces command as excessive in terms of the opposition it generated. Krieger Vasena and the entire national cabinet would resign almost immediately following the events. The *Cordobazo* also demonstrated the rift between massive sectors of Argentine society and a state which was increasingly isolated, arrogant and lacking in legitimacy. The dangers of such a rift were symbolised by Córdoba's devastated central area.

Perhaps most disquieting for the armed forces was the unpredictability, ferocity and uncontrolled nature of the upheaval. While the events had formally occurred within the framework of calls by the labour movement and opposition political parties the mobilisation had clearly escaped the confines of normal channels of protest and opposition. The experience of the following years was to further demonstrate the difficulty of channelling and institutionalising this mobilisation and protest. Faced with this situation the armed forces would in the 1969–73 period undertake a slowly accelerating search for a political solution aimed at taming the unrest they had unleashed. The implications for the union hierarchy of the *Cordobazo* were equally ominous. Taken by surprise by the events, they had attempted to take advantage of the upsurge in protest and the uncertainty of the regime to put themselves at the head of the mobilisation and thus reestablish their credibility and bargaining power with the authorities at a national level. Yet, the years following the *Cordobazo* saw an intensification of the crisis of the Peronist union leadership as their position was challenged by the emergence of new actors and currents.

New actors: rebellion of the rank and file

The wave of working-class protest which began in 1969 and grew in the following years was related to longer-term structural factors which had been undermining the union hierarchy's power and facilitating the emergence of new opposition forces within the labour movement. The centre of these new forces was the industries established by Frondizi, principally vehicle production, steelmaking and petro-chemicals. Geographically these industries were centred on Córdoba, the industrial belt running along the Paraná river south from Rosario, and the suburbs of Gran Buenos Aires. In the 1969–73 period militant protest movements emerged primarily in Córdoba and the Paraná industrial belt. The emergence of workers in these new industrial sectors as important challengers to both government and union leaders came as a profound suprise to both.

For nearly a decade after their establishment, the labour force in the new industries was quiescent, largely isolated from the turmoil of the mainstream labour movement. This was the result of a variety of factors. The companies, often multi-nationals, operating in these sectors were able, and willing, to pay higher than average wages to assemble and keep an adequately trained and docile labour force. There was also, in general, far greater stability of employment in these sectors than in the more traditional economy.[7] In addition they adopted a labour policy which provoked far-reaching changes in the structure of collective bargaining in Argentina.

They insisted on, and won, first from Frondizi and later from Illia two crucial innovations. First, they gained government permission in certain cases to establish company unions (*sindicatos por empresa*) something unheard of in the traditional Peronist union structure. Thus, for example, the four Fiat plants established in Argentina, three of which were in Córdoba and one in Buenos Aires, each had separate, company-inspired unions.[8] Similarly, the massive petro-chemical concern, PASA, founded in 1958 in San Lorenzo, a northern suburb of Rosario, set up its own plant union which was granted juridical bargaining status (*personería gremial*) by Frondizi. Where plant unions were not considered to be feasible, as in the rest of the automobile industry, union jurisdiction was granted to weaker, existing unions. In automobiles, for example, the Sindicato de Mecanicos y Afines del Transporte Automotor (SMATA), a small union made up largely of garage mechanics, was granted organising rights over the claims of the powerful metal workers' union, the Unión Obrera Metalúrgica (UOM). This policy enabled the companies to isolate the new workforce from the national labour movement, and implement modern labour relations strategies stressing company paternalism, social benefits and leisure facilities. This strategy seemed successful. The workers in these industries played no part in the reestablishment of the CGT in 1963, nor in the factory occupations of the *Plan de Lucha* in 1964.

The other, related, innovation in labour policy was the insistence of companies in these new sectors on company-level bargaining. An increasing number of these plant contracts (*convenios por empresa*), were authorised by a succession of Ministers of Labour in the 1958–66 period, undercutting the system of industry-wide national contracts embodied in the Law of Professional Associations. Such contracts were not restricted to the new, dynamic sector. The most modern companies in the traditional industries, such as textiles, were insisting on them by the early 1960s. Companies pressed for this change because it meant that they could negotiate wages and conditions in accordance with their individual productivity levels and production needs. Issues such as payment systems and job classifications could be settled in accordance with individual company needs, rather than be subject to industry-wide bargaining where a wide variety of political and institutional pressures came to bear on the final contracts. Moreover, the employers reasoned that such decentralised bargaining would also inevitably fragment wage negotiations and hinder a unified worker response on wages and conditions.

Decentralised collective bargaining certainly helped produce initially a docile labour force in the dynamic sector of the Argentine economy. It also weakened the power of the national union structure since it moved the centre of wage bargaining in crucial areas of the economy away from the national negotiations and back to the company level. While in some industries such as textiles the national union still bargained for these local contracts, in the vast majority of the new industrial sectors the traditional, mainly Peronist national unions were unrepresented. The impact of this transformation of the bargaining structure on the national union hierarchy was not unintended, either on the part of the state or employers. Indeed, the Illia government responded to the hostility of the Peronist unions by encouraging precisely the trends we have been describing and launching a rigorous programme of state overseeing of union affairs, designed to encourage greater local union autonomy and weaken the hold of the hierarchy on the union apparatus. Thus, the union leadership which was plunged into crisis by the Onganía regime had already in the preceding years seen its position in the collective bargaining system weakened and its control of the union apparatus partially threatened.

Another, unintended, consequence of this policy became increasingly clear after 1969. The displacement of bargaining over wages and conditions from the national to the company level helped revive local sections and unions in those industries affected. Plant bargaining, in the long run, strengthened the initiative and capacity of the rank and file to act and pressure both employers and unions. The fact that conditions and wages were determined at plant level provided a focus for rank-and-file activity which was missing where such issues were determined at national level and then simply transmitted to local units. It meant that autoworkers, for example, could credibly hope to influence and even determine issues of crucial importance to their working lives; their own activity and choices could have an impact on their wages and conditions. As we have seen in an earlier section of this work, it was the absence of such a concrete focus for rank-and-file involvement following the defeats of the Frondizi era which partly underlay the demobilisation of the rank and file in the Peronist unions for much of the 1960s.

The economic policy of Krieger Vasena helped, too, to break the quiescence of the workers in these industries. Strict wage controls directly affected the relatively privileged levels of their salaries. While they remained above those in the more traditional industries, they lost more heavily in comparison with lower-paid workers.[9] At the same time grievances over issues associated with modern production technology also came to the fore, as companies increased production speeds and introduced rationalisation schemes. All of these factors coalesced in the period following the *Cordobazo* and laid the basis for rank-and-file movements which challenged first their own employers and unions, then the national union apparatus and, finally, the military regime itself.

In 1970 over 5,000 Fiat Córdoba workers overthrew the compliant leaders of their company unions and elected new radical leaderships. In the same year, too, the workers in PASA rebelled against their company-appointed leaders and elected rank-and-file delegates to control their union. In the largest union in the modern sector, SMATA, which had over 30,000 members by 1970, the national leadership had been under increasing pressure since before the *Cordobazo*. Rank-and-file opposition delegates were in control in many of the major companies such as Chrysler, Peugeot and Citroën. In 1972 opposition militants won control of the Córdoba branch, representing some 7,000 IKA–Renault workers. Many other workers in the modern sector followed suit in these years.

The ability of the rank-and-file opposition to successfully challenge the existing leaderships was facilitated by the particular nature of these unions in terms of the internal control they could exercise over their members. While the labour policy of companies in the dynamic sector ensured that their workforce would remain largely isolated from the traditional national unions, it also meant that when the period of docility was shattered these companies were left with unions which had great difficulty in controlling a rebellious rank and file, since they did not have at their disposal the sort of apparatus of internal control which existed in traditional Peronist unions such as the UOM, construction and textile unions.

This was evidently the case with company unions like those in Fiat. Here again, company policy established in the late 1950s backfired in the post-1969 period. The elimination of the national unions, and the restricted scope of company unions, proved a great advantage to the rank-and-file opposition. It was clearly easier to challenge a union leadership which was restricted to one enterprise, and which did not have a strong apparatus of internal control, than it was to take on the might of a national union hierarchy like that of the UOM. Even in national unions like SMATA, there did not exist the sort of long established internal 'machinery' of control characteristic of the older industrial unions. They were effectively newcomers who had only succeeded in establishing their presence in the mid 1960s. The generally harmonious labour relations in the modern sector had made the construction of such a *maquina* unnecessary. Moreover, workers in both company unions and in those branches of national unions which rebelled against their national leaders, like SMATA and the light and power union in Córdoba, were aided by provisions in labour law which granted them control of their own finances and considerable organisational autonomy. National unions like SMATA and the light and power union corresponded to the federative structure rather than the highly concentrated union structure characteristic of unions in traditional industries such as metal working and textiles. As such, their ability to curb fractious local branches was severely restricted.

The labour opposition which flourished after 1969 remained essentially confined to the interior of the country. In Buenos Aires itself the labour movement in both the modern and traditional sectors remained, prior to 1973, largely outside the upheaval of the interior. This can be explained, in part, by factors alluded to above. In Buenos Aires the traditional mechanisms of repression and cooption remained largely intact; the opportunities for asserting local organisational autonomy were far less. The very size and extent of the metropolitan industrial belt gave the union bureaucracy greater room for manoeuvring and atomising working-class opposition. This in turn was related to what one author has described as a radically different labour climate in the interior.[10] In the urban settings of the interior where the new industries were installed, the social conflict generated by factory life was prolonged outside the factory and reinforced by forms of social and spatial segregation. Social opposition emerging from these modern industries was not obfuscated by the wider urban setting but rather made more transparent. A close physical proximity between place of work and place of abode – particularly in many of the single-industry towns of the interior – also helped reinforce the internal solidarity of working-class communities.

In Buenos Aires the factory simply did not have a comparable centrality, but was part of a huge urban structure in which social contrasts, and solidarities, formed at the workplace were diluted. This was clearly reflected in a lower level of community solidarity available to particular working-class mobilisations. Grievances and collective consciousness formed at the point of production were diluted within the urban conglomeration of the metropolis. This meant that while the emerging opposition forces could find an echo in Buenos Aires, they were unable to successfully challenge either employers or their union leaders in the sort of generalised community protest of the interior. In the automobile industry, for example, opposition groupings were present in the plants of Buenos Aires and led many strikes. They were not, however, able to successfully challenge employers or their unions in the way that Renault or Fiat workers in Córdoba were able to do.[11]

Clasismo and *sindicalismo de liberación*: the meaning and limits of the new union opposition

The militancy which swept the cities of the interior in the years following 1969 helped to destabilise both governments and established union leaderships. The centre of this militancy remained in Córdoba, though its ramifications spread far beyond. In Córdoba the vanguard of this movement lay in the light and power workers' union led by Agustín Tosco, the two largest Fiat plant unions Sitrac and Sitram, and the IKA–Renault plant.[12] The activities of these workers had, however, a city-wide impact, and their influence spread to other workers in the interior who engaged in similar actions.

One of the distinguishing features of this militancy was its frequent recourse to direct action and the adoption of other non-conventional tactics of labour mobilisation. Active strikes, *paros activos*, became the most common form of labour activity in Córdoba. In the course of 1971 some twelve active strikes were launched by the Córdoba CGT. Conflicts also often involved plant occupations and the taking of management hostages. An active strike implied a conscious policy of breaking with the passivity associated with traditional labour protest. It implied, for example, an attempt to involve the workforce on a daily basis in demonstrations aimed at taking the conflict to the wider community. The culmination of such forms of activity came in March 1971 in a second city-wide upheaval in Córdoba, known as the Viborazo.[13]

While the forms of labour activity adopted by these workers represented a radical departure from more traditional labour practices, the most important characteristic of this wave of militancy was its anti-bureaucratic nature. Above all, it defined itself in terms of its opposition to existing models of union leadership and forms of internal government. Indeed, as we have seen, the origins of many of these movements lay in just such a questioning of existing leaderships. The typical scenario for their emergence involved an initial challenge to managerial policy, usually involving issues of labour conditions, which then rapidly expanded to a questioning of existing leaders who were perceived as being too closely identified with the companies. Out of this experience came a more general attack on the *burocracia sindical*. A bureaucrat was, in Agustín Tosco's words: 'someone without vocation, without ideals, who converts himself into a typical "administrator" of a union post, who uses it for his personal satisfaction and from his position starts to "rule" over his comrades'.[14]

In contrast, the new militants offered 'honest leadership'. This implied personal probity and a commitment to internal democracy on the part of the new militant leaderships. The importance of these issues for workers, and the support they offered militants who were sensitive to them, was clearly articulated by an electrical supply worker in Córdoba, speaking of his support for Agustín Tosco:

The union sees that its money is turned into social works, that Tosco doesn't put his hand in the till, doesn't take any for himself and people feel safe because the leaders keep their promises, not like in other unions where they betray strikes and sell out to the bosses, and live in luxury like potentates, with a house in the mountains, fast cars, women... Here they consult the union in assemblies and there are no thugs like in the UOM, where they throw you out if you oppose them.[15]

The issue of 'honest leadership' became a constantly reiterated theme of the labour protest of these years and helped give the protest its anti-bureaucratic nature. Neither the theme nor the target were new in the Argentine labour movement. As we have described, it emerged during the Resistance period and had gone on to become a part of the Peronist left's critique of Vandorism. Yet, never before had it been an issue of such central importance, so clearly and concretely posed. 'Honest leadership' implied, above all, democracy and responsiveness to the rank and file's needs. A deliberate policy was adopted by the militants of preventing the formation of professional bureaucracies in the traditional Peronist style. Emphasis was placed on the need for the leadership to have worked its way up from below. In the elections which overthrew the existing leadership of SMATA Córdoba, in March 1972, for example, thirty of forty-five candidates were shop-floor delegates.[16] A common policy of these leaderships was membership rotation. Periodically in SMATA Córdoba, for example, the leaders would return to their trades in the plants and other militants would take their place.[17]

Constant consultation with the membership was also emphasised and steps taken to limit the executive autonomy of leadership bodies. Much of this responsiveness to the issue of internal democracy may well have been generational. Many of these militants were young with little of an older generation of militants' experience of the demoralising impact of bureaucratic power. The average age of the SMATA Córdoba leaders elected in 1972 was thirty, and most of the formative experience of this new generation had come in the period after 1966.[18]

The issues which formed the centre of union activity and concern were also distinctive. The new leaderships in the modern sector industries directed much of their energy toward the quality of working life inside the plants. This was a concern which directly challenged rationalisation schemes aimed at intensifying production and questioned management prerogatives and authority within the labour process. Line speed ups had constantly fuelled the emerging discontent of the IKA–Renault workers in the late 1960s, and managerial insistence on its right to unilaterally determine production speeds had been a major issue leading to the revolt of Fiat workers in 1970. Once they had established their control the new militants set about confronting companies on these issues. In their negotiations with Fiat in July 1971, for example, Sitrac and Sitram demanded the abolition of the company's incentive scheme, arguing that it enabled the company to pay low basic wages and to increase exploitation by constantly increasing production targets and line speeds. Bonuses, they argued, should be incorporated into basic wage rates and increased production should be derived from new technology, not from intensified effort. They also suggested a reduction of job categories in order to create a more united work force, and demanded worker participation in fixing production targets.[19]

The resurgence of issues concerned with labour conditions and managerial authority in this new wave of labour protest represented the first time in nearly a decade that such issues had been raised within the labour movement. We have documented in an earlier chapter the way in which the defeats of the Frondizi era had rolled back a wide spectrum of shop-floor gains in this field. As the internal commissions were weakened in the 1960s, and with an official union leadership economically on the defensive and concerned to protect wages above all else, the issue of labour conditions had effectively vanished from the agenda of the national union movement and the shop floor. The impact of this newly rediscovered concern amongst the labour opposition of the late 1960s and early 1970s should not be underestimated. When coupled with the emphasis on internal democracy it helped define, in concrete terms, the wider significance of the militant upsurge of these years. A Fiat worker from the Materfer plant in Córdoba was quite explicit about the significance of this experience:

Those fifteen months of union democracy left an enormous legacy for Fiat workers ... we showed what we could do to better our working conditions when we organise and the leaderships that we elect authentically carry out the mandate of the rank and file ... We got wage increases, upgrading of categories, improvements in the canteen, in medical attention, we stopped arbitrary firings. But more important than all this was the total change in life in the plants. Delegates defended us from foremen in all problems which arose at work. We controlled production speeds which had previously been terrible. We eliminated the oppressive climate which had existed within the factory and we could claim our rights as human beings.[20]

In a more general sense, the leaderships which came to the fore in the modern sector in the 1969–73 period also sought to frame their labour protest in terms of wider, ideological concerns. *Clasismo, sindicalismo de liberación*, as it was variously called, implied, at the level of leadership ideology, an identification of the working-class movement with the suppression of capitalism and the creation of a socialist society. The programme of Sitrac and Sitram, issued in May 1971, proposed massive nationalisation of production and workers' control of industry. This evidently entailed a broad definition of the function of trade unionism. Agustín Tosco consistently rejected a purely economic definition of union action:

The trade unionist must struggle with all his conviction, all his efforts to change the system ... the union leader must know that in spite of a 'good economy', if there is no just distribution of wealth, exploitation continues. And he must, therefore, struggle for 'social liberation'. He must also know that there will never be good labour contracts with the country's economy dominated by the monopolies. And therefore they must struggle for national liberation.[21]

A leader of Sitrac–Sitram asserted that 'the supporters of a *clasista* union orientation are perfectly aware of the natural incompatibility between their own class interests and those of the dominant classes'.[22] One of the principal functions of a union was precisely to inculcate such convictions amongst its rank and file. The union thus had a vital consciousness-raising task to prepare the working class for what would ultimately be a political battle against employers and the state.

Clasismo evidently carried potentially profound implications for the Peronist union bureaucracy, Argentine employers and, ultimately, the state. For the national union hierarchy its fiercely anti-bureaucratic emphasis on internal democracy and mass participation posed a clear threat in terms of influence and example. It presented workers confronted with the spectacle of a traditional union leadership in crisis with a viable alternative model of union action. For employers, the new union opposition's championing of issues centred on labour conditions represented a direct challenge to authority relations inside the factories. For both unions and employers, *clasismo's* recognition of the irreconcilable nature of class interests implied a constant battle between the two, and the denial of the common ground for compromise so essential for both traditional trade unionism and employers. The threat posed to the military regime was also clear. The movement had repeatedly demonstrated its capacity to challenge public order well beyond the factory gates. Its capacity to articulate a wide spectrum of social and political grievances, its claims to redefine the role of unionism and its ability to adopt radical forms of activity, presented a consistent threat to political stability which the Argentine state could ill afford to ignore.

Yet, it became equally clear that this opposition movement had limitations and internal contradictions. Certainly, its failure to become a true national force and expand its influence to Buenos Aires proved to be a considerable weakness. The weight of state repression was important, too. In October 1971, for example, the national government dissolved the Sitrac–Sitram unions and imprisoned their leaders. Many other militants also suffered the effects of government and managerial repression as the state moved to contain and isolate the movement. The state's relative success in achieving this after 1971 was aided by weaknesses within the opposition movement.

Most crucially, the political project associated with *clasismo*, the broader claims of the militant leaderships concerning the ultimate goal of the anti-bureaucratic movement, were not necessarily completely shared by their rank and file. For the majority of the rank and file the basic feature of the new movement was not the theory of *sindicalismo de liberación*, nor the goal of a socialist society, but rather union combativity and 'honest leadership' which translated into meaningful changes in their working lives. A militant from the Chrysler plant in Buenos Aires was quite frank when discussing this issue:

They're with whoever defends them; in Chrysler the rank and file knew our political line ... for them it mattered little if we are *guerrilleros* or communists, what was important was that we defended them, and so they defended us ... the rank and file don't respond to an ideology, they respond to honest leadership, nothing else.[23]

The crisis of both the military regime and the union leadership following the *Cordobazo*, together with the radicalisation of the rank and file, particularly in the interior, provided a space into which radical political activists could move and achieve an influence among important sectors of the working class they had been denied for thirty years. Maoists, revolutionary Peronists, communists and a variety of new left Marxist groups achieved a considerable influence in the union opposition movement of the 1969–73 period. Many of the leaderships which emerged were a coalition of leftist tendencies who saw, apparently for the first time in Argentina, the emergence of a new proletariat not dominated and manipulated by Peronism and its union bureaucracy. The rank-and-file rebellion of the interior seemed to herald the arrival of a proletarian vanguard capable of launching both an economic and political assault on capitalism.

The specific national conjuncture of the post-*Cordobazo* period certainly gave ground for such hopes. These times were heady ones indeed for radical activists. The capacity of the working class to challenge and undermine the regime seemed self-evident. The *Cordobazo* had removed Onganía from power; the *Viborazo* had likewise been the death knell for his successor, Levingston. At the same time the military regime and the broad opposition it had generated had radically simplified political and social activity. Opposition to the military was widespread and broad based, and subsumed within it a wide range of political tendencies. Within the working class, opposition to the regime's economic policy and crude repression seemed a sufficient strategy, and those who most consistently and courageously carried this through established a credibility and were granted a broad-based support which was largely independent of a commitment to the details of their radical political ideology. In the situation created by the regime's policies the line between union and political activity and loyalty, always blurred in Argentina, disappeared as the new union opposition expressed the generalised rejection by their rank and file of the *Revolución Argentina*.

This is not to suggest that Marxist activists foisted their political concerns on an unwilling membership. The labour protest of this era had its origins in authentic rank-and-file mobilisations, and was not the work of external agitators as the regime and union leadership maintained. Radical leftist groups helped provide links between plant agitation and the wider community. In addition, they provided many of the new working-class activists thrown up by this mobilisation with a broader political identity at a time when many of them were seeking an alternative to both simple union militancy and an increasingly defensive traditional Peronism. Militants such as René Salamanca, the leader of SMATA Córdoba and Carlos Masera, a leading figure in Sitrac–Sitram, adopted an explicit Marxist identity both because of the practical help offered by radical groups inside the plants and because they offered them a broader vision of social change and regeneration. Such a vision had until then been a monopoly of Peronism and one of *clasismo's* enduring legacies was to have at least partially broadened the spectrum of political ideologies available in working-class discourse.

The point which must be emphasised, however, is that this was only a partial breach in Peronism's monopoly. The political loyalties of workers in these unions remained overwhelmingly Peronist and, while this working-class Peronism remained open to a variety of new inputs and counter-discourses, in the most immediate political sense their support for the new leaderships was not based on political identification. A militant from the light and power union in Córdoba explained the union's support for Tosco, a non-Peronist, in these terms: 'The majority of the union is Peronist, but they voted for Tosco as a union leader. We've known him for fifteen years, he's honest, capable and has proved himself in struggles against the bosses.'[24]

This implied that the strategy adopted by the militant opposition was a precarious one. They were able to mobilise their membership and adopt a political role which challenged the regime and advocated a socialist revolution. Yet, this mobilisation was based largely on a loyalty toward the combativity and honesty of the leaders rather than on specifically ideological factors. The consciousness-raising function of the union was, in these circumstances, of very limited success. For most of this period the discrepancy between the political pretensions of the militant leadership and the political loyalties of the rank and file remained muted. But, as the regime began, after 1971, under the leadership of General Lanusse, to moderate its policies and prepare the return of traditional political activity, the potential conflict became more apparent. The reemergence of a credible political option for the working class embodied in a resurgent political Peronism and the possible return of Perón himself clearly exposed the limits of political radicalisation.

Some currents within the union opposition were aware of the weakness of their position. Tosco in the light and power workers' union was constantly aware of the problem and lamented the rank and file's apathy toward the broader, revolutionary concerns. He was also aware of the need to avoid offending the Peronist predisposition of many in his union. However, a majority of the new wave of militants took the reality of labour protest and social conflict and made the leap of faith that this would inevitably be translated into a revolutionary political maturing of the working class. Drawing from the *Cordobazo* its legacy of elemental social upheaval, they glorified the spontaneity and explosive potential of the masses. In this way they intended to resolve the dilemma of the gap between their revolutionary ideology and the actual political state of the working class.

Such a strategy inevitably isolated the new wave of militants. This was particularly evident in their relationship with Peronist activists who were by 1971 following Perón's orders to unify the movement behind the union leadership, and thus prevent internal divisions which would hinder his negotiations with the regime. This meant that the militant unity in action which had been characteristic of the preceding years became more difficult to achieve. The failure of the *clasista* militants to formalise such a unity at the *Plenario Nacional de Sindicatos Combativos, Grupos Clasistas, Obreros Revolucionarios*, held in August 1971, amply reflected this, as did the lack of response to the crushing of Sitrac–Sitram in October of the same year. Yet, as the working class looked increasingly by 1971 to the electoral return of Peronism as a solution to their problems, the radical opposition launched their slogan 'Ni golpe, ni elección: revolución!'[25]

The continuing crisis of the union leaders: from *Cordobazo* to the return of Perón

The period from 1969 to 1973 saw the gradual dismantling of the *Revolución Argentina*, culminating in the return of Peronism to political power in the elections of March 1973. In the years following the *Cordobazo* the armed forces' high command tried with varying degrees of success to put the lid back on the Pandora's box of social and political upheaval that had been opened by the Córdoba events. The first casualty of this policy was Onganía himself who, unwilling to make the necessary compromises, was ousted in June 1970. Under his successor General Levingston some first steps were taken toward a return to institutional normality. In July 1970 the CGT was normalised under newly elected authorities. Levingston, however, balked at further significant concessions to the social and political opposition. The isolation of his government became more apparent as popular discontent continued, accompanied by an increasingly daring series of guerrilla actions. In March 1971 a second city-wide upheaval shook Córdoba. Provoked by an unpopular, military-appointed governor, this second *Cordobazo* involved the same *ad hoc* alliance between workers, students and wide sectors of the local population. To this was now added, however, a leadership role for the radical Sitrac–Sitram unions and a widely reported intervention of guerrilla groups. The *Viborazo* galvanised the high command. By the end of March Levingston had been summarily dismissed and replaced by the head of the Junta de Comandantes, General Alejandro Lanusse.

Alarmed by what they regarded as the growing threat of social disintegration and chaos, worried by the demoralising impact of the increasing use of the armed forces to police the nation's citizenry, the military commanders considered it imperative to dismantle, in a controlled fashion, the most provocative aspects of the *Revolución Argentina* and prepare the ground for an orderly transition to civilian rule. The *Gran Acuerdo Nacional*, launched by Lanusse, encapsulated this military strategy. It proposed the reestablishment of the traditional institutions of civic and political life in order to defuse the social upheaval inundating Argentina, and channel it into acceptable paths. In July 1971 the proscription of political parties decreed by Onganía in 1966 was lifted and elections promised. Discussions between the major political forces and the leaders of the armed forces began in earnest, to establish the basis for the proposed national consensus. Clearly, this would have to involve a recognition of Peronism as a political force. Lanusse and the high command realised that any attempt to institutionalise and head off the popular discontent they had unleashed would be doomed to failure without the at least tacit support of Peronism. In a significant break with the traditional anti-Peronism of the armed forces, Lanusse began talks with Peronist figures. Hints were even dropped about the possible return of Perón himself. At the same time, Lanusse continued a policy, begun under Levingston, of dismantling many of those aspects of Krieger Vasena's economic policy which had so offended important entrepreneurial sectors.

The concrete political solution originally envisaged by the military as

emerging from the *Gran Acuerdo Nacional* involved the electoral legitimation of a military-backed candidate, Lanusse himself, in the elections promised for 1973. Such a candidate would be accepted by
Peronists and Radicals, they reasoned, as a necessary cost of the transition to democracy. Their support for such a solution would evidently
have to be won in return for programmatic concessions and political
guarantees. The social basis of this solution was to be furnished
through the support of the Peronist unions. The union leadership
would be attracted by the offer of a close relationship with a sympathetic military figure. After the trauma of the Onganía regime, and under
continued attack from new opposition forces, the unions would welcome the opportunity afforded by a state which had courted their support to reestablish their control and their credibility as a major factor of
power in Argentina. These populist aspirations of Lanusse were to be
buttressed by a determined effort to expand the government's popular
support through social welfare measures. At the same time as this moderate path was to be followed, a policy of repression was to be directed
at all 'subversive' forces, whether radical unionists or guerrilla militants.

Lanusse's strategy was partially successful. The reconvening of political parties and the reopening of the political option, which culminated in the 1973 elections, managed to contain the radical opposition
within the unions. A recurrence of the *Viborazo* was avoided. Nevertheless, the final terms of the political solution which emerged in the
course of 1972 differed dramatically from that originally envisaged by
the strategists of the *Gran Acuerdo Nacional* and represented an at least
partial defeat for their plans.

Several factors undermined the success of Lanusse's plan. On the one
hand, Perón himself astutely countered one of its principal goals: the
political incorporation of Peronism into the new institutional opening
which would, at the same time, reduce Perón's own authority and limit
his role in the emerging consensus. He was able to take advantage of the
new context to reestablish his own preeminence. Refusing to commit
himself to the military's scheme he kept his lines of communication
open to other political forces. Through the coalition called the Hora del
Pueblo he maintained contact with the Radical Party and a wide range
of democratic forces advocating a direct return to electoral democracy.
By March 1972 Peronism had established its own electoral front, the
Frente Justicialista de Liberación (FREJULI), and affirmed its intention to contest the elections in its own right. Perón's success in asserting his preeminence was a logical consequence of Lanusse's

reopening of party politics. Perón, as the ultimate arbiter of Peronist votes, inevitably became more powerful as other political actors bargained for his support and these votes in the upcoming elections.

Perón's ability to outmanoeuvre Lanusse was also due to the social and civic crisis which continued to rend Argentine society. While the regime had some success after 1971 in repressing and controlling the labour rebellion in the interior, and while the prospect of elections in 1973 helped assuage the democratic yearnings of large sectors of Argentine society, the mobilisation of important segments of the urban middle class, particularly its youth, continued unabated. Children of Onganía's insensitive and ruthless authoritarianism, their rebellion had first erupted in 1969 and continued in the following years in a society which seemed to offer them diminishing economic opportunities. Its scope came to extend far beyond the initial grievances of its university environment. These middle-class youths adopted a radical anti-imperialist ideology and many turned increasingly toward Peronism or the guerrilla groups as a channel for their aspirations. This youthful rebellion was clearly not readily assimilable within the reborn system of traditional political parties.

This was most dramatically symbolised by the ever-increasing intensity of guerrilla actions. By 1970 there were four major guerrilla groups operating in Argentina: the Fuerzas Armadas Peronistas, the Fuerzas Armadas Revolucionarias, the Ejército Revolucionario del Pueblo, and the Montoneros. Between 1970 and 1973 these groups, and a number of smaller imitators, embarked on a wave of actions which included direct attacks on military installations, the kidnapping and killing of industrialists and political figures, spectacular bank robberies and hijackings, and the assassination of leading military figures.[26] Such actions found an often explicit support among the youth who were flooding into the Peronist movement at this time. The threat that this challenge posed to political and social stability gradually changed the terms of the negotiations between Perón and the military. By 1972 Perón and Peronism were seen by many in the armed forces as the only viable hope to reestablish social order and control the threat posed by a radicalised youth and radicalised labour protest. A city-wide upheaval in Mendoza in February 1972, which was very similar in its form to the *Cordobazo*, convinced the military that they had far more to lose from a continued delay in reaching a political solution than did Perón. Once Perón had accepted, by the end of 1972, the military's one remaining stipulation – a proscription on his own personal candidature – the way was cleared for the return of Peronism to political power.

Ultimately, too, the regime's assumption that it would be able to enrol a significant proportion of the union leadership as a partner within a revived military reformism proved to be overly optimistic. The crisis provoked by the Onganía regime could not be overcome by government fiat. As was the case with the political parties, the simple act of resurrecting the union movement could not undo the damage done to its credibility and morale. Would the union leadership be able to direct and channel a social protest which had arisen outside its control and independent of its wishes? The more moderate government economic policy adopted by Onganía's successors, together with the return of some sort of limited collective bargaining, did hold the prospect of a certain rehabilitation for the union leadership. They were not, however, able to win sufficient concessions from the regime to win back all the lost ground. While the economic policy under Lanusse introduced sufficient flexibility in wage policy to prevent explosive unrest, the authorities were not willing to reintroduce unrestricted collective bargaining, and thus give the union leaders the tools with which to reassert their unquestioned hegemony over their rank and file and embark their unions on the path toward compromise and alliance envisioned in the *Gran Acuerdo Nacional*. This implied that although the Peronist union leadership had the capacity to maintain its control of the national union apparatus centred in Buenos Aires it no longer enjoyed in these years the ability to mobilise and lead its members in the impressive fashion it once had during the apogee of Vandorism.

Most importantly for the calculations of the military strategists, the union hierarchy's position within Peronism was an increasingly beleaguered one. This threat to their position came from two sources. First, it was a consequence of the rehabilitation of the political system and traditional political actors. The reestablishment of traditional political activity deeply disturbed and divided many Peronist union leaders. Even under as astute a tactician as Vandor we have seen how ambiguous were the results of union incursions into the political arena in the mid 1960s. With Vandor's murder, and the increasing uncertainties of the early 1970s, union prospects within a restored democratic politics looked murky at best. The union hierarchy was aware that any political opening would tend to strengthen Perón's position and weaken its own, and this was especially true in a context which promised the formal legalisation of political Peronism, and even the possible return of Perón. The union leaders were also aware of the distrust and resentment felt by Perón and his entourage toward themselves.

While many of the Peronist leaders were, therefore, concerned by

Perón's tactical manoeuvres, they were, in their weakened circumstances, unable to adopt a unified response. One faction, headed by the secretary general of the CGT, José Rucci, adopted a policy of complete compliance with Perón's political tactics, openly subordinating the CGT to his bargaining needs with the regime and political parties. In July 1971, however, a group of some sixty Peronist unions, many of which had formerly been within the 'participationist' current, issued a public statement denouncing traditional political parties, attacking the growing political activity of the CGT, and calling for a 'revolution within the revolution' to return the *Revolución Argentina* to its true, corporatist path. Most union leaders considered such a barely disguised attack on Perón's tactics to be unwise, particularly as they saw the inexorable move toward elections in the course of 1972. Their chief concern became their ability to assert their claims to their share of the spoils offered by the political resurgence of Peronism.

The fact that the union leadership was so pessimistic about its prospects within a revitalised Peronism reflected its concern over the growing influence of new forces within the movement. Increasingly it felt isolated and under attack from an emerging leftist current within Peronism. This left differed considerably from the traditional union left of the early 1960s. The traditional union *duros*, now enrolled in Peronismo Combativo, were still a critical force within the CGT and the councils of the 62 Organisations. They were, however, limited in their influence to a number of small unions. The CGT de los Argentinos, which had briefly seemed to promise a real influence for this tradition had by 1969 disappeared as an effective force. Revolutionary Peronism centred on organisations such as Peronismo de Base, achieved a considerable influence among rank-and-file workers, particularly in the interior in the years after 1969. They were active within the new union opposition movements and adopted similar positions to other *clasista* currents. Their influence, too, was a limited one within Peronism and the national unions.

Of far greater concern to the union leaders were the Peronist youth and guerrilla groups, in particular the Montoneros. The threat they posed was both physical and political. Starting with the assassination of Augusto Vandor in July 1969, and continuing with the murder of José Alonso a year later, the Peronist guerrillas began a campaign of selective physical elimination of union leaders. As they flocked into the youth organisations of Peronism, and to a lesser degree the guerrilla groups, in the years following the *Cordobazo*, the young, mainly middle-class recruits espoused a radical anti-imperialism which drew on a wide range of third-world nationalist figures for inspiration. Identifying Peronism as a national liberation movement, they declared its goal to be the establishment of a national form of socialism. The strategy which would lead to this goal was that of armed struggle. They proclaimed the main obstacle to Peronism's pursuit of this goal to be the union bureaucracy. The bureaucracy was, for these newcomers, a corrupt caste whose function was to repress and manipulate the Peronist masses, and divert them from the struggle for the creation of a new Argentina. As such it was objectively an ally of the oligarchy and imperialism, which would either be physically eliminated from Peronism, or surpassed by the entry into the movement of new revolutionary blood which would mature into the future leadership.

The threat posed by these sectors to the union bureaucracy was not, therefore, simply a physical one. It was above all ideological and political. At no time in the years 1969–73 did they pose an institutional threat to the leadership within the unions, as, for example, the labour insurgents of the interior potentially did. Indeed, they made no attempt to create a specifically working-class organisation to compete within the unions. The working class was assumed to be, *per se*, revolutionary, and once the bureaucracy had been removed it would reestablish its true relationship with the revolutionary leader, Perón, and the new revolutionary leadership of Peronism. The Peronist youth and guerrilla groups represented above all a challenge to the entire trajectory of the union movement within Peronism and, indeed, the identity they held of Peronism as a movement. The reformist nationalism they had identified with Peronism, and the pragmatism and compromise that had come to imply after 1955, were now assailed in terms of a moral crusade launched by newcomers with no traditional standing within the movement. These new arrivals now sought to redefine Peronism in terms of a revolutionary creed which could have little meaning for the union leaders. A fundamental part of this redefinition involved, moreover, the denial of the legitimacy of the union leadership's very presence within the new Peronist movement envisaged by the young radicals.

In calmer times such threats to their traditional standing within Peronism from outside the unions could have been dismissed. In the years of mass mobilisation and heightened social conflict, with the attendant influx of radicalised sectors into Peronism, such threats had to be taken seriously. The reopening of the political system clearly made the union leadership far more vulnerable to political attack from outside the strictly union field. Nor did Perón assuage these fears. He perceived that the youth sectors of the movement clearly reflected a prevalent popular mood of resentment and hope for renewal in Argentine society far more authentically than could an insecure union leadership. They were capable of organising the popular mobilisation made possible by the reemergence of mass politics. They were, in addition, an important bargaining tool for him; a reminder of Peronism's capacity to destabilise if it were not reintegrated into Argentine society.

Throughout 1972 Perón entertained leaders of the Peronist youth in Madrid, and praise for the *muchachos* and criticism of the union bureaucracy were frequently found in his public comments. The Montoneros were granted recognition as 'special formations' of the movement. Taking Perón's assurances that the youth would inherit the movement at face value, the leaders of the Juventud Peronista and the Montoneros chose to ignore potential differences between their strategy and that of Perón. Given the generalised euphoria which engulfed the movement as the election campaign got under way, the indications which already existed of the commitments and compromises Perón was prepared to embark upon were interpreted as masterly tactical ruses on the part of the veteran leader. For the union leaders the frightening influence of the new pretenders seemed palpable enough. As FREJULI chose its candidates in early 1972 the union leadership was reminded of its reduced weight within the movement. In contrast to 1962 and 1965 where they had imposed their candidates at will, they were now forced to accept an equal proportion of candidacies with other sections of Peronism. Not a single ticket for a provincial governor was offered to a union figure; the most they achieved was the vice-gubernatorial nomination in some provinces. Nor were they consulted over Perón's choice of Hector Campora as the Peronist presidential candidate. Perhaps most ominously, the entire tone and organisation of the election campaign were set by the youth sectors who succeeded in mobilising vast sectors of the population and in targeting both the military regime and the union bureaucracy for special execration. Thus, the results of the 11 March elections which gave Peronism a clear and impressive victory were regarded with little enthusiasm by the union leaders. After eighteen years of formal commitment to Peronism's regaining of state power, the reality which confronted them when Campora was inaugurated as president on 25 May offered little ground for optimism and security.

On 3 October 1973 Juan Perón stood on the balcony of the CGT headquarters in downtown Buenos Aires. He was surrounded by the elite of the Peronist union leadership; Lorenzo Miguel, Adelino Romero, Casildo Herreras were all present. From mid-day onward, and for most of the afternoon, Perón waved his greetings to a seemingly endless procession of workers, bused in by their unions for the occasion, as they marched passed chanting his name and singing Peronist anthems such as the Muchachos Peronistas. As the afternoon wore on a growing crescendo of noise percolated through from the adjacent area and began to drown out the traditional anthems broadcast on the official loudspeaker system. The source of the noise soon became apparent as observers reached the foot of Avenida Belgrano where it meets with Paseo Colón, some 500 metres from the CGT headquarters. Looking up the slope one could see an apparently endless mass of humanity covering the entire breadth of the avenue and stretching back as far as the eye could see. Three huge banners were stretched out at the front of this mass. One bore the legend 'Montoneros – FAR', another 'Juventud Peronista' and the third proclaimed 'Perón en el poder para el Socialismo Nacional'. The demonstrators were overwhelmingly young, and for what seemed like hours on end they waited, arms linked, as the sun lowered on a perfect *porteño* spring afternoon. Finally, in their hundreds of thousands they, too, were allowed, grudgingly, to march past the CGT. The homage they payed was somewhat different, the chants were not those of traditional Peronism but, rather, proclamations in favour of the 'Patria Socialista', and by the time the majority of them marched past the balcony Perón had long since left.

The symbolism inherent in the event could hardly be missed. For the first time in eighteen years Perón received the traditional gesture of homage surrounded by leaders of the labour movement in their headquarters. More was at stake than this, however. The clear gesture of support Perón offered the union leadership, and the equally evident snub for the radical sectors of Peronism symbolised the dramatic turn of fortunes for both under the new government. The euphoria of the days following the inauguration of Hector Campora was rapidly fading. The resignation of Campora, the growing campaign in the weeks after his resignation against the 'infiltrators' within the movement, the role played by the unions in the election campaign which brought Perón the presidency in September, all heralded a shift of influence within Peronism. The popular feeling of hope and renewal present in the first six months of 1973 had been palpable. It had been clearly reflected in the crowds which had stormed Villa Devoto prison on the day Campora was inaugurated and released the political prisoners held there. It was also evident in the marked democratisation of the state apparatus during Campora's brief rule. A sense of the possibility of participating in the proclaimed 'national reconstruction' was all-pervasive among the Peronist youth of this era.

Yet, with hindsight, Perón's choice of the union bureaucracy over the more radical sectors of his movement seems predictable and certainly consistent with his overall strategy. The cornerstone of this strategy was the *Pacto Social*. The pact was, essentially, an agreement between employers and unions which froze wages and prices. Overseen by the state as part of a general plan of national reconstruction, the agreement had the binding status of law. It formed part of a wider strategy to achieve social and political conciliation. On the political level Perón reached a series of understandings with the Radical Party to prevent inter-party strife in the newly elected congress. Socially, the principal institutions of the Argentine employers and unions were given privileged access to the state. The head of the Confederación General Económica, José Gelbard, became the Minister of the Economy; the CGT likewise became an integral part of the administration of government policy. In the breathing space this would achieve, Perón hoped to redirect the Argentine economy toward a new era of growth based on Argentina's emergence as an industrial exporter. Inflation would be controlled as the sectional claims of employers and workers were kept in abeyance. This would stimulate both domestic and foreign investment which would generate the modernisation necessary to compete on the world market. On the basis of this renovated economy a future stage of income redistribution would be contemplated.[27]

The success of such a strategy depended on several factors. First, the weight of Perón's personal prestige and commitment to the plan was crucial in giving it legitimacy and inducing respect for it. Second, the plan depended on the ability of key representative institutions such as the CGE and the unions to translate the formal commitments into the active respect of their members. Finally, much depended on the existence of an international economic context which would make Perón's economic plans for the Argentine economy feasible. Within this context Perón's preference for the union bureaucracy over the radical youth sectors of Peronism was logical. Ultimately, both his vision of the future Argentine society and the needs of his immediate strategy pointed toward his rehabilitation of the union hierarchy.

The implications of this choice for the Peronist youth and the Montoneros soon became evident. Within a year they were to be driven into sullen compliance or into clandestine opposition. Increasingly marginalised and thrown on the defensive even before Perón's death in July 1974, many would enter into open, armed opposition to his political heir and widow, Isabel. At the same time, the position of the union leadership was, in formal terms, immeasurably strengthened both within the Peronist movement and within the working class. Bathed in the newly reacquired aura of Perón's blessing, their isolation within the movement broken, the union leaders became, ironically, the chief exponents of *verticalismo* – the campaign for unquestioning respect for hierarchical authority within the movement. By late 1974 they had driven their young opponents from the mainstream of the movement. They had also, with the aid of the emerging extreme right of Peronism, succeeded in removing all of the figures of political Peronism who had shown sympathy for the radical sectors. Even before Perón's death the governors of Buenos Aires, Córdoba and Mendoza had been forced to resign. In Buenos Aires the new governor was Victor Calabró, a leader of the metal workers. Between July and October 1974 the union bureaucracy also settled their scores with the *clasista* union opposition. They made use of the greatly enhanced powers granted them by a new Law of Professional Associations passed in November 1973 and semi-official terrorism directed at these unions. The militant leaderships of SMATA Córdoba, the Buenos Aires print workers, and finally the Córdoba light and power workers were in rapid succession legally removed from their posts and then declared to be outlaws.

Yet, the position of the Peronist union leadership was in fact rather more fragile than these appearances suggested. They had overcome the isolation of the early 1970s and established themselves as legitimate interlocutors with the government, on an equal footing with employers and political parties. However, the price demanded was a high one: adherence to the *Pacto Social* with the severe limitations this implied for their role as spokesmen for the working-class demands in the economic arena. The risk involved would have been lessened if the pact had been respected and if its economic results had been those envisaged for it. But in the last resort neither the CGT nor the CGE had the credibility necessary to enforce the compliance of their followers.[28]

The election victory and the expectations it had generated provoked a wave of factory rebellions which for the first time inundated the industrial belt of Gran Buenos Aires. While Perón's prestige prevented an explicit rejection of the pact's wage controls, workers found a thousand ways to translate the political victory at the polls into gains on the shop floor. Conditions of work, health and safety, back pay, job reclassifications and new, authentic plant leaderships, emerged as issues as innumerable scores accumulated in the pre-1973 period were now settled. Thus, despite an offical policy of consensus and conciliation at the political level, in social terms the period saw a heightening of class conflict.[29]

This situation inevitably disturbed the union leadership since they were burdened with the responsibility for enforcing compliance with an unpopular wage freeze which was in effect being by-passed by large sections of their rank and file. Nor did the employers make their task any easier. The CGE was equally ineffective in enforcing its price restraint. By late 1973 employers were unofficially raising prices and charges of stockpiling and black marketeering became rampant. The international economic situation further added to Perón's economic problems. The *Pacto Social* coincided with a contracting world market and a leap in international inflation triggered by the oil price rise. The costs of Argentine industrial imports rose drastically. Employers clamoured to pass these increases on to the consumers. By early 1974 the impact of this situation on the balance of payments and on inflation was becoming apparent, as was the general lack of confidence of entrepreneurs as they refused to invest in new plant and expenditures.

The union leadership attempted to minimise the costs of their new position of co-sponsors of wage controls and social harmony. After Perón's death they pressured Isabel Perón to reestablish free collective bargaining. They were also able to defeat their opponents within the Peronist movement and in the union opposition. The reasons for this success in eliminating their competitors within Peronism and the working class were several. Most simply, they were able to use the enormous resources of the state to isolate and terrorise potential opponents. Any analysis of this period which fails to take sufficient note of the intensive, all-pervasive impact of both official and para-police repression inevitably misses a crucial component of the everyday experience of political and union militants, particularly in the period after Perón's death. The personal risks involved in militant activity became terrifyingly high.

Perhaps more fundamentally still, both the Peronist and non-Peronist left found themselves politically isolated within the working class. In the case of the Peronist youth and guerrilla formations such isolation seemed at times almost wilful. Their declaration of war against Perón's successor implied a disregard for the millions of votes cast by Peronist workers less than a year earlier. Whatever the eventual collapse of her government it seems clear that she still enjoyed, at least until June 1975, a strong degree of residual political legitimacy in the eyes of Peronist workers. Thus, both the Peronist and non-Peronist guerrillas were doomed to fight out a tragic and uneven battle largely isolated from the working class who formed the central subject of their radical rhetoric. Increasingly, by 1975, they were involved in a bloody battle for survival which profoundly shook Argentine civil society and had little relevance for the working class. The macabre tit for tat of escalating assassinations had a deep impact on the rank-and-file militants who, bereft of the benefit of a clandestine infrastructure, found themselves the favoured target of right-wing death squads.

For the *clasista* union opposition the situation was more complex, if in the end no less personally tragic. The dissociation between the level of social struggle and the political loyalties of the rank-and-file Peronists, which had been apparent prior to 1973, became a critical factor in these years and profoundly impacted on the development of the union opposition movement. The discrepancy between the political ideology of an Agustín Tosco or a René Salamanca and the political allegiance of their overwhelmingly Peronist rank and file had not been critical under the military regime. With the new Peronist government, however, such a discrepancy inevitably created confusion and defeated their attempts to build a radical political alternative to Peronism in government. To oppose the economic policy of the Peronist government implied a political challenge, and while on the strictly economic terrain the workers would follow radical leadership this was never translated into a transformation of their political allegiances. Indeed, even strictly union loyalties to radical leaders became more ambivalent. It was now much more difficult for workers to defend radical leaderships under attack from a Peronist state for which the working class had fought since 1955. The appeals launched by the state and union leaders based on orthodoxy and loyalty were, therefore, both confusing and effective. The union leadership was, thus, ultimately able to benefit from the reality of the working class's political identification with Peronism and the legitimacy that this bestowed on them.

The inability of the Peronist and non-Peronist left to construct a viable alternative leadership cleared the way for the emergence of the union bureaucracy as the dominant force within the Peronist government during its last eighteen months in power. The victory was, however, a pyrrhic one. While they were able to repress and marginalise competitors within the working class and within Peronism they were unable to reestablish their hegemony over their rank and file, or establish their credibility as a dominant force within Argentine society. In part this resulted from the ferocious battle launched by Isabel and her personal circle to diminish their influence. The union leaders were involved in a debilitating battle against the president and her advisers throughout her government.

Partly, too, this reflected the rapidly deteriorating economic situation. As the last vestiges of the *Pacto Social* crumbled and the Argentine economy entered a deepening recession, accompanied by spiralling inflation, the dangers of rank-and-file discontent reemerged in full force. In June 1975 this discontent erupted in a massive popular protest against the drastic economic stabilisation plan decreed by Isabel's Minister of Economy, Celestino Rodrigo. The *Rodrigazo* which involved a spontaneous general strike, factory occupations and demonstrations which continued for nearly a month was a crushing blow to Isabel's government. Although the union leadership had willingly put itself at the head of this upsurge and negotiated the annulment of the economic measures and the resignation of Rodrigo and Lopez Rega, the *Rodrigazo* had also exposed the precariousness of its own position. Able to defeat opponents of both right and left within Peronism they were still vulnerable to the unpredictability of working-class responses in a deteriorating economy. Moreover, though they could clearly veto economic and political arrangements they themselves had nothing to offer by way of coherent alternatives. As the economic crisis deepened, and with unrivalled influence over the state after the *Rodrigazo*, their policy amounted to *ad hoc* crisis management combined with calls for a return to traditional reformist economic measures which Argentina's situation made patently untenable.

In this context, deprived of effective leadership, the Argentine working class waited out the long agony of Isabel Perón's government. Within the factories and *barrios* attempts began to emerge to fill the vacuum created by Peronism's internal implosion and the crushing of the organised opposition movements. Coordinating committees, the *coordinadoras*, emerged in the wake of the *Rodrigazo* in an attempt to meet a need felt by both activists and rank and file for structures which would bring workers together to coordinate activity and discussion among workers in different industries in a particular zone. They were not able, however, to fully develop in the time left between the June mobilisation and the military coup of March 1976. The impact of economic crisis and the demoralisation induced by the collapse of the Peronist movement combined to produce a fatalism in the face of the long rumoured miliary coup.

10

Conclusion

Of course, the terms of the problem are clear: class manifests itself not only as institutionalised apparatus, but also as an ensemble ... of direct action groups, and as a collective which receives its statute from the practico-inert field (through and by productive relations with other classes) ... And these three simultaneous statutes arise in practical and dialectical connection with one another, through a process which is itself conditioned by the historical conjuncture as a whole. In fact, language *always* presents class too simply, either as always united, and ranged against the exploiters, or as temporarily demobilised (having completely relapsed into seriality). May it not be that these imperfect and incomplete concepts are an accurate reflection of our inability to understand this unique triple reality of a developing historical class?

Jean-Paul Sartre, *Critique of Dialectical Reason*, vol. 1, p. 685

The decades following the overthrow of Juan Domingo Perón in 1955 saw the reemergence of Peronist unionism as the dominant organised expression of the Argentine working class, and the confirmation of Peronism as the dominant political and ideological loyalty of that class. Having survived a systematic attempt in the period immediately following the 1955 coup to legally dismantle the centralised union movement built by Perón, and to forcibly eradicate its influence within the working class, the union movement had by the mid-1960s emerged as an organism of great social and political power. Together with the armed forces they were, indeed, the two fundamental poles around which Argentine society seemed to revolve. One of the principal themes of this work has been to chart this transformation and to understand the nature of this union movement, and its leadership.

While we have outlined some of the elements of a firmly entrenched union bureaucracy these are not in themselves necessarily a sufficient explanation of the power of such a leadership, its survival, or its continuing ability to influence and dominate its rank and file. There are, certainly, a number of interpretations available from both academic and more public sources. It would not be an exaggeration to say that the union bureaucracy, and in particular Vandor, have simultaneously fascinated and repelled most commentators on Argentine society. The isolated elements of a general picture presented by these observers seems evident enough and was reinforced by the general image propagated by the media. *Matonaje*, *pistolerismo*, corruption, fraud, collaboration with employers, negotiation with the state, bargaining with the armed forces, have all been intrinsically bound up with both the image and interpretation of this leadership. They have acquired the status of almost self-evident truths, social facts which common-sense observation confirms and whose simple relating implies a series of connotations. While this has certainly been true of the role of the union leadership in public discourse it has been no less evident in more formal academic interpretations. Most of these interpretations of union development and behaviour can, with little exaggeration, be regarded as falling within a paradigm dominated by what Alvin Gouldner has called 'the pathos of pessimism'.[1]

At its most simplistic this paradigm has involved an explanatory framework which looks primarily to the existence of fraud, corruption, and violence for its key elements. With these the union leadership has pursued its goal of accumulating and protecting its own power and wealth through the incorporation of Peronist unionism within 'the system' and, ultimately, of integrating it within the strategic needs of international capitalism. Within this perspective the unions have become almost entirely subservient to the interests of the ruling class, and the leadership has imposed this subservient status on its members by a mixture of violence and fraud. This approach, it should be clear by now, dominated the Peronist left's view of Vandor and Vandorism and, indeed, much of the non-Peronist left's analysis as well.[2] This analysis has been presented with varying degrees of complexity. It can be seen at its crudest in the press of the Peronist Youth in the 1969-74 period, when the struggle against the 'traitors' of the union bureaucracy became both an ideological and tactical obsession.

Yet, it could be argued that even a work as nuanced and as rich in insights into the nature of the union bureaucracy as Rodolfo Walsh's *Quién mató a Rosendo?* still remains fundamentally within this simplistic paradigm. By centering his analysis of Vandor on an investigation of one of the most notorious cases of union gangsterism, Walsh inevitably makes this stand as a symbol of Vandorism's profoundest meaning. The murder of Domingo Blajaquis and his companions, and of Vandor's own protégé and putative rival, Rosendo García, dominate, as they are indeed intended to, the readers' understanding of the Peronist union hierarchy. In the penultimate chapter of the book Walsh does attempt to provide a wider context by detailing the loss of jobs in the metal-working industry and the drop in union membership, but this is attributed to Vandor's 'sell out' to the employers and the state and serves largely to reinforce the dominant image of the work. Now it is not my intention to minimise or deny the existence and increasing use of violence and corruption by the Peronist union leadership. Indeed, the increasing resort to such instruments of internal control was a major trend documented in this work. But it is also clear that such factors cannot be taken in isolation; they must be seen as *elements* of a wider social and historical process if they are to have analytical usefulness in explaining the nature of Peronist union leadership power.

A more academic version of the 'pessimistic' approach – and certainly one with a more respectable sociological pedigree – is that with its intellectual ancestry in the works of Robert Michels, and ultimately Max Weber. This has regarded the development of bureaucracy and oligarchy as an inevitable tendency within labour organisations – an 'iron law of oligarchy' in Michels's words.[3] The incorporating effect of an advanced society on the individual union leader is often emphasised, as is the growing dominance of the institutional needs of the union over the less 'rational' wishes of the members. This leads to a situation where, in the words of the sociologist José Luis de Imaz, 'functional criteria prevail over ideological passions'.[4] Imaz saw this process as a reflection of the growing status aspirations of both union leaders and their constituents in an increasingly socially-mobile society. Although Imaz's approval of this process has not generally been shared by other writers the tendency he was describing has not been questioned. Another Argentine sociologist, Francisco Delich, has expressed a reluctant verdict which can be regarded as representative of the consensus view:

In Buenos Aires the most important unions have been transformed into true machines of social integration, into poles of transmission between the political power and the working-class base. A caste of functionaries, the providing of a broad range of social services which include health, education, leisure and housing, among other things allows the union leadership a permanent manipulation of the rank and file.[5]

Such a view is clearly a logical extension of earlier characterisations of the nature of trade unionism under populist regimes. Indeed, one could scarcely wish for a more explicit application of Michels's general analysis to a modern labour movement.

Evidently there existed a basis for this sort of analysis in the social reality of post-1955 Argentina. Indeed one of the crucial concerns of this work has been to analyse the process of 'integration', the growing dominance of the 'logic of institutional pragmatism' within the Peronist unions. Many of the issues dealt with in the extensive literature on the sociology of trade unions in Western Europe and the United States concerning the incorporation thesis have relevance to Argentina.[6] It is clear, for example, that what have been described as the 'socialising influences' at work on trade union leaders played, as we have shown, an important role in Argentina too.[7] Constant bargaining with employers and discussions with governments inevitably had a 'corrupting' effect in terms of fostering a tendency to consider the point of view of management rather than of their members, as well as pandering to the status yearnings of working-class leaders. This in turn can be traced in the adoption of new life styles: the acquisition of fast cars, *barrio norte* apartments and invitations to fashionable dinner parties, all of which distanced them from their members' feelings and interests.

Similarly, the emphasis in much sociological analysis on the overall integrating function of unions within modern capitalism is clearly pertinent to the Argentine case.[8] The Peronist union leadership played an important functional role within the process of restructuring of Argentine capitalism in the 1950s and 1960s. The average productivity of Argentine industry between 1953 and 1964 has been estimated to have increased by some 62%.[9] CONADE figures which take 1960 as a base of 100 show a rise in average productivity to 118 by 1966.[10] Real wages on the other hand did not recover to pre-1959 levels until the end of the 1960s.[11] The fact that working-class resistance to the increased exploitation and lowered standard of living indicated by these figures was kept within 'acceptable' levels was due in no small part to the ability of the union leadership to control its members; they undoubtedly fulfilled a role as regulators of social conflict – the 'managers of discontent' in C. Wright Mills's famous phrase.[12] It is here that the union leaderships' purging of the activists from the factories and unions after the defeats of 1959, and their collaboration in controlling the internal commissions, acquires its true significance, as too does the growth of the social service function of Argentine unions. The opposition to the Peronist union hierarchy, either in the form of the *duros* of the mid 1960s, or the Peronist youth and guerrilla formations of the late 1960s and early 1970s, took this reality at face value and fashioned their tactics accordingly.

Yet, the analysis we have presented cautions against a too facile acceptance of this apparently self-evident reality of union incorporation and leadership collaboration. We have suggested, for example, that the union leadership's integrationist project must be analysed without recourse to the sinister moral implications traditionally associated with the term *integracionismo* in Peronist discourse if we are to assess this process and its limits adequately. The moral affront and sense of betrayal felt by many militants of the Resistance generation, and later by the Peronist youth, must be recognised and understood but this should not blind us to the fact that in the situation which existed in the 1960s the logic of 'institutional pragmatism' was as inescapable, *for both leaders and led*, as the logic of rationalisation.

Within an overall context shaped by an employer and state offensive the union membership expected its leaders to take advantage of whatever leeway the state was prepared to offer in order to maintain basic organisation and conditions. As the *caso Cardoso* demonstrated, for all the emotional difficulty they felt in accepting Cardoso's talk of the need to take advantage of legality, even the most intransigent of Peronist unionists could in reality offer no viable alternative. Similarly, while it is easy for sociologists to talk despairingly of unions being no more than 'machines of social integration' by providing health, education, leisure and housing services the fact remained that in a society where the state provided very few of these basic needs workers tended, not unreasonably, to look to their unions for such things. In this sense, it could be plausibly argued that much of what is talked of as integration in the Argentine context was in fact no more than a normal result of the intrinsically interrelated relationship between unions and capitalism; a development all the more to be expected in a society with as high a level of industrialisation and unionisation as Argentina's.

Beyond this it is surely legitimate to question whether any analysis of the development of Peronist unionism after 1955 which is based on an almost exclusive emphasis on integration within the system is an adequate description of reality. Contrary to the apparently self-evident image of Vandorism which is generally elaborated I would argue that rather than emphasise the extent of incorporation we could with perhaps greater profit insist on its limits. At the level of union-employer relations, for example, too much should not be made of talks between the CGT and the CGE. While they remained an important programmatic goal, in reality harmonious relations between unions and employers were severely restricted. One author very sympathetic to goals of class harmony has described industrial relations in Argentina in these years in the following terms:

If we want to place collective bargaining in one of these categories [armed peace, harmony at work, cooperation between unions and management] we would undoubtedly have to opt for the first: armed peace. Our industrial system has not reached the state of complete maturity ... necessary to stabilise the relations between labour and capital.[13]

Clearly, the overall economic context is of importance here. Integration as a viable strategy depends crucially on the capacity of an economy to provide the goods in terms of wages and conditions. In a situation such as existed in Argentina after 1955, with the deterioration of both wages and conditions, a union leadership had to oppose, or at least be seen to oppose, management and the state on this basic issue of vital importance to its membership. The 'managers of discontent' had also to be, as Wright Mills recognised, the organisers of discontent. Nor was this simply a fear of being outflanked by a rank and file dissatisfied with the performance of its leaders. A labour leader like Vandor also needed, as we pointed out, from the point of view of his own bargaining needs with management and other political forces, to be able to mobilise his members when necessary. This mobilisation might be of an overwhelmingly controlled, limited nature but it was still sufficient to render problematic the basis of any incorporation strategy.

While it is true that the union leadership played a crucial role in confining working-class discontent within limited parameters this was a reformism which could still engender such 'unincorporated' actions as the factory occupations of the *Plan de Lucha* in 1964. As one author has written while analysing the incorporation debate in sociological literature: 'If excessive discontent and conflict is disruptive of established bargaining relations, excessive passivity is equally unpalatable – depriving the whole institution of unionism of its basic *raison d'être*. The union official ... his task is to sustain a delicate balance between grievance and satisfaction, between activism and quiescence.'[14] This is, of course, an extremely ambivalent, and potentially risky process, from the union leaderships' point of view, but it was just this ambivalence that was at the core of Vandorism and which, once recognised, must modify any simple incorporation thesis.

At the level of union–state relations a similar conclusion emerges from our analysis. What strikes one about the decades following the fall of Perón is the fact that despite the evidently increased weight of the Peronist unions within the socio-political system there was, in fact, a marked paucity of formalised, institutional expressions of state–union collaboration. This indeed was precisely one of the major complaints of the unions, a major point of unfavourable comparison with the Perón era, and one which was consistently emphasised in CGT propaganda. A comparison with other industrialised nations with similar rates of unionisation underlines the point. A writer assessing the role of the unions in post-war British society has described it in the following terms:

The unions have become in a very real sense part of the 'establishment'. Their association with the government and employers on scores of committees of all kinds, and their accepted right to be consulted on any subject made them an important influence on the nation's councils ... They had become a part of the body of the state in many of its intricate ramifications.[15]

To relate the position of British unions is to be struck immediately by the contrast with the Peronist union situation. In no sense, even at its apogee, could one really talk of Vandorism as part of the 'establishment', associated with government and management 'on scores of committees', 'a part of the body of the state'. For all its talks with generals, its open-shirted bonhomie with presidents, the Peronist unions' influence on the nation's councils was grudgingly recognised and strictly limited by the restricted tolerance for all things Peronist and working class. A scotch with the Secretary of Labour was, ultimately, a poor substitute for genuine institutions of integration. The ambiguity to which we frequently referred in the last part of this work in relation to the union leadership's power and position was thus both a source of strength, but also, ultimately, a source of weakness and frustration.

The fine line that any union leadership walks between integration and opposition was made even finer in the case of the Peronist union leaders by the meagre nature of real gains that could be made. It was frustration with a system which offered the facade, and potential, of integration without the substance, which offered this leadership a certain toleration in its political and economic activities while ensuring that it could never finally take advantage of the power this toleration bequeathed, which led them to welcome an end to this debilitating game in the form of a military coup in 1966.

Yet, the support for Onganía's coup was a crucial error since it removed even the limited space for manoeuvre which had existed. In Onganía's brave new world there was only room for outright opposition or complete subservience. The crucial ambivalence which was characteristic of the pre-1966 period was now abolished and with it the source of Vandorism's strength and weakness. Its ability to bargain, negotiate and occasionally mobilise, which was a vital part of its relationship with its members, was now undercut and the way cleared for new forces which years of demobilisation and acquiesence had held back to emerge to challenge, albeit incompletely, this leadership.

There is, nevertheless, a further, and I think more important, caveat which emerges from this work and which must be placed on an uncritical acceptance of the integration paradigm. The elements of leadership power, its use of coercive measures of internal control, its adoption of an integrationist project, must be placed within a wider social context if they are to have genuine analytical usefulness, and that context must be the general history and experience of the Argentine working class, and in particular the union rank and file, in the post-1955 era. The power of the Peronist union leadership cannot be viewed as distinct from that history; it must ultimately be seen as a specific historical development arising out of a general class experience which was itself related to a particular project of economic development and the options and limitations this presented to organised workers bargaining over their material conditions of work and life. In this context bureaucracy and rank and file are not necessarily diametrically opposed poles, but are rather intricately interrelated, the one with the other. It is evident, for example, from our analysis of the Frondizi period that while elements such as fraud, corruption and violence were increasingly used by union leaderships to maintain their internal control, they could only be used to the extent that they were because of the acquiesence of the rank and file; they were not imposed on an entirely unwilling working class.

The issue of fraudulent union elections and the lack of rank-and-file participation must be viewed in this light. Juan Carlos Torre's elaboration of electoral participation rates in major unions shows rates ranging from 20% to 40% on average.[16] Thus, even with growing fraud by the leaderships a not insignificant proportion of union members did participate in the electoral process. In part this was due, we may suggest, to their recognition that while union bureaucratisation might represent the 'sanctification of inertia' implicit in the consolidation of the Peronist union leadership, the unions nevertheless represented, in Sartre's phrase, 'an abstract skeleton of the united class ... a permanent invitation to unity', a unity which represented a basic core of the working class's self-identity and self-defence in what was clearly perceived as an increasingly hostile and insecure environment.[17]

In a related fashion we may suggest that this recognition was also a reflection of a basic reservoir of support that had its roots in the working-class experience of demobilisation, resignation, and *accept-*

ance of the prevalent style of union government. This resignation and acquiescence were not, however, absolute, given characteristics, in the sense that for Michels and Weber mass membership apathy was *the* inevitable corollary of oligarchic control and bureaucratisation in modern organisations. The burden of our argument in this work has been that this acquiescence was a relative phenomenon arising out of the concrete social experience of workers in the defeats of 1959 and 1960, and the consequent demoralisation that followed, together with the effects of the government's economic offensive – unemployment, rationalisation and lower real wages. This resulted, we have argued, in a growing lack of belief for much of the 1960s in the efficacy of militant collective action as workers sought either an individual accommodation with forces they felt they could no longer effectively confront or were disposed to increasingly trust in the formalised bargaining power of their union leaders.

While this applied to both activists and rank and file, it was particularly important among the former. Here we find an increasing privatisation of attitude, a turning inward away from public engagement in the early and mid 1960s. It will be recalled that Jorge Di Pascuale spoke of the 'hard times that were wearing out many people' and of how 'the majority began to separate themselves from combative positions and dedicate themselves exclusively to their own affairs'. Alberto Belloni, too, captured this process when he described his former activist comrades who 'now began to isolate me, to treat me with suspicion' and who were, he noted, 'becoming bureaucrats too in a small way'. It was these former activists who formed the basis of the local union hierarchies, and who were often coopted onto the national union leaderships. It was, therefore, one of the peculiar strengths of the Peronist union leadership that it was largely made up of, and used as instruments of its domination, activists drawn from the working class. Those militants who stood out against this tide inevitably found themselves isolated from their constituency, their members in the factory. Jean-Paul Sartre has captured the essence of the militant's isolation in this type of situation: 'He is a leader when they are on the move; when they scatter he is nothing ... he cannot realise his personal ambition, if he has any, except by inspiring in the masses a confidence renewed from day to day: and he will only inspire confidence in them if he agrees to lead them where they are going.'[18] The early and mid 1960s were not auspicious times for inspiring daily confidence among the Argentine working class and militants like José Vazquez, Domingo Blajaquis, Alberto Belloni and Raimundo Villaflor were to suffer bitterly for this.

We must also question the extent to which objective conditions existed, by the 1960s, for the development of an autonomous rank-and-file
organisational alternative within the unions. In a general sense it is clear
that the collective bargaining system in Argentina had a built-in bias
against the development of such organisation; it militated against the
rank-and-file worker's involvement in those areas of most immediate
concern to him. Bargaining was generally done at the national level, as
we have seen, between central union negotiators and the central
employers' federation for a particular industry. The very most plant organisation could do was to monitor the implementation of the central
agreement. Even union dues were collected by a check-off system.
Meaningful, independent shop-floor organisation would thus have
been difficult to sustain at the best of times since there was little to concretely centre activity around. The flourishing of shop-floor organisation during the Resistance had been partly due to the dismantling of
this centralised system by the military regime. The restructuring of a
centralised system after 1958 was accompanied by a series of contracts
imposed in the wake of working-class defeat. As we saw in Part Three
these contracts greatly enhanced employers' freedom concerning production arrangements and work systems. In doing this, we argued,
they removed a whole series of issues around which membership interest and rank-and-file organisation could have been built, as indeed it had
been in the 1955–9 period. It was only in the late 1960s and early 1970s
that the demobilising impact of this situation was overcome and rank-
and-file opposition reemerged, primarily in the new modern industries of the interior. In Part Five, we detailed the reasons for this
emergence and the limits of its challenge to both union hierarchy and
the state.

Now, this clearly has important implications for any discussion of
rank-and-file apathy and acquiesence, since we are dealing with a
system which clearly tended to foster rank-and-file passivity, and yet
which was independent of the specific, anti-democratic machinations
of Peronist union leaders. As we have pointed out, union leaders saw
the mutual benefit to be derived from such a system, but its development cannot be simply ascribed to leadership 'betrayal'. It, too, must
be placed within the context of the demobilisation, and demoralisation
which we are describing. For many Argentine workers the logic of
rationalisation and incentive schemes seemed, by 1962/3, to be inescapable given the lack of a viable strategy of rejection; most would seem to
have agreed, perhaps reluctantly, with the sale of what control they had
within the workplace in return for wage increases achieved for them by
their union leaders.

Thus, the relationship between Peronist union leaders and their rank and file was far more complex and symbiotic than, certainly, the simple integration paradigm put forward by both analysts and the media would lead us to believe. The problem with this image, I would suggest, is that it creates two metaphysical abstractions, apparently polar opposites but in fact one the corollary of the other: a working class that always struggles and aspires to independent collective action regardless of context and experience and a bureaucracy which always betrays and represses those struggles and aspirations.

Beyond these abstractions lurks, I suspect, a deeper concern which has to do with notions concerning the ontological status of the working class. Argentine working-class history has been frequently perused, analysed and used in order to explain an apparent lack, a failure of the working class to act in a fashion in keeping with its allotted historical destiny. Deviations from a path in keeping with its historical essence have taken various forms, whether in terms of its original commitment to a populist regime or in terms of the failure of the Resistance struggle to break the hold of populist commitment and the continued Peronist allegiance of the working class throughout the 1955–73 period. The union leadership has, in this sense, provided a convenient *deus ex machina* for disillusioned leftist intellectuals seeking an explanation of the working classes' failure to measure up to their hopes for it and for radicals within Peronism seeking to understand the reasons for Peronism's failure to transform itself into a movement of national and popular liberation. The apathetic workers dominated by corrupt bureaucrats bent on integrating them into Argentine capitalism associated with the integration paradigm are counterposed to the inherently militant workers seeking to overcome such domination and fashion a uniquely Argentine socialism. This 'romantic' image, which has involved a kind of glorification of the presence of the masses within populism, an estimation of the 'revolutionary' potential of such movements simply because they did involve the 'working class', is, in this way, the mirror image of the pessimistic approach.

Rather than draw sustenance from either of these approaches we have tried in this study to avoid an essentialist notion of the working class. Claude Lefort analysing the general problem of the submittance of the working class to a variety of state and social bureaucracies has argued:

The proletariat is not *automatically* revolutionary. To the extent that its objective situation ties it to an organised collectivity it tends to think of its own liberation in the context of a general social liberation. But as an individual the worker can at any moment refuse to assume the destiny of his class and try to find an individual solution to his problems ...[19]

Such a recognition entails an understanding of the complex, multi-faceted variety of working-class action and consciousness and a denial of a single, and essential, working-class nature.[20] The implications of such an understanding are evident in relation to the dyad resistance/integration whose apparently radically opposed terms have dominated much analysis of the Argentine working class's history in the post-1955 era. This work has documented the remarkable capacity of the Argentine working class to act for itself, to create rank-and-file organisation, to organise resistance against social and political repression; indeed we have argued that development of the working-class movement and of Peronism in the post-1955 era is incomprehensible without understanding this rank-and-file experience. Nevertheless, it is also clear from our study that such vitality and resistance did not preclude demobilisation, passivity and the acceptance of the need, albeit temporarily, to achieve an integration within the status quo as circumstances and experience dictated.

The legitimacy of the union hierarchy and structure derived from its capacity to express and reflect both aspects of this working-class experience and consciousness. Yet, if this was a source of the bureaucracy's legitimacy it was also a potential source of insecurity and fragility. As we have seen, the fine line between articulating the demands of mobilised sections of the working class and acting as agents of social control was frequently subject to pressures from the state which were beyond the ability of the union leadership to control. The period of the *Revolución Argentina* was characterised precisely by such a crisis of legitimacy brought about by the emergence of sectors of the working class who broke from their previous passivity and accepted forms of action. Once again, however, we emphasised the complexity of this crisis and the limits of the radical challenge to the union leadership's legitimacy.

This sort of analysis also has implications for our understanding of the relationship between Peronist ideology and the working class. Generally speaking the ideological elements of Peronist discourse have been taken at face value, as univocal and unambiguous. Notions such as nationalism, class harmony, the paternalistic state and the role of the leader have been described and then assigned positive or negative values according to the ideological predilections, reformist or revolutionary, of the investigator. The possibility of different meanings being attached to the same, discreet ideological elements is thus rarely allowed for in these analyses. Evidently, there were notions in Peronism which did function to help ensure the reproduction of the dominant capitalist social relations. The formal rhetoric of Peronism was not one which saw society in primarily class terms; one of the essential notions present in that language was 'the people', the critical division in society between 'the people' and 'the oligarchy', the corrupt few who for their own selfish ends were exploiting the many, 'the nation'. It has frequently been emphasised that such a concept had reformist implications, a non-class potential appropriate to a movement led by dissident elite sectors which functioned primarily as a channel for integrating the emerging urban masses within an expanded polity without fundamentally altering the class relations of such a society.

Yet it is also clear from this work that such notions coexisted and were interrelated with elements which made the consolidation of capitalist ideological hegemony extremely problematic. We have argued that these elements could at times be explicitly denying of capitalist values and needs, posing an alternative reading of reality as part of an emerging counter-discourse. This we have suggested could be seen during the Resistance period. At other times, in different conjunctures, these elements were more likely to be found in the form of tensions, implicit assumptions involved in social practice, values condensed from the 'lived experience' of the working class. We have used Raymond Williams's term 'structure of feeling' to refer to these tensions. Often, we have suggested, there was a complex mixture of the two processes.

A recognition of this complexity enables us to interpret some of the standard, apparently reformist slogans of Peronism in a more sensitive light. A belief in the essential virtue of 'the people' still left open to question the issue of who formed part of this category; as we have commented there was a tendency from the beginning of the Peronist experience for *el pueblo* to become transformed into *el pueblo trabajador*. Similarly, as we have pointed out, a commitment to a formal belief in the ultimate possibility of the 'good', 'beneficent' state where social justice could be located did not preclude a recognition of the oppressive character of the existing state. Perón himself became a mythologised figure for many Argentine workers in this period, but the myth had both regressive and positive potential. Finally, working-class nationalism was itself a complex, paradoxical phenomenon. By taking seriously, and insisting on, the relevance of notions of economic nationalism which it had imbibed in the Perón era, and by envisaging itself as the only social force sincerely committed to defence of the nation's interest, the working class laid the groundwork for a series of confrontations with the governing forces within Argentine society which stretched from the Lisandro de la Torre occupation of 1959 to the conflict with the military governments of the 1966–73 era.

The nationalist notion of a harmonious and united national community could itself become a source of antagonism as it embodied both a utopian commitment to a society based on greater social justice and an end to class conflict and a painful point of comparison with everyday injustice and oppression.[21] Thus, a formal commitment by Argentine workers to the tenets of traditional Peronist ideology need not be taken exclusively at face value. Such tenets were mediated by class experience and practice and reinterpreted in the light of this changing experience. The result was a frequently paradoxical working-class consciousness. The allegiance to a movement whose formal ideology preached the virtue of class harmony, the need to subordinate the interests of workers to those of the nation and the importance of a disciplined obedience to a paternalistic state did not eliminate the possibility of working-class resistance and the emergence of a strong oppositional culture among workers. Certainly, such a consciousness was far more complex than would be indicated by a simple characterisation of it as a form of reformist, 'false consciousness'. On the other hand, this resistance could not be reduced to a pristine, unambiguous revolutionary ideology of class conflict. It inevitably contained strong elements which promoted integration and cooptation.

The closer attention to the complexity of ideological process which we have attempted to outline in this work should also help us to better approach one of the apparent conundrums of modern Argentine history: the persistence of Peronism's domination of the working class as a political and social actor. A pervasive form of explanation has been one which has emphasised the continued adherence of workers to populist ideology. Since these ideological maxims were originally formulated in a socio-economic conjuncture which radically altered in the post-1955 period, a conjuncture which had facilitated a state-sponsored income redistribution, it has been assumed that the working class must have had an inadequate perception of these changes. Workers have continued to espouse these maxims despite their failure to correspond to social reality. We are back once more to a theory of working-class populism as a form of social pathology so prevalent in early analyses of the relationship of the working class and Peronism. The continued adherence of workers to these tenets has clearly implied irrationality, emotionalism and 'false consciousness'.

Yet, as we have argued, this paradox lessens once we look behind the surface gloss of formal ideology and recognise the ambivalent way in

which workers could at times recast traditional tenets of Peronist ideology to express their changing needs and experience. In looking for explanations of Peronism's continued weight within the working class in
the post-1955 era we could more profitably perhaps emphasise the importance and meaning of the original Peronist experience for workers.
It is easy to overlook the all-embracing nature of this experience, its
erasure of prior working-class tradition and allegiance. The Perón era
saw the formation of a dominant working-class tradition and a profound recasting of the historical memory of Argentine workers. Their
experience of the post-1955 era was to be framed within the parameters
established by this memory and tradition.

Once again, however, the pervasiveness of this tradition after 1955
should not be ascribed merely to irrational nostalgia. Memory and tradition were not ossified but were rather reinvented and reinterpreted
selectively in accordance with new needs. This was made possible
because of the continued relevance of the core of this historical experience. Peronism did not only represent higher wages, its historical
meaning for workers was embodied also in a political vision which entailed an expanded notion of the meaning of citizenship and the
workers' relations with the state, and a 'heretical' social component
which spoke to working-class claims to greater social status, dignity
within the workplace and beyond, and a denial of the elite's social and
cultural pretensions. These elements were most concretely embodied in
the new power and status of the union movement. It should be clear
from the narrative of the post-1955 period contained in this book that
the essence of this historical experience continued to have relevance for
Argentine workers. The insistent attempts of the dominant forces in
Argentine society to exclude, or at best limit, Peronist participation within the political system, and to attack certain fundamental economic and
social gains, seemed to symbolise their unwillingness to fully recognise the
working-class claims embodied in its original commitment to Peronism.

In this context it could be said that Peronism's continued vitality in
the 1955–73 period was at least partly due to its ability to express these
original working-class claims and their still 'heretical' status. John William Cooke frequently referred to Peronism as the 'hecho maldito' of
Argentine society which constantly bedeviled attempts of the ruling
elite to establish arrangements which excluded it. But what was the essence of this 'damnable' quality? Not, it would seem, in a particularly
radical formal ideology, or political programme, many of whose essential tenets it shared with other political forces by the 1960s, nor in the
revolutionary nature of its policies while in office. Partly it lay in its primary embodiment in a strong union movement, which however 'prag-

matic' its leadership, represented a considerable stumbling block to the needs of Argentine capitalism. In part it also lay in the continued identification, in however ambivalent a fashion, with the legacy of Peronism's original 'heretical' appeal to workers.

This presented considerable problems for Peronism's rivals for working-class allegiance in the 1955–73 period. As we have seen, the new wave of *clasista* militants who emerged after 1969 were constantly confronted with this issue. It was on the ground established by the working class's pre-1955 experience that left-wing appeals fell in the post-1955 era. Many of the basic elements of leftist rhetoric had already found echo in the Peronist experience. The contestatory, oppositional credentials of Peronism were moreover reinforced by the Resistance period, which is clearly of crucial importance in this process. Given this situation what need was there for working-class adherence to a more formal leftism symbolised by left-wing political parties? In this situation, too, it was meaningless to expect workers to simply abandon a tradition and experience which, for better or worse, they felt was *their* experience and tradition, not that of a particular political party. Peronism had become by the late 1950s a sort of protean, malleable commonplace of working-class identification. In the course of researching this book I was constantly struck by the seemingly unquestioning, identification, particularly amongst militants, of working-class activism, resistance and organisation with being a Peronist. It seems to have become almost an accepted part of working-class 'common sense' in the 1955–73 period.

Finally, this was, I think, compounded by a perception of Peronism as not primarily a political doctrine, nor a sectarian political party. Its quest for social justice and a recognition of the working class's rights as citizens and workers was viewed as beyond the pettiness of party-political strife. In a system where the legitimacy of party-political activity was constantly being undermined by institutional upheaval and restrictions placed on the political expression of working-class interests, this perception of the apolitical status of Peronism was a great advantage. Osvaldo Soriano in his fine evocation of the tragedy of Perón's return in 1973 as experienced by a small town in the province of Buenos Aires has captured this element. The mayor of the town, Don Ignacio, a life-long Peronist, arrives one day to work in the town hall to find that he has been denounced by rivals as a communist. When he informs his assistant, Mateo, of the charges against them the latter replies: 'Bolsheviks? But how? I was always a Peronist ... I never got involved in politics.'[22]

Notes

1 Peronism and the working class, 1943–55

1 For the military background to the coup of 1943 see Robert Potash, *The Army and Politics in Argentina, 1928–1945, Yrigoyen to Perón* (Stanford, 1969). For a general analysis of the 1943–55 era see Peter Waldmann, *El peronismo, 1943–1955* (Buenos Aires, 1981). For developments in the labour field see Samuel L. Baily, *Labor, Nationalism and Politics in Argentina* (New Brunswick, 1967); also Hugo del Campo, *Sindicalismo y peronismo* (Buenos Aires, 1983).

2 The rural elite's economic interests were safeguarded by the Roca–Runciman treaty of 1933 which guaranteed continued access to British markets for Argentine beef in return for major concessions concerning the status of British imports into Argentina. Effectively the treaty ensured the maintenance of Argentina's traditional position within the British sphere of the international economy and as such it was denounced by nationalists and others. See Miguel Murmis and Juan Carlos Portantiero, 'Crecimiento industrial y alianza de clases en la Argentina, 1930–40', *Estudios sobre los orígenes del peronismo*, vol. 1 (Buenos Aires, 1972).

3 These figures are calculated on the basis of data in the Economic Commission on Latin America, *El desarrollo económico en la Argentina* (Buenos Aires, 1959), cited in Miguel Angel García, *Peronismo: desarrollo económico y lucha de clases* (Llobregat, 1979), p. 54.

4 This peaked in 1943 when these non-traditional manufacturing exports accounted for some 19.4% of total exports. It has been estimated that some 180,000 new jobs had been created by this export-led industrial growth in the war years. See Juan José Llach, 'El Plan Pinedo de 1940: su significación histórica y los orígenes de la economía política del peronismo', *Desarrollo Económico*, vol. 23, no. 92 (1984), pp. 515–58.

5 García, *Peronismo*, p. 62.

6 Gino Germani, *Política y sociedad en una época de transición* (Buenos Aires, 1962), p. 307.

7 Ruben Rotundaro, *Realidad y cambio en el sindicalismo* (Buenos Aires, 1972), p. 128.

8 Alejandro Bunge, *Una nueva Argentina* (Buenos Aires, 1940), p. 372.

9 For a detailed analysis of the internal divisions within organised labour in this period see Hiroschi Matsushita, *Movimiento obrero argentino: 1930–*

45: sus proyecciones en los orígenes del peronismo (Buenos Aires, 1983); David Tamarin, *The Argentine Labor Movement, 1930–45: a study in the origins of Peronism* (Albuquerque, 1985).

10 See Miguel Murmis and Juan Carlos Portantiero, 'El movimiento obrero en los orígenes del peronismo', *Estudios*, p. 80.

11 For Perón's personal background and ideas see Joseph Page, *Perón: a biography* (New York, 1983). For an analysis of Perón's labour policy and its impact in the 1943–5 period see Walter Little, 'La organización obrera y el estado peronista', *Desarrollo Económico*, vol. 19, no. 75 (1979), pp. 331–76.

12 On the background to the October events see Felix Luna, *El 45, crónica de un año decisivo* (Buenos Aires, 1969).

13 See Louise Doyon, 'El crecimiento sindical bajo el peronismo', *Desarrollo Económico*, vol. 15, no. 57 (1975), pp. 151–61.

14 See Louise Doyon, 'Conflictos obreros durante el regimen peronista, 1946–55', *Desarrollo Económico*, vol. 17, no. 67 (1977) pp. 437–73.

15 See Juan Carlos Torre, 'La caída de Luis Gay', *Todo es Historia*, vol. 8, no. 89 (1974). One of the last symbols of *laborista* autonomy was Cipriano Reyes, the meatpackers' leader, who remained in congress as a *laborista* representative until 1948 when his mandate expired. Perón then had him arrested and he remained in prison until the end of the regime. For *laborismo* see Cipriano Reyes, *Qué es el laborismo?* (Buenos Aires, 1946).

16 See Rotundaro, *Realidad y cambio*, ch. 4. The Fundación Eva Perón was established by an act of congress and was entirely under the control of Eva Perón. It acted as a huge patronage machine and distributor of social welfare resources.

17 Economic Commission for Latin America, *El desarrollo económico*, pp. 122ff.

18 See Jorge Abelardo Ramos, *Historia del Stalinismo en la Argentina* (Buenos Aires, 1974), for a highly critical account. For an official communist version see *Esbozo de la historia del Partido Communista Argentino* (Buenos Aires, 1947). Also Rubens Iscaro, *Historia del Movimiento Sindical*, vol. 1 (Buenos Aires, 1974).

19 For examples of this approach see Germani, *Política y sociedad*; Rodolfo Puiggros, *El peronismo: sus causas* (Buenos Aires, 1965); Alberto Belloni, *Del anarquismo al peronismo* (Buenos Aires, 1960). For a critical review of some of the basic assumptions see Walter Little, 'The popular origins of Peronism' in David Rock, ed., *Argentina in the Twentieth Century* (Pittsburgh, 1975).

20 For a review of this revisionist literature see Ian Roxborough, 'Unity and diversity in Latin American history', *Journal of Latin American Studies*, vol. 16, part 1 (1984), pp. 1–26. Revisionist interpretations have not gone entirely unchallenged. Gino Germani in his last contribution to the debate on the origins of Peronism restated his basic arguments concerning the weight of the new migrants in the formation of Peronism and the importance of traditional psycho-social cultural patterns, see 'El rol de los obreros y de los migrantes internos en los orígenes del peronismo', *Desarrollo Económico*, vol. 13, no. 51 (1973), pp. 435–88. For critical comments see Tulio Halperin Donghi, 'Algunas observaciones sobre

Germani, el surgimiento del peronismo y los migrantes internos', *Desarrollo Económico*, vol. 15, no. 56 (1975), pp. 765–81.

21 Gareth Stedman Jones, 'Rethinking Chartism', *Languages of Class: studies in English working class history* (Cambridge, 1984), p. 97.

22 For the Radical Party see David Rock, *Politics in Argentina, 1890–1930: the rise and fall of Radicalism* (Cambridge, 1975)

23 For Perón's recognition of the importance of the Yrigoyenist heritage see Felix Luna, *El 45: crónica de un año decisivo* (Buenos Aires, 1969), p. 205 and passim.

24 The term was coined by the nationalist historian, José Luis Torre, and became widely used in the nationalist and opposition literature of the time.

25 For a political history of the 1930s see Alberto Ciria, *Parties and Power in Modern Argentina, 1930–46* (Albany, 1969); for examples of the specific mechanisms of fraud see Felix Luna, *Alvear* (Buenos Aires, 1958).

26 See Norberto Folino, *Barceló, Ruggierito y el populismo oligarquico* (Buenos Aires, 1966).

27 For an account of this corruption see Luna, *Alvear*, pp. 196–234.

28 *ibid.*, p. 232.

29 *El Laborista*, 24 January 1946, cited in Dario Canton, *Elecciones y partidos políticos en la Argentina* (Buenos Aires, 1973), p. 227.

30 The issue of the different categories of rights associated with a developing concept of citizenship has been analysed in T. H. Marshall, *Citizenship and Social Class*, London, 1947. Marshall makes the distinction between civil and political rights associated with formal democracy and the gradual enlargement of this notion of citizenship to embrace 'social rights'. For an outline and critique, see Anthony Giddens, 'Class divisions, class conflict and citizenship rights', *Profiles and Critiques in Social Theory* (Berkeley, 1982). An attempt to develop such concepts for developing nations is to be found in Gino Germani, 'Clases populares y democracia representativa en América Latina', *Desarrollo Económico*, vol. 2, no. 2 (1962), pp. 23–43.

31 The conservative politician Marcelo Sanchez Sorondo's comment on the speeches of Alvear could with justification be extended to the politicians of the Unión Democrática: 'His speeches seem plucked out of an anthology of democratic commonplaces.' Cited in Ciria, *Parties and Power*, p. 128. See also Luna, *El 45*, pp. 108ff for an examination of the political rhetoric of the anti-Peronist opposition in 1945/6.

32 Luna, *El 45*, p. 206.

33 Cited in Carlos Fayt, *La naturaleza del peronismo* (Buenos Aires, 1967), p. 143.

34 Cited in Luna, *El 45*, p. 192.

35 See *Primera Plana: historia del peronismo*, 31 August 1965.

36 Julio Mafud, *Sociología del peronismo* (Buenos Aires, 1972), p. 107.

37 See Rock, *Politics in Argentina*, p. 59: 'As the activities of the committees illustrate, the Radicals relied a great deal on paternalistic measures. The main advantage of this was again that it could be used to break down the divisive interest group ties by atomising the electorate and individualising the voter.'

38 Perón's principal speeches from this era were collected and published in Juan D. Perón, *El pueblo quiere saber de que se trata* (Buenos Aires, 1957).

39 Guita Grin Debert, in *Ideología e populismo* (São Paulo, 1979), presents an interesting analysis of the role of individuals, classes and the state in different forms of populist discourse. Her analysis of a quintessential populist rhetoric of a populist leader such as Adhemar de Barros makes an instructive contrast with Perón's political discourse.

40 The principal group which influenced Peronism was FORJA, the Fuerza de Orientación Radical de la Joven Argentina, made up primarily of dissident Radical Party intellectuals. While its political influence was limited, the status of intellectuals like Raul Scalabrini Ortiz, Arturo Jauretche, Luis Dellapiane and others was considerable. *Cipayo* literally meant sepoy and implied a servile instrument of a colonial power. The fact that the reference was directly taken from British colonial history clearly implied that Argentina under its traditional elite was as equally subservient to British interests as colonial India. *Vendepatria* was an invented epithet meaning literally 'a seller of one's country'.

41 See Llach, 'El Plan Pinedo de 1940', for the different political responses to the issue of industrialism.

42 Milciades Peña, *El peronismo: selección de documentos para la historia* (Buenos Aires, 1973), p. 10.

43 Stedman Jones, *Languages of Class*, p. 96.

44 See, for example, Juan D. Perón, *Doctrina peronista* (Buenos Aires, 1973), pp. 51–83.

45 Luis Franco, *Biografía patria* (Buenos Aires, 1958), p. 173.

46 Eduardo Colom, *17 de octubre, la revolución de los descamisados* (Buenos Aires, 1946), pp. 106–7.

47 For a study of such themes in tango see Judith Evans, 'Tango and popular culture in Buenos Aires' (unpublished paper presented to the American Historical Association conference, Washington, 1980). For an analysis of the subtext of Peronist discourse as manifested by Perón's speech on 17 October see Emilio de Ipola, 'Desde estos mismos balcones', *Ideología y discurso populista* (Buenos Aires, 1983).

48 Colom, *17 de octubre*, p. 107.

49 From the socialist newspaper, *La Vanguardia*, cited in Angel Perelman, *Como hicimos el 17 de octubre* (Buenos Aires, 1961), p. 78.

50 See Anson Rabinach, 'Bloch's theory of fascism', *New German Critique* (Spring 1977).

51 Pierre Bourdieu, *Outline of a Theory of Practice* (Cambridge, 1977), p. 178.

52 Cited in Manuel Gálvez, *En el mundo de los seres reales* (Buenos Aires, 1955), p. 79.

53 Ernesto Goldar, 'La literatura peronista' in Gonzalo Cárdenas et al., *El peronismo* (Buenos Aires, 1969), p. 151.

54 Cipriano Reyes, *Como yo hice el 17 de octubre* (Buenos Aires, 1973), p. 144.

55 Perelman, *Como hicimos el 17 de octubre*, p. 12.

56 Mafud, *Sociología del peronismo*, p. 107.

57 See for example the classic tangos of Discépolo, 'Qué vachaché', 'Yira, yira'. Similar themes can be found in other forms of popular culture of the 1920 and 1930s such as *grotesco* theatre. See Noemi Ulla, *Tango, rebelión y*

nostalgía (Buenos Aires, 1967); Norberto Galaso, *Discépolo y su época* (Buenos Aires, 1967); Gustavo Sosa-Pujato, 'Popular culture' in Ronald Dockhart and Mark Falcoff, *Prologue to Perón: Argentina in depression and war* (Berkeley, 1975).

58 From Discépolo's tango 'Qué vachaché'. The lyrics can be found in Osvaldo Pelletieri, *Enrique Santos Discépolo: obra poética* (Buenos Aires, 1976), p. 80.

59 See Julio Mafud, *La vida obrera en la Argentina* (Buenos Aires, 1976), p. 241.

60 The phrase is Osvaldo Pelletieri's, in Pelletieri, *Discépolo*, p. 63.

61 Jacinto Cimazo and José Grunfeld, *Luis Danussi en el movimiento social y obrero argentino* (Buenos Aires, 1976), p. 93.

62 *ibid.*, p. 86.

63 Perelman, *Como hicimos el 17 de octubre*, p. 12.

64 See del Campo, *Sindicalismo y peronismo*. Also of interest is Ricardo Gaudio and Jorge Pilone, *Estado y relaciones obrero-patronal en los orígenes de la negociación colectiva en Argentina*, CEDES, Estudios Sociales, no. 5 (Buenos Aires, 1976).

65 Cimazo and Grunfeld, *Luis Danussi*, p. 103. See also Tamarin, *Argentine Labor Movement*, especially chapter 7. Tamarin stresses the importance of communist organising activity in moving beyond the boundaries of the traditional organised sectors of the working class, though he notes that the increase in union membership in the late 1930s and early 1940s scarcely kept pace with the increase in the labour force, or succeeded in penetrating those areas of greatest industrial expansion.

66 Interview with Don Ramiro González, Rosario, November 1976.

67 Interview with Lautaro Ferlini, Buenos Aires, November/December 1976.

68 Bourdieu, *Outline*, p. 170.

69 According to Felix Luna this term was first used by the socialists in their paper, *La Vanguardia*, to refer to Perón's supporters. Luna, *El 45*.

70 See Julie M. Taylor, *Eva Perón: the myths of a woman* (Chicago, 1979). The most complete biography of Evita is that of Nicholas Fraser and Marysa Navarro, *Eva Perón* (New York, 1981).

71 A point made by Dario Canton in Fayt, *La naturaleza del peronismo*, p. 343.

72 José Gobello, *Diccionario lunfardo y otros términos antiguos y modernos usados en Buenos Aires* (Buenos Aires, 1975). The exception was the use of *negra* among the poor as a term of affection between a man and a woman.

73 Luna, *El 45*, p. 350.

74 Quoted in Perelman, *Como hicimos el 17 de octubre*, p. 78.

75 The phrase is Leopoldo Marechal's: 'It was the invisible Argentina that many had announced in literature without even knowing or loving their millions of concrete faces.' See Elbia Rosbaco Marechal, *Mi vida con Leopoldo Marechal* (Buenos Aires, 1973), p. 91.

76 Luna, *El 45*, p. 350.

77 For the notion of 'counter-theatre' see E. P. Thompson, 'Eighteenth-century English society', *Social History* (May 1978).

78 Luna, *El 45*, p. 397.

79 Cited in Monica Peralta Ramos, *Etapas de acumulación y alianzas de clase*

en la Argentina, 1930–1970 (Buenos Aires, 1972), p. 120. For justicialist ideology see Alberto Ciria, *Perón y el justicialismo* (Buenos Aires, 1974).

80 Peralta Ramos, *Etapas de acumulación*, p. 120.

81 Servicio Internacional de Publicaciones Argentinas, *Emancipation of the Workers* (Buenos Aires, 1952), pp. 27–30.

82 Goldar, 'Literatura peronista', p. 155.

83 Cited in Dario Canton, *El parlamento argentino en épocas de cambio, 1890, 1916, y 1946* (Buenos Aires, 1966), p. 168.

84 *Argentina de Hoy*, August 1953.

85 Sylvia Sigal and Juan Carlos Torre, 'Reflexiones en torno a los movimientos laborales en América Latina' in Ruben Katzman and José Luis Reyna, eds., *Fuerza de trabajo y movimientos laborales en América Latina* (Mexico City, 1969), p. 145.

86 The concept of *disponibilidad* (availability) occurs in many of Germani's key works. See especially *Política y sociedad* and 'Clases populares y democracia respresentativa'. While it seems to me that criticisms of this and other concepts in the work of Germani in terms of their implications of passivity and manipulation are justified, Germani's work does, nevertheless, contain many fundamental insights into the specificity and peculiarity of a movement such as Peronism which are in tune with the general drift of the argument in this chapter. In particular his insistence concerning the uniqueness of Peronism as a form of political mobilisation seems to me to be of continuing relevance. His insistence that this should be viewed within the framework of a traditional/modern dichotomy would seem to me to be both wrong and unnecessary, a point astutely made by Tulio Halperin Donghi in 'Algunas observaciones'.

2 The survival of Peronism

1 *Crítica*, 19 September 1955.

2 *Crítica*, 21 September 1955.

3 Santiago Sénen González and Juan Carlos Torre, *Ejército y sindicatos* (Buenos Aires, 1969), p. 12.

4 *ibid.*, p. 33.

5 *El Obrero Ferroviario*, October 1955. A similar pattern occurred in the petrol workers', meatpackers', and garment workers' unions.

6 *CGT*, 7 October 1955.

7 *ibid.*

8 *La Vanguardia*, the socialist newspaper, carried a report in late October on the state of union affairs in Rosario in which it bitterly attacked the action of local authorities who had handed back the local CGT to Peronists after it had been taken over by a local socialist/syndicalist committee. See *La Vanguardia*, 27 October 1955.

9 See Sénen González and Torre, *Ejército y sindicatos*, pp. 87–90, for the different civilian backers of the distinct military tendencies.

10 *Crítica*, 2 November 1955.

11 See Cerrutti Costa's statement to this effect in Sénen González and Torre, *Ejército y sindicatos*, pp. 137–43. On Lonardi's thought and actions in this

period see Luis Ernesto Lonardi, *Dios es justo* (Buenos Aires, 1958) and Marta Lonardi, *Mi padre y la revolución del 55* (Buenos Aires, 1980).

12 Sénen González and Torre, *Ejército y sindicatos*, p. 97.

13 *ibid.*, p. 97.

14 *La Nación*, 24 September 1955, mentions shooting in Avellaneda involving 'undisciplined elements'. For details of the Lanus demonstration see Roberto, 'De la resistencia peronista a las elecciones de 11 de marzo', *Peronismo y Socialismo*, no. 1, September 1973.

15 *La Nación*, 26 September 1955.

16 Interview with Alberto Belloni, Buenos Aires, 14 January 1974. Belloni was at this time a worker in the port of Rosario.

17 *New York Times*, 25 September 1955. This is one of the best sources for events in Argentina at this time; certainly many events which never penetrated the Argentine press are to be found there.

18 Juan M. Vigo, *La vida por Perón: crónicas de la Resistencia* (Buenos Aires, 1973), p. 54.

19 *ibid.*, p. 50.

20 *New York Times*, 20 October 1955.

21 Interview with Alberto Belloni,

22 *New York Times*, 4 November 1955. The *New York Times* gave a figure of 65% absenteeism nationally, reaching 100% in the most industrially concentrated *barrios*.

23 Roberto, 'De la resistencia peronista'.

24 Vigo, *La vida por Perón*, p. 55.

25 See Sénen González and Torre, *Ejército y sindicatos*, p. 54.

26 *New York Times*, 15 November 1955.

27 Vigo, *La vida por Perón*, p. 69.

28 *La Nación*, 16 November 1955. Only those unions already taken over by anti-Peronists such as the shop clerks and the bank workers, and public services forcibly kept open by the military, failed to respond.

29 *New York Times*, 16 November 1955.

30 Miguel Gazzera, 'Nosotros los dirigentes' in Norberto Ceresole and Miguel Gazzera, *Peronismo: autocrítica y perspectivas* (Buenos Aires, 1970), p. 61.

31 Statement of the Minister of Labour, Raul Migone, *La Nación*, 17 November 1955.

32 Decree 14.190 which modified the previous decree 7107 spoke of rehabilitating some 92,000 persons. Even after this, however, some observers maintained that upward of 50,000 remained legally proscribed from union activity. *Qué*, 26 August 1956.

33 This happened for example in the SIAM di Tella plants. See *La Verdad*, 28 November 1955.

34 *Qué*, 21 December 1955.

35 *La Verdad*, 2 January 1956.

36 *La Vanguardia*, 5 January 1956.

37 See the speech of José Gelbard, the head of the Confederación General Económica, at the Congress of Productivity and Social Welfare held in March 1955. 'Report of the proceedings of the *Congreso Nacional de Productividad y Bienestar*', *Hechos e Ideas* (Buenos Aires, 1955), p. 282.

38 *ibid.*, p. 280.
39 For details of this resistance see Daniel James, 'Rationalization and working class response: the limits of factory floor activity in Argentina', *Journal of Latin American Studies*, vol. 3, part 2 (1981), pp. 375–402.
40 See Doyon, 'Conflictos obreros'.
41 *Qué*, 25 April 1956.
42 Ministerio de Trabajo y Previsión, *Nuevo régimen de remuneraciones y de las convenciones colectivas de trabajo* (Buenos Aires, 1956).
43 *La Nación*, 20 February 1956. A new decree, 6121, April 1956, specifically said that in the event of modernisation of a factory provisions which stipulated the number of workers to a job would not apply.
44 *La Vanguardia*, 21 June 1956.
45 Pamphlet, no date but probably late 1956, in author's files.
46 Interview with Alberto Belloni, Buenos Aires, January 1974. *Gorila* was the term of contempt used by Peronists to describe anti-Peronists.
47 *Qué*, 25 April 1956.
48 The arbitration award in the meatpacking industry stated that the existing norms concerning sick leave were an 'indirect hindrance' to productivity as defined in decree 2739. Ministerio de Trabajo y Previsión, *Laudo del tribunal arbitral*, no. 63/1956 (Buenos Aires, 1956).
49 Interview with Alberto Belloni, Buenos Aires, January/February 1974.
50 *El Vitivinícola*, February 1956.
51 Interview with Alberto Belloni, Buenos Aires, January/February 1974.
52 *Lucha Obrera*, 22 December 1955.
53 Interview with Sebastian Borro, Buenos Aires, January 1974.
54 *Unidad Obrera*, June 1956.
55 See *La Vanguardia*, 17 May 1956, for a bitter denunciation by the socialists of this trend.
56 *Unidad Obrera*, June 1956.
57 *Qué*, 9 October 1956.
58 The most prominent examples were Angel di Giorgio, interventor of the bus and tramdrivers' union and Francisco Péréz Leirós at the head of the municipal workers union.
59 *La Vanguardia*, 31 May 1956.
60 *La Vanguardia*, 16 August 1956.
61 In fact the party was allowed to participate in the elections to the constituent assembly in July 1957. There was a noticeable decline in its union militancy at this time.
62 The Peronists won in the industrial unions, the *libres* in some white-collar unions such as the shop clerks. The garment workers also elected a socialist list and the print workers a syndicalist headed list.
63 Economic Commission for Latin America, *Economic Development and Income Distribution in Argentina* (New York, 1969) p. 254.
64 R. Mallon and Juan Sourrouille, *Economic Policy Making in a Conflict Society* (Cambridge, Mass., 1975), p. 18. One author calculates that the share of wages in the gross national income declined from 49.5% in 1955 to 47.3% in 1957. See Clarence Zuvekas, Jr, 'Economic growth and income distribution in post-war Argentina', *Inter-American Economic Affairs*, vol. 20, no. 3 (1966), pp. 19–39.

65 Interview with Ernesto González, Buenos Aires, February 1974.
66 Leaflet in author's possession, no date but issued by rank-and-file groups in early January 1957. The incident is confirmed by a report in *La Vanguardia*, 3 January 1957.
67 Rodolfo Walsh, *Quién mató a Rosendo?* (Buenos Aires, 1969), p. 19.

3 Commandos and unions

1 Interview with Sebastian Borro, Buenos Aires, January 1974.
2 *ibid.*
3 Interview with Alberto Belloni, Buenos Aires, January/February 1974. Belloni contrasted this to the thirty or so members who attended meetings prior to 1956.
4 See *Qué*, 16 April 1957, for the programme of the Intersindical.
5 *Mayoría*, 17 July 1957.
6 *Perón–Cooke correspondencia*, vol. 1 (Buenos Aires, 1972), p. 151.
7 Details of this attempt can be seen in *Mayoría*, 24 June 1957 and 6 January 1958. In effect 358 delegates were allocated to ten organisations and 311 to eighty-seven; of the ten unions six were anti-Peronist. See *Qué*, 22 August 1957.
8 *Noticias Gráficas*, 7 January 1956.
9 *Noticias Gráficas*, 7 February 1956.
10 *Noticias Gráficas*, 18 February 1956.
11 *Noticias Gráficas*, 10 February 1956.
12 *Noticias Gráficas*, 7 February 1956.
13 *La Razón*, 3 April 1956.
14 *Noticias Gráficas*, 18 March 1956.
15 *Noticias Gráficas*, 14 February 1956.
16 *La Razón*, 7 March 1956.
17 Vigo, *La vida por Perón*, p. 175.
18 *ibid.*, p. 149.
19 *Noticias Gráficas*, 25 February 1956.
20 *Noticias Gráficas*, 21 February 1956.
21 *Noticias Gráficas*, 22 February, and 2 March 1956.
22 Leaflet in author's possession, no date but probably mid 1956.
23 Vigo, *La vida por Perón*, p. 24.
24 *La Razón*, 16 March 1956.
25 The rising led by Valle was based on the few remaining Peronist officers, particularly among the lower ranks and the non-commissioned officers, together with some disillusioned nationalist officers who had been part of Lonardi's faction. The rising was doomed from the beginning since its plans were known to military intelligence. It seems that Aramburu deliberately let it continue in order to have a pretext for an exemplary purge. The execution of officers and NCOs who had taken part was unprecedented in Argentine military history and was to become an important part of the popular culture of the Resistance. For the civilian repression which followed the rising see Rodolfo Walsh, *Operación Masacre* (Buenos Aires, 1963).
26 See *Perón–Cooke correspondencia*, vol. 2, p. 391.
27 Vigo, *La vida por Perón*, p. 31.

28 *Frente Obrero*, August 1956.

29 Crónica por un resistente: crónicas de la Resistencia', *Antropología del Tercer Mundo*, August 1972.

30 Neo-Peronists were chiefly politicians from the pre-1955 era who had held posts within the Peronist Party. Their post-1955 careers were usually based on their potential ability to call on the loyalty of part of the political apparatus in their particular region.

31 *Perón–Cooke correspondencia*, vol. 2, p. 11.

32 *ibid.*, p. 35.

33 *Perón–Cooke correspondencia*, vol. 1, p. 144.

34 *ibid.*, p. 227.

35 *Soberanía*, 4 June 1957.

36 *Perón–Cooke correspondencia*, vol. 2, p. 8.

37 For details of these negotiations which culminated in the agreement to throw the Peronist vote behind Frondizi, see Ramón Prieto, *El Pacto* (Buenos Aires, 1965).

38 'Continuist' was the name given to the candidacy of Ricardo Balbín of the Unión Cívica Radical del Pueblo, because it was assumed that the military saw in the radicals a means of continuing the post-1955 anti-Peronist policies.

39 Another important issue for unionists was the parlous financial state of the unions after military interventions. This badly affected the services offered by the unions to their members. This gave a particular urgency to the issue of the full recuperation of the unions.

40 Interviews with Alberto Belloni and Sebastian Borro, Buenos Aires, January/February 1974.

4 Ideology and consciousness in the Peronist resistance

1 Ministerio de Trabajo y Seguridad Social, *Conflictos de trabajo* (Buenos Aires, 1961).

2 *Crisol del Litoral*, no. 2, November 1955.

3 *El Cuarenta*, no. 1, April 1957.

4 *Palabra Argentina*, 10 December 1957.

5 *Azul y Blanco*, 26 December 1956.

6 *Palabra Argentina*, 10 December 1957.

7 *ibid.*

8 See Marilena Chauí, 'O discurso competente', *Cultura e democracia, o discurso competente e outras falas* (São Paulo, 1982).

9 Cited in Roberto Carri, 'La Resistencia peronista: crónica por los resistentes', *Antropología del Tercer Mundo*, June 1972.

10 *Crisol del Litoral*, no. 1, October 1955.

11 *ibid.*

12 *ibid.*

13 Leaflet in author's possession.

14 *Crisol del Litoral*, no. 4, December 1955.

15 Leaflet in author's possession, probably from late 1956, simply addressed to 'Obreros argentinos'.

16 *El Cuarenta*, no. 2, May 1957.

17 Raymond Williams, *Marxism and Literature* (Oxford, 1977), p. 130.
18 Carri, 'La Resistencia peronista'.
19 Ernesto Laclau, 'Towards a theory of populism', *Politics and Ideology in Marxist Theory* (London, 1977), pp. 143–200.
20 Williams, *Marxism and Literature*, p. 132.
21 *Juancito*, Rosario, 18 September 1967.
22 *Juancito*, Rosario, October 1957.

5 Resistance and defeat

1 *Línea Dura*, 25 June 1958.
2 In July they had refused to become involved in a campaign against Frondizi's refusal to nationalise the foreign-owned utility companies, DINIE and CADE. In August they had compromised in a strike involving medical personnel in the union health services. They had also refused to call a strike for 17 October.
3 *Clarín*, 8 November 1958.
4 *Palabra Obrera*, 20 November 1958.
5 *Qué*, 25 November 1958.
6 *Línea Dura*, 4 November 1958.
7 For Frondizi's economic ideas see Rogelio Frigerio, 'Morfología del subdesarrollo', *Introducción a los problemas nacionales* (Buenos Aires, 1965). Also Clarence Zuvekas, 'Argentine Economic Policy 1958–62: the Frondizi government's development plan', *Inter-American Economic Affairs*, vol. 22, no. 1 (1968), pp. 45–75.
8 These contracts had represented part of the Peronist regime's opening to foreign capital in its last years. For Frondizi's criticism see Arturo Frondizi, *Petróleo y política*, 3rd edn (Buenos Aires, 1960).
9 During the election campaign Frondizi continued to attack foreign intervention in the oil industry. Given the emotive symbolic power of this issue the *desarrollistas* were reluctant to extend their new realism concerning foreign capital to this area. However, there was no logical reason why oil should be excluded from this analysis. A similar change in Frondizi's thinking occurred with agrarian reform. Under Frigerio's influence this was transformed from a demand for change in the structure of landownership to an emphasis on technical improvement. These changes caused growing friction within the UCRI. Frondizi had brought with him in his split from the Radical Party an important number of younger militants who took the more radical strands of the UCRI platform seriously. See Ismael Viñas, *Orden y progreso: análisis del frondicismo* (Buenos Aires, 1960), pp. 173 ff.
10 Juan José Real, *30 años de historia argentina* (Buenos Aires, 1962), p. 172.
11 *ibid.*, p. 172.
12 Gómez Morales, the Minister of Economic Affairs, estimated that more than $100 million of foreign investment was needed to meet steel expansion targets, $200 million for petroleum production. Contracts with Fiat, Kaiser, and Standard Oil had reflected this concern as did the friendly reception given to Milton Eisenhower, the American president's brother, on an official visit in 1953.

13 In his book *La fuerza es el derecho de las bestias* (Montevideo, 1957), Perón defended the contracts and denounced those who opposed foreign investment in any circumstances as *nacionalistas de opereta* (p. 91).
14 Decree 14,780 gave foreign investors the same rights as domestic investors. It also allowed the completely free remittance of profits. Other measures included income tax deductions of up to 100% on new investments in machinery and transport equipment.
15 See Zuvekas 'Economic growth and income distribution in post-war Argentina'; also Mallon and Sourrouille, *Economic Policy Making*, p. 72.
16 Zuvekas, 'Argentine economic policy 1958–1962'.
17 Ministerio de Trabajo, *Conflictos de trabajo*.
18 In the last months of 1958 Peronists won in textiles, telephone and communications, metal working, meatpacking, food processing, transportation, docks, light and power, and shoe making.
19 Figures are taken from *Mayoría*, 20 November 1958. It must be said that figures for union elections are notoriously difficult to be precise about in Argentina. However, these figures seem to me to be about right and there was very little accusation of fraud in the non-Peronist press.
20 Ministerio de Trabajo, *Conflictos de trabajo*, table 25. According to the International Labour Organisation this was also the highest strike figure in the world in 1959.
21 The best account of the negotiations between the union and Frondizi over this issue is the interview with Sebastian Borro, *En Lucha*, 2nd epoch, February 1974. Borro confirmed the details in my interview with him, Buenos Aires, January 1974.
22 For an account of the build up of the strike see *Mayoría*, 29 January 1959.
23 *Palabra Obrera*, 29 January 1959.
24 *Mayoría*, 29 January 1959.
25 Report issued by the Comando Nacional Peronista, a clandestine group, *El Soberano*, 2nd epoch, 9 March 1959.
26 Interview with Tito Dragovitch, Buenos Aires, 10 September 1976. Dragovitch was a militant in the edible-oil processing union which had its stronghold in Avellaneda.
27 Interview with Alberto Belloni, Buenos Aires, January 1974.
28 The new committee consisted of Castillo of the San Martín regional CGT, Jonch (telephone workers), Poccione (leather workers), Racchini (glass workers), Garcia (rubber workers), Orellano (flour milling), Dominguez (Chaco), Dotan (Santiago del Estero), and Gazzera (pasta makers). For accounts of the meeting see *Clarín*, 30 January 1959, *Palabra Obrera*, 4 February 1959.
29 *Palabra Obrera*, 4 February 1959.
30 *Pueblo Unido*, 12 March 1959.
31 *ibid*.
32 *Documentos del Plenario Nacional de las 62 Organizaciones*, Buenos Aires, December 1959, in mimeo.
33 *ibid*.
34 Interview with Sebastian Borro.
35 *AOT*, 19 September 1959.
36 *Mayoría*, 29 September 1959.

37 Ministerio de Trabajo, *Conflictos de trabajo*.
38 Puente's speech was to the Círculo Argentino de Estudios sobre Organización Industrial; its text was included in the *Documentos del Plenario Nacional de las 62 Organizaciones*, Buenos Aires, May 1960. One of the main demands of the 62 Organisations at this time was for Puente's removal.
39 Walsh, *Quién mató a Rosendo?*, p. 20.
40 *La Democracia*, 22 May 1960.
41 Interview with Alberto Belloni, Buenos Aires, January 1974.
42 Interview with Jorge Di Pascuale, *En Lucha*, 2nd epoch, February 1974.
43 Interview with Herminio Alonso, Buenos Aires, December 1976. The phrase 'the face of God' ('la cara de Dios') refers to female genitalia in *porteño* slang.
44 *Palabra Obrera*, 12 April 1960.
45 *Palabra Obrera*, 2 February 1961.
46 *Palabra Obrera*, 1 September 1960.
47 *Palabra Obrera*, 11 May 1960.
48 Interview with Alberto Bordaberry, Buenos Aires, October 1976.
49 *ibid.*
50 Walsh, *Quién mató a Rosendo?*, p. 37.
51 *ibid.*, p. 36.
52 *ibid.*, p. 37. The *quiniela* was a form of numbers game played daily for a small initial stake.
53 Quoted in *Palabra Obrera*, 12 January 1961.
54 *Palabra Obrera*, 13 April 1961.
55 *Palabra Obrera*, 20 September 1961.
56 Interview with Alberto Belloni.
57 *ibid.*
58 *ibid.*
59 Interview with Sebastian Borro.
60 *Perón–Cooke correspondencia*, vol. 2, p. 147.
61 *El Trabajador de la Carne*, August 1960.
62 Interview with Jorge Di Pascuale, Buenos Aires, January 1974. Di Pascuale confirmed to me the dilemma the hardline activists found themselves in. They recognised the full implications of accepting back the CGT on Frondizi's terms but they could not ignore the opportunities provided by Frondizi.
63 *Documentos del Plenario Nacional de las 62 Organizaciones*, Buenos Aires, May 1960.

6 The corollary of institutional pragmatism

1 *Documentos del plenario nacional de las 62 Organizaciones*, Buenos Aires, May 1960.
2 *ibid.*
3 *Documentación e Información Laboral*, no. 1, March 1960.
4 *ibid.*
5 *ibid.*
6 *Palabra Obrera*, 19 February, 1960.

7 *ibid.*

8 *El Alpargatero*, June 1960.

9 *ibid.*

10 For the debate concerning the extent of plant modernisation under Frondizi see Zuvekas, 'Argentine economic policy, 1958–1962'; Mallon and Sourrouille, *Economic Policy Making*.

11 *El Alpargatero*, September 1960.

12 *Alpargatas al desnudo*, June 1961. Edited by the Centro Comunista, Barracas, Buenos Aires. An advert for labour issued by the company in June 1960 carried a tacit admission of the importance of increased physical effort. It advised those interested that: 'Alpargatas needs labourers from 21 to 35 years of age: a minimum weight of 65 kilos – anyone under this need not apply.' *La Prensa*, 9 June 1960.

13 Ministerio de Trabajo y Seguridad Social, *Convención Colectiva de trabajo de la industria textil*, 155/60 (Buenos Aires, 1960).

14 *Palabra Obrera*, 2 March 1961.

15 Ministerio de Trabajo y Seguridad Social, *Convención Colectiva de trabajo de la industria metalúrgica*, 55/1960 (Buenos Aires, 1960).

16 *Palabra Obrera*, 22 October 1959.

17 Ministerio de Trabajo, *Convención colectiva de la industria metalúrgica*.

18 Taking 1950 as a base of 100 the productivity per hour worked in the textile and metal-working industries rose from 114.1 in 1956 in the case of metal working to 150.3 in 1961; in textiles the increase was less dramatic, from 127.6 to 130.2. Manufacturing industry in general increased from 113.8 in 1956 to 141.4 in 1962. See CGE–Consejo Federal de Inversiones, *Programa Conjunto*, vol. 3 (Buenos Aires, 1964), p. 115.

19 *AOT*, 18 January 1961.

20 For a typical statement of this sort of thinking see Hamilton Alberto Diaz, *Curso de guerra contrarevolucionaria: lucha contra el terrorismo*, Servicio de Información del Ejercito (Buenos Aires, Escuela Superior de Guerra, 19 October 1961). This was a lecture delivered to selected army officials.

21 *ibid.*, p. 14.

22 Juan Carlos Brid, 'Quince años de resistencia,' *Nuevo Hombre*, 12 September 1971.

23 Diaz, *Curso de guerra*, p. 13.

24 Directive, no. 1, February 1960. Purportedly from Perón, circulated in leaflet form.

25 This list was compiled from Diaz, *Curso de guerra*, and from newspapers of the time.

26 Diaz, *Curso de guerra*, p. 10.

27 *ibid.*, p. 14.

28 Roberto Carri, 'La Resistencia peronista'.

29 Diaz, *Curso de guerra*, p. 14.

30 Brid, 'Quince Años'.

31 'Crónica por un resistente'.

32 See Richard Gillespie, *Soldiers of Perón* (Oxford, 1983).

33 Diaz, *Curso de guerra*, p. 22.

34 See *En Lucha*, 2nd Epoch, June 1974.

35 See *Perón–Cooke correspondencia*, vol. 2 (Buenos Aires, 1973), pp. 372–3.

36 Interview with Alberto Bordaberry, Buenos Aires, October 1976.
37 Interview with Daniel Hopen, Buenos Aires, March 1974. Hopen had been a student leader in the University of Buenos Aires and involved in support operations.
38 Diaz, *Curso de guerra*.
39 *Noticias Gráficas*, 9 January 1962.
40 *La Nación*, 17 June 1961.
41 *Palabra Obrera*, 16 March 1961.
42 Vicente Solano Lima claimed for example that 'Perón did not want to take part in the elections. He preferred to support another party. He had chosen the Partido Conservador Popular.' *Cuestionario*, no. 20, December 1974.
43 *Noticias Gráficas*, 11 February 1962.
44 *Noticias Gráficas*, 11 January 1962.
45 *Noticias Gráficas*, 13 January 1962.
46 Gazzera, 'Nosotros los dirigentes', p. 119.
47 Interview with Jorge Di Pascuale, Buenos Aires, February 1974.
48 Gazzera, 'Nosotros los dirigentes', p. 120.

7 The *burocracia sindical*

1 *El Popular*, 4 December 1963.
2 The regional committees of the CGT had been returned to the unions by Frondizi in 1958 as a first step in the process of normalisation of the CGT.
3 The principal independent unions were: print workers, La Fraternidad (the locomen's union), shop workers, merchant seamen, municipal employees, paper workers, commercial travellers.
4 For details of congress see, *Documentación e Información Laboral, Informe Especial*, no. 1/2, 25 February 1963.
5 Interview with Alberto Bordaberry, October 1976. Bordaberry recalled José Rucci, one of Vandor's lieutenants and an activist in the Resistance, organising the *barra* at meetings of the 62. Rucci would hand out money for meals after the *barra* had performed well, i.e. after they had successfully prevented any opposition voices from being heard.
6 See Carlos Diaz Alejandro, *Essays on the Economic History of the Argentine Republic* (New Haven, 1970), pp. 218ff.
7 The Consejo Nacional de Desarrollo (CONADE) estimated that unemployment increased from 2.7% in 1960 to 7.5% in 1964. Manufacturing production declined by 10% between 1961 and 1963. While the CGT's figures on the trend of real wages differed somewhat from that of the government even the latter's best case scenario allowed for stagnation of real wages between 1960 and 1964. See CGT, *La CGT y el Plan de Lucha, cuarta etapa*, Buenos Aires, November 1964, p. 22.
8 CGT, *Ocupación por 3,913,000 trabajadores de 11,000 establecimientos*, Buenos Aires, June 1964. For a general study of the *Plan de Lucha* see Guy Bourdé, 'Les occupations des usines en Argentine', *Le Mouvement Social*, April–June 1978.
9 Francois Gèze and Alain Labrousse, *Argentine: révolution et contrerévolution* (Paris, 1975), p. 153.
10 *Estatuto de la Asociación Obrera Textil*, Buenos Aires, 14 December 1966.

11 Ministerio de Trabajo y Seguridad Social, *Censo nacional de asociaciones profesionales* (Buenos Aires, 1965), table 16, p. 24.
12 *Estatuto del Sindicato Unido de Petroleros del Estado*, Buenos Aires, 1965.
13 See Ministerio de Trabajo, *Censo*, table 13, p. 21.
14 *ibid.*, table 12, p. 21.
15 It is important to distinguish between the *cuota sindical y asistencial* and the *cuota extraordinaria*. Since article 2 of law 14,455 established the principle of the right to chose to be affiliated or not to a union there was no legal obligation on a non-union member to pay basic union dues. However, article 8 of law 14,250 of 1953 established the right of unions to negotiate with employers the retention of the extraordinary quotas which were to be specified in the collective contracts signed every two years. These were to apply to union and non-union members alike. They were, however, to be the result of bargaining with employers and were not an automatic right. The legal rationale behind this was that since by law all wages and conditions negotiated by the union were applicable to members and non-members alike the union was entitled to recompense for its efforts from those who benefited from the contracts it negotiated. The confusion on this topic had some basis in the very vagueness of article 33 of law 14,455 which gave the unions the right to receive dues retained by employers from workers' wages without specifying whether non-affiliates were to be included. Resolution 253/60, 12 May 1960, dealt with this confusion and underlined the non-compulsory nature of the *cuotas sindicales y asistenciales*.
16 Ministerio de Trabajo, *Censo*, p. 6.
17 *ibid.*, table 2, p. 12.
18 See Jorge Correa, *Los jerarcas sindicales* (Buenos Aires, 1972), for a collection of the best-known cases.
19 *Memoria y Balance, XI Congreso Nacional de la AOT*, 22, 23 and 24 March, 1968.
20 *ibid.*
21 Gazzera, 'Nosotros los dirigentes', p. 116.
22 See Correa, *Los jerarcas sindicales*, pp. 84–90, for documentation of some of the most blatant cases.
23 *Documentación e Información Laboral*, no. 70, January 1966.
24 Torre, *El proceso político interno*, p. 13. As Torre points out, given the fact that elections were held every two years in the fifteen-year period there were 175 elections in these unions.
25 See *AOT*, July 1963; also *Primera Plana*, 27 November 1962.
26 Roberto Carri, 'Sindicalismo de participación, sindicalismo de liberación', unpublished appendix to *Sindicatos y poder* (Buenos Aires, 1967).
27 *Descartes*, 18 April 1962.
28 Villalón was a political maverick of rather obscure background. He was rumoured to have good contacts with the Cubans, from whom he had a concession to import Havana cigars. He had no background or base within the traditional Peronist movement.
29 *Primera Plana*, 19 November, 1963.
30 *Primera Plana*, 7 July 1964.

31 *ibid.*

32 See *Primera Plana*, 23 March 1965.

33 *Primera Plana*, 6 April 1965. All these figures, apart from Framini, were supporters of Vandor. Lascano was official head of the Justicialist Party. José Alonso, the head of the CGT and one of the CGT's delegates on the body, while not a willing Vandorist, owed his position in the CGT to Vandor's support.

34 *Primera Plana*, 7 September 1965.

35 *Primera Plana*, 9 November 1965.

36 *ibid.*

37 The line up between the two 62 Organisations was fairly equal numerically, the Vandorists keeping some 233 CGT delegates, the 62 *de pie* some 225. The Vandorists did, however, have an advantage among those Peronist unions who had not declared themselves one way or the other.

38 See Bourdé, 'Les occupations des usines'.

39 V. L. Allen, *The Sociology of Industrial Relations* (London, 1971), p. 53.

40 For the calculations behind the *Plan de Lucha* see *Documentación e Información Laboral, Informe Especial*, no. 7, May 1964. Vandor used the CGT and the 62 Organisations to follow a hard line and maintain strikes and social conflict at the same time as he negotiated over the full acceptance of Peronism within the political system.

41 The 'juego imposible' is Guillermo O'Donnell's expression in *Un juego imposible: competicion y coaliciones entre partidos politicos en Argentina, 1955–66*, Documento de Trabajo, Instituto Torcuato Di Tella (Buenos Aires, 1972).

42 Interview with Enrique Pavón Pereyra, 1968, appeared in *Siete Días*, no. 312, 1973.

43 Letter to Don Antonio Caparros, July 1969. In author's files.

44 Cited in Walsh, *Quién mató a Rosendo?*, p. 171. The weight of Perón's personal condemnation was considerable. The weight such a condemnation would carry even with a union leader of Vandor's independent resources can be gauged by the fact that when *Primera Plana* ran a headline to an article called 'La gran carrera: Perón o Vandor', Vandor immediately took out full-page announcements in the press replying: 'Vandor contesta: Perón'.

8 Ideology and politics in Peronist unions

1 *Justicialismo*, October 1963. The document was issued by the Mesa Coordinadora of the 62 Organisations on 23 August 1963.

2 *ibid.*

3 *ibid.*

4 *ibid.*

5 See, for example, the CGE programme of November 1962. This proposed a new expansionist impulse based on state provision of credit facilities. This contrasted sharply with the more orthodox concern with budget deficits and control of inflation expressed by the traditional representative of large industry, the Unión Industrial Argentina. See *Primera Plana*, 13 November 1962.

6 CGT, *El porqué de la Semana de Protesta*, May 1963.
7 CGT, *La CGT en marcha hacia un cambio de estructuras*, January 1965, p. 25.
8 *Primera Plana*, 11 March 1965.
9 *Documentación e Información Laboral*, no. 29, July 1962.
10 CGT, *La CGT convoca al pueblo a Cabildo Abierto, terceta etapa del Plan de Lucha*, July 1964.
11 *Dínamis*, 13 January 1966.
12 *Palabra Argentina*, 4 February 1960.
13 *AOT*, December 1961.
14 'Business unionism' was the term originally coined by R. F. Hoxie in *Trade Unionism in the United States* (New York, 1923), and referred to the exclusive concentration on collective bargaining, the negotiation over the price of labour on the labour market. It specifically denied the validity of participation in political or social activity, e.g. the provision of welfare facilities.
15 CGT, *Boletín Informativo Semanal de la CGT*, no. 64, 7 June 1964.
16 For an example of the first reaction see Ricardo Otero, *Augusto Vandor* (Buenos Aires, 1970). Otero who had been a relatively minor figure within the UOM apparatus became Minister of Labour in 1973. For the demonological approach, virtually any issue of the Peronist left press would serve as an illustration. But see in particular the issue of *La Causa Peronista*, 3 September 1974. Also *El Descamisado*, 10 February 1974, describing the 'execution' of Vandor in 1969. For the Peronist guerrilla factions his killing was intended to be the exorcism Peronism needed to purge its prime source of moral corruption and ideological degeneration.
17 Gazzera, 'Nosotros los dirigentes', p. 113.
18 *ibid.*, p. 114.
19 Walsh, *Quién mató a Rosendo?*, p. 175.
20 *ibid.*, pp. 175–9.
21 *Primera Plana*, 19 December 1967.
22 The term *clasista* was a term generally used by the Peronists to refer to a Marxist conception of politics and society. The term implied an emphasis on class conflict and the organising of the working class in its own independent party to achieve its specifically class goals.
23 Asociación de Trabajadores de la Sanidad Argentina (ATSA), *Curso de capacitación sindical*, 25 November 1966.
24 *Dínamis*, 13 January 1966.
25 *Petróleo Argentino*, November/December 1965.
26 *ibid.*, May/June 1965.
27 See *Primera Plana*, 5 February 1964.
28 *ibid.*, 11 May 1965.
29 *Petróleo Argentino*, June/July 1966.
30 CGT, *La CGT en marcha*, p. 65.
31 *ibid.*, p. 71.
32 *Dínamis*, 14 July 1966.
33 CGT, *Boletín Informativo Semanal*, no. 64, 7 June 1964.
34 ATSA, *Curso de capacitación sindical*, p. 17.
35 This was confirmed to me by Enrique Micó, Alonso's successor as leader

of the garment workers, in an interview in February 1974. The Catholic provenance of some crucial strands in Peronist ideology has been frequently commented on, not least by Perón himself.

36 *Documentación e Información Laboral*, no. 60, February 1965.

37 *Primera Plana*, 8 October 1963.

38 Interview with Sebastian Borro, Buenos Aires, February 1974.

39 Interview with Jorge Di Pascuale, Buenos Aires, February 1974.

40 *Compañero*, 21 June 1963.

41 *Primera Plana*, 8 October 1963.

42 It was during the *giro a la izquierda* that Framini became the most prominent *duro* figure, making a number of revolutionary-sounding speeches emphasising that 'there is no solution within the capitalist system'. Part of Perón's 'turn' was symbolised in a sympathetic attitude to the non-Peronist left, especially the Communist Party and the Vanguard Socialist Party. Also notable were some sympathetic statements about Castro and the Third World in general. It was in this period that Cooke was urging Perón to make Cuba his base.

43 For the programme of the MRP see 'Peronismo: el exilio (1955–73), *Cuadernos de Marcha*, no. 71 (Montevideo, 1973).

44 *Primera Plana*, 11 August 1964. For details of the MRP conference as well as a later critique by one of its leading participants, Gustavo Rearte, see *En Lucha, órgano del Movimiento Revolucionario 17 de octubre*, no. 13, December 1973.

45 *Compañero*, 21 June 1963.

46 *Perón–Cooke correspondencia*, vol. 2, p. 189.

47 *ibid.*, p. 190.

48 'A los compañeros de la carne, Agrupación Blanca y Negra, Rosario,' letter of Cooke's, 1965, in mimeo in the author's files.

49 Interview with Jorge Di Pascuale, Buenos Aires, February 1974; interview with Sebastian Borro, Buenos Aires, February 1974. Borro's response when I asked how he came to terms with so many defeats and setbacks was to shrug his shoulders and say: 'Hay que tener fe en Perón y el pueblo.'

9 The Peronist union leaders under siege

1 For a discussion of the union leaders' calculations concerning the June coup see Carri, *Sindicatos y poder en la Argentina*, pp. 145–7.

2 See Juan Carlos Portantiero, 'Clases dominantes y crisis política en la Argentina actual' in Oscar Braun, ed., *El capitalismo argentino en crisis* (Buenos Aires, 1973). Also see Guillermo O'Donnell, *Estado y alianzas en la Argentina, 1956–1976*, CEDES, doc. no. 5 (Buenos Aires, 1976).

3 For Onganía's economic policy see Oscar Braun, 'Desarrollo del capitalismo monopolista en la Argentina' in Braun, ed., *El capitalismo argentino*. Also see Peralta Ramos, *Etapas de acumulación*.

4 For an overview of the Onganía regime see Gregorio Selser, *El Onganiato: la llamaban Revolución Argentina*, 2 vols. (Buenos Aires, 1973).

5 For the impact of Krieger Vasena's economic policy on real wages see Peralta Ramos, *Etapas de acumulación*.

6 The Córdoba events lack a definitive study. See Francisco Delich, *Crisis y*

protesta social:Córdoba, Mayo 1969 (Buenos Aires, 1970); Beba Balvé *et al., Lucha de calles, lucha de clases* (Buenos Aires, 1974).

7 For an analysis of intersectorial differences see Pablo Gerchunoff and Juan Llach, 'Capitalismo industrial, desarrollo asociado y distribución del ingreso entre dos gobiernos peronistas, 1950–1972', *Desarrollo Económico*, vol. 15, no. 57 (1975), pp. 3–54.

8 The four Fiat plants, all established in the mid and late 1950s, were Fiat Concord, Fiat Materfer, Grandes Motores Diesel in Córdoba, and Fiat Concord in Buenos Aires. The Córdoba plants employed a total of 5,665 workers in the mid 1960s. 'Informe preliminar sobre el conflicto en Fiat', *Pasado y Presente*, vol. 11, no. 2 (1965).

9 Peralta Ramos, *Etapas de acumulación*, p. 147.

10 Juan Carlos Torre, *Los sindicatos en el gobierno, 1973–1976* (Buenos Aires, 1983), p. 86.

11 For a more detailed analysis of the emergence of the automobile workforce see Judith Evans and Daniel James, 'Reflections on Argentine automobile workers and their history' in Richard Kronish and Kenneth Mericle, eds., *The Political Economy of the Latin American Motor Vehicle Industry* (Cambridge, Mass., 1984).

12 Sitrac and Sitram were the acronyms used to refer to the Sindicato de Trabajadores de Concord and the Sindicato de Trabajadores de Materfer, respectively.

13 The *Viborazo* took its popular name from a boast made by the extreme conservative governor of Córdoba appointed by Levingston who had declared that he would root out subversives from Córdoba as one would root out a nest of vipers.

14 I. M. Roldan, *Sindicatos y protesta social en la Argentina: un estudio de caso el Sindicato de Luz y Fuerza de Córdoba, 1969–1974* (Amsterdam, 1978), p. 198.

15 *ibid.*, p. 274.

16 Interview with SMATA Córdoba leaders, Córdoba, August 1973.

17 *Intersindical*, no. 3, October 1972. The same was also true in the Córdoba light and power union.

18 Interview with SMATA Córdoba leaders.

19 *La Opinión*, 13 July 1971.

20 *Ya!*, 29 June 1973.

21 Roldan, *Sindicatos y protesta*, p. 199.

22 *Los Libros*, no. 3 (1971). Also see Elizabeth Jelin, 'Spontaneité et Organisation dans le mouvement ouvrier: le cas de l'Argentine, du Bresil et du Mexique', *Sociologie du Travail*, vol. 18, no. 2 (1976), pp. 139–69.

23 *Avanzada Socialista*, January 1972.

24 Roldan, *Sindicatos y protesta*, p. 273.

25 For a stimulating critique of the opposition see *Pasado y Presente*, New Series, vol. 1, no. 1 (1973).

26 For a general outline of the development of the guerrilla phenomenon in Argentina see Richard Gillespie, *Soldiers of Perón* (Oxford, 1982).

27 For the economy of the Peronist government, 1973–6 see Guido Di Tella, *Perón–Perón, 1973–1976* (Buenos Aires, 1983); Adolfo Canitrot, 'La viabilidad economica de la democracia: un analisis de la experiencia

peronista, 1973–1976', CEDES, *Estudios Sociales*, no. 11 (Buenos Aires, 1978).

28 For an account of the complex interrelationship between union leaders and other forces in this period see Torre, *Los sindicatos en el gobierno*.

29 See Elizabeth Jelin, 'Los conflictos laborales en Argentina, 1973–1976', CEDES, *Estudios Sociales*, no. 9 (Buenos Aires, 1977).

10 Conclusion

1 Alvin Gouldner, 'Metaphysical pathos and the theory of bureaucracy' in L. A. Coser and B. Rosenberg, eds., *Sociological Theory* (New York, 1964), p. 507.

2 See for example Correa, *Los jerarcas sindicales*. Correa presents a Communist Party analysis entirely devoted to the corruption, fraud and violence of the Peronist leadership. The difference between his analysis and that of the Peronist left was that Correa viewed these features as a largely inherent consequence of Peronism's nature as a movement and an ideology.

3 Robert Michels, *Political Parties* (Glencoe, 1958).

4 José Luis de Imaz, *Los que mandan* (Albany, 1976), p. 220.

5 Delich, *Crísis y protesta social*, p. 33.

6 See Richard Hyman, *Marxism and the Sociology of Trade Unionism* (London, 1972), for a résumé of this predominantly 'pessimistic' literature.

7 See V. L. Allen, *Militant Trade Unionism* (London, 1976), p. 26.

8 See Hyman, *Marxism*, pp. 20–3.

9 Miguel Angel García, *Peronismo: desarrollo económico y lucha de clases en Argentina* (Llobregat, 1979), p. 125.

10 Sindicato Luz y Fuerza, *Pautas para una política nacional* (Buenos Aires, 1970), p. 34.

11 Cited in Peralta Ramos, *Etapas de acumulación*, p. 75.

12 C. Wright Mills, *The New Men of Power* (New York, 1948), p. 7.

13 Rotundaro, *Realidad y cambio*, p. 388.

14 Hyman, *Marxism*, p. 37.

15 E. L. Wigham, *What's wrong with British unions?* (London, 1961), p. 11, cited in Hyman, *Marxism*, p. 23.

16 Juan Carlos Torre, *El proceso político interno de los sindicatos argentinos*, Instituto Torcuato di Tella, Documento de Trabajo, no. 89 (Buenos Aires 1974), p. 5.

17 Jean-Paul Sartre, *Critique of Dialectical Reason*, vol. 1 (London, 1976), p. 683.

18 Jean-Paul Sartre, *The Communists and Peace* (London, 1969), p. 194.

19 Claude Lefort, *Qué es la burocracia?* (Paris, 1970), p. 95.

20 Such an understanding is present in Jean-Paul Sartre's work in the *Critique of Dialectical Reason* with his preoccupation with the emergence and interplay of the fused group, the organised group and the institution and the ever-present danger of the relapse into seriality, passivity. Sartre insists too that the institutionalisation of individual praxis and the emergence of bureaucracy respond to both personal and organisational needs, and can, potentially, be reversed by the reemergence of individual praxis. Hence:

'The working class is neither pure combativity, nor pure passive dispersal nor a pure institutionalised apparatus.' Sartre, *Critique*, p. 690.

21 See Tom Nairn's assessment of the intrinsic duality of nationalism: 'The task of a theory of nationalism ... must be to embrace both horns of the dilemma. It must be to see the phenomenon as a whole, in a way which rises above these "positive" and "negative" sides ... Such distinctions do not imply the existence of two brands of nationalism, one healthy and one morbid. The point is that, as the most elementary comparative analysis will show, all nationalism is both healthy and morbid. Both progress and regress are inscribed in its genetic code from the start.' Tom Nairn, *The Break-up of Britain* (London, 1977), pp. 347–8.

22 Osvaldo Soriano, *No habrá mas penas ni olvido* (Buenos Aires, 1984).

Select bibliography

Newspapers, journals and reviews

Dates in general refer to years consulted and are not synonymous with the actual publishing span. Most of the Peronist press published in the 1955–9 period operated under, at best, semi-clandestine conditions with many restrictions. Hence publication was often sporadic and sometimes lasted for no more than one or two issues.

Argentina en Marcha, 1960, pro-Frondizi weekly
Así, 1970, weekly review
Avanzada Socialista, 1972–74, weekly paper of Partido Socialista de los Trabajadores
Azul y Blanco, 1956–8, nationalist, anti-Aramburu
La Causa Peronista, 1974, Peronist Youth/Montoneros weekly
Che, 1961, Partido Socialista de la Vanguardia weekly
Clarín, national daily newspaper
Compañero, 1963, pro-*línea dura*, independent Peronist
Crisol del Litoral, 1955, independent, pro-Peronist newssheet produced by rank-and-file activists in Puerto General San Martin, Santa Fe
Crítica, national daily newspaper
El Cuarenta, 1957, independent, pro-Peronist newssheet produced in Rosario area.
Cuestionario, 1974, weekly review
La Democracia, 1960, pro-Frondizi daily
El Descamisado, 1973–4, Peronist Youth/Montoneros weekly
Descartes, 1962, Peronist weekly controlled by the 62 Organisations
En Lucha, órgano del Movimiento Revolucionario 17 de octubre, 1974, revolutionary Peronist
Frente Obrero, 1956, Peronist
Intersindical, 1972, pro-communist
Juancito, 1957, Peronist *barrio* newssheet, Rosario
Justicialismo, 1963, Peronist weekly, pro-62 Organisations
Línea Dura, 1958, semi-official Peronist weekly, edited by John William Cooke
Lucha Obrera, 1955, Trotskyist/Peronist
Mayoría, 1957–9, pro-Frondizi weekly

Militancia, 1973–4, revolutionary Peronist
La Nación, national daily newspaper
New York Times
Noticias Gráficas, 1955–62, national daily newspaper
Nuestro Pueblo, 1959–60, pro-Frondizi weekly
Nueva Era, 1955–8, monthly journal of the Argentine Communist Party
Nuevo Hombre, 1971, pro-guerrilla weekly linked with Catholic left
Palabra Argentina, 1955–9, pro-Peronist weekly
Palabra Obrera, 1958–63, Trotskyist, pro-Peronist
'Peronismo: el exilio, 1955–73', *Cuadernos de Marcha*, no. 71, 1973 (special issue)
El Popular, 1963–4, pro-communist weekly
Primera Plana: historia del peronismo, 1965–6
Pueblo Unido, 1959, Peronist weekly
Qué pasó en siete días (Qué), 1955–9, pro-Frondizi weekly
La Razón, national daily
Review of the River Plate, weekly review
Siete Días, 1973, weekly review
El Soberano, 1959, pro-clandestine groups
Unidad Obrera, 1956, Trotskyist, pro-Peronist
La Vanguardia, 1955–7, daily newspaper of the Socialist Party
La Verdad, 1955–6, Trotskyist, pro-Peronist
Ya!, 1973, pro-Peronist Youth

Union materials

Agrupación Obrera, 'Obreros Argentinos', rank-and-file leaflet, no date, author's files
Agrupamiento Sindical Argentino, leaflet, no title, no date, in author's files
El Alpargatero, 1960, rank-and-file newspaper, Alpargatas textile plant, Barracas, Buenos Aires
AOT, 1955–66, newspaper of the Asociación Obrera Textil
Boletín de Huelga, December 1956, Unión Obrera Metalúrgica
Confederación General de Trabajo, *Boletín Informativo Semanal*, 1963–6, weekly information bulletin published under editorship of Luis Angheleri
  CGT, 1955, newspaper of the GCT under Peronist regime. Three issues appeared in September/October, 1955
  El porqué de la Semana de Protesta, May 1963, pamphlet
  La CGT convoca al pueblo a Cabildo Abierto, tercera etapa del Plan de Lucha, July 1964, pamphlet
  La CGT y el Plan de Lucha, cuarta etapa, November 1964, pamphlet
  Ocupación por 3,913,000 trabajadores de 11,000 establecimientos, June 1964, pamphlet
  La CGT en marcha hacia un cambio de estructuras, January 1965, pamphlet
Curso de capacitación sindical, 25 November 1966, Asociación de Trabajadores de la Sanidad Argentina (ATSA)
Dinamis, 1965–6, journal of Sindicato de Trabajadores de Luz y Fuerza
Documentación e Información Laboral, 1960–6, monthly bulletin of union affairs, edited Leonardo Dimase

Documentos del Plenario Nacional de las 62 Organizaciones, December 1959
Documentos del Plenario Nacional de las 62 Organizaciones, 20 May 1960
Estatuto de la Asociación Obrera Textil, 14 December 1966
Estatuto del Sindicato Unido de Petroleros del Estado, 1965
Memoria y Balance, XI Congreso Nacional de la AOT, 22, 23 and 24 March 1968
El Obrero Ferroviario, 1955, paper of Unión Ferroviaria
Pautas para una política nacional, Sindicato de Trabajadores de Luz y Fuerza, 1970
Petróleo Argentino, 1960–6, paper of the Federación de Sindicatos Unidos de Petroleros del Estado (SUPE)
El Trabajador de la Carne, 1958–60, paper of the Federación de Trabajadores de la Industria de la Carne
El Vitivinícola, 1957, paper of the Unión Obrera Vitivinícola

Official government sources

Banco Central de la Nación, Origen del producto y distribución del ingreso, 1950–1969, suplemento del boletín estadístico, no. 1, January 1971
CGE–Consejo Federal de Inversiones, programa conjunto, vol. 3, 1964
Consejo Nacional del Desarrollo, Plan nacional de desarrollo, Buenos Aires, 1970
Ministerio de Trabajo y Previsión, *Nuevo régimen de remuneraciones y de las convenciones Colectivas de trabajo*, Buenos Aires, 1956
   Laudo del tribunal arbitral, no. 63/1956, Buenos Aires, 1956
Ministerio de Trabajo y Seguridad Social, *Conflictos de trabajo*, Buenos Aires, 1961
   Convención colectiva de la industria textil, no. 155/1960, Buenos Aires, 1960
   Convención colectiva de la industria metalúrgica, no. 55/1960, Buenos Aires, 1960
   Censo nacional de asociaciones profesionales, Buenos Aires, 1965
Ministerio de Trabajo, *Asociaciones profesionales de trabajadores*, law 14,255, decree 969/66 and 2477/70, Buenos Aires, 1970
'Report of the proceedings of the *Congreso Nacional de Productividad y Bienestar Social*', Buenos Aires, March 1955, *Hechos e Ideas*, 1955
Servicio Internacional de Publicaciones Argentinas, 'Emancipation of the Workers', Buenos Aires, 1953

Interviews

Herminio Alonso, Buenos Aires, December 1976
Alberto Belloni, Buenos Aires, January/February 1974
Alberto Bordaberry, Buenos Aires, October 1977
Sebastian Borro, Buenos Aires, February 1974
Tito Dragovitch, Buenos Aires, September 1976
Lautaro Ferlini, Buenos Aires, November/December 1976
Don Ramiro González, Rosario, November 1976
Ernesto González, Buenos Aires, February 1974

Daniel Hopen, Buenos Aires, March 1974
Enrique Micó, Buenos Aires, February 1974
Jorge Di Pasquale, Buenos Aires, February 1974

Secondary sources: books, articles, pamphlets

Allen, V. L., *Militant trade unionism*, London, 1971
Bourdieu, Pierre, *Outline of a Theory of Practice*, Cambridge, 1977
Braun, Oscar, *El capitalismo argentino en crisis*, Buenos Aires, 1973
Brid, Juan Carlos, 'Quince años de resistencia', *Nuevo Hombre*, 8 August 1971, 12 September 1971
Cabo, Dardo, and Roa, Ricardo, 'Duros y negociadores en el movimiento peronista', *Nuevo Hombre*, 15 September 1971
Canton, Dario, *Elecciones y partidos politicos en la Argentina*, Buenos Aires, 1973
    El parlamento argentino en épocas de cambio, 1890, 1916 y 1946, Buenos Aires, 1966
Carri, Roberto, *Sindicatos y poder en Argentina*, Buenos Aires, 1967
    'La Resistencia peronista: crónica por los resistentes', *Antropología del Tercer Mundo*, June 1972
Chauí, Marilena, *Cultura e democracia, o discurso competente e outras falas*, São Paulo, 1982
Cimazo, Jacinto, and Grunfeld, José, *Luis Danussi en el movimiento social y obrero argentino*, Buenos Aires, 1976
Ciria, Alberto, *Parties and Power in Modern Argentina, 1930–1946*, Albany, 1969
    Perón y el justicialismo, Buenos Aires, 1974
Colom, Eduardo, *El 17 de octubre, la revolución de los descamisados*, Buenos Aires, 1946
Cooke, John William, 'Peronismo y lucha de clases' *Cristianismo y Revolución*, October/November 1966
Correa, Jorge, *Los jerarcas sindicales*, Buenos Aires, 1972
'Crónica por un resistente: crónicas de la Resistencia', *Antropología del Tercer Mundo*, August 1972
Delich, Francisco, *Crisis y protesta social: Córdoba, mayo 1969*, Buenos Aires, 1970
Diaz, Hamilton Alberto, *Curso de guerra contrarevolucionaria: lucha contra el terrorismo*, Servicio de Información del Ejército, Escuela Superior de Guerra, Buenos Aires, 19 October 1961
Doyon, Louise, 'El crecimiento sindical bajo el peronismo', *Desarrollo Económico*, vol. 15, no. 57 (1975), pp. 151–61
    'Conflictos obreros durante el régimen peronista, 1946–1955', *Desarrollo Económico*, vol. 17, no. 67 (1977), pp. 437–73
Economic Commission for Latin America, *Economic Development and Income Distribution in Argentina*, New York, 1969
Evans, Judith, 'Tango and popular culture in Buenos Aires', paper presented to American Historical Association conference, Washington, 1980
Evans, Judith, and James, Daniel, 'Reflections on Argentine automobile workers and their history', in Richard Kronish and Kenneth Mericle, eds.,

The Political Economy of the Latin American Motor Vehicle Industry, Cambridge, Mass., 1984

Fayt, Carlos, *La naturaleza del peronismo*, Buenos Aires, 1967

Franco, Luis, *Biografía patria*, Buenos Aires, 1958

Frigerio, Rogelio, *Los cuatro años*, Buenos Aires, 1962
  Introducción a los problemas nacionales, Buenos Aires, 1965

Frondizi, Arturo, *Petróleo y política*, 3rd edn, Buenos Aires, 1960
  Política económica nacional, Buenos Aires, 1963

Gálvez, Manuel, *En el mundo de los seres reales*, Buenos Aires, 1955

García, Miguel Angel, *Peronismo: desarrollo económico y lucha de clases en Argentina*, Llobregat, 1979

Gazzera, Miguel, 'Nosotros los dirigentes' in Norberto Ceresole and Miguel Gazzera, *Peronismo: autocrítica y perspectivas*, Buenos Aires, 1970

Germani, Gino, *Política y sociedad en una época de transición*, Buenos Aires, 1962
  'El rol de los obreros y de los migrantes internos en los orígenes del peronismo', *Desarrollo Económico*, vol. 13, no. 51 (1973), pp. 435–88

Gèze, Francois, and Labrousse, Alain, *Argentine: revolution et contrerévolution*, Paris, 1975

Gobello, José, *Diccionario lunfardo y otros términos antiguos y modernos usados en Buenos Aires*, Buenos Aires, 1975

Goldar, Ernesto, 'La literatura peronista' in Gonzalo Cárdenas et al., *El peronismo*, Buenos Aires, 1969

Gouldner, Alvin, 'Metaphysical pathos and the theory of bureaucracy' in L. A. Coser and B. Rosenburg, eds., *Sociological Theory*, New York, 1964

Halperín Donghi, Tulio, 'Algunas observaciones sobre Germani, el surgimiento del peronismo y los migrantes internos', *Desarrollo Económico*, vol. 15, no. 56 (1975), pp. 765–81

Hyman, Richard, *Marxism and the Sociology of Trade Unionism*, London, 1972

Imaz, José Luis de, *Los que mandan*, Albany, 1976

Iscaro, Rubens, *Historia del Movimiento Sindical*, vol. 1, Buenos Aires, 1974

Jelín, Elizabeth, 'Los conflictos laborales en Argentina, 1973–1976', CEDES, *Estudios Sociales*, no. 9, Buenos Aires, 1977

Laclau, Ernesto, *Politics and ideology in Marxist theory*, London, 1977

Lefort, Claude, *Qué es la burocracia?* Paris, 1970

Little, Walter, 'Political integration in Peronist Argentina', Ph.D. thesis, University of Cambridge, 1971
  'La organización obrera y el estado peronista', *Desarrollo Económico*, vol. 19, no. 75 (1979), pp. 331–76

Llach, Juan José, 'El Plan Pinedo de 1940: su significación histórica y los orígenes de la economía política del peronismo', *Desarrollo Económico*, vol. 23, no. 92 (1984), pp. 515–58

Luna, Felix, *El 45: crónica de un año decisivo*, Buenos Aires, 1969
  Alvear, Buenos Aires, 1958

Mafud, Julio, *Sociología del peronismo*, Buenos Aires, 1972
  La vida obrera en la Argentina, Buenos Aires, 1976

Mallon, Richard and Sourrouille, Juan, *Economic Policy Making in a Conflict Society*, Cambridge, Mass., 1975

Matsushita, Hiroschi, *El movimiento obrero argentino, 1930–1945: sus proyecciones en los orígenes del peronismo*, Buenos Aires, 1983

Michels, Robert, *Political Parties*, Glencoe, 1958

Murmis, Miguel, and Portantiero, Juan Carlos, 'El movimiento obrero en los orígenes del peronismo', *Estudios sobre los orígenes del peronismo*, vol. 1, Buenos Aires, 1972

'Crecimiento industrial y alianzas de clase en la Argentina, 1930–40', *Estudios sobre los orígenes del peronismo*, vol. 1, Buenos Aires, 1972

O'Donnell, Guillermo, *Un juego imposible: competición y coaliciones entre partidos políticos en la Argentina, 1955–1966*, Documento de Trabajo, Instituto Torcuato di Tella, 1972

Pelletieri, Osvaldo, *Enrique Santos Discépolo: obra poética*, Buenos Aires, 1976

Peña, Milciades, *El peronismo: selección de documentos para su historia*, Buenos Aires, 1973

Peralta Ramos, Monica, *Etapas de acumulación y alianzas de clase en la Argentina, 1930–70*, Buenos Aires, 1972

Perelman, Angel, *Como hicimos el 17 de octubre*, Buenos Aires, 1961

Perón, Juan Domingo, *La fuerza es el derecho de las bestias*, Montevideo, 1957

Letter to the 62 Organisations, 25 June 1960, published as pamphlet by the 62 Organisations

Interview with Enrique Pavón Pereyra, 1968, published in *Siete Días*, no. 312, 1973

Letter to Don Antonio Caparros, July 1969

Perón–Cooke correspondencia, 2 volumes, Buenos Aires, 1972

Prieto, Ramón, *El Pacto*, Buenos Aires, 1965

Real, Juan José, *30 años de historia argentina*, Buenos Aires, 1962

Reyes, Cipriano, *Como yo hice el 17 de octubre*, Buenos Aires, 1973

Rock, David, *Politics in Argentina: the rise and fall of Radicalism, 1890–1930*, Cambridge, 1975

Roldan, I. M., *Sindicatos y protesta social en la Argentina: un estudio de caso el Sindicato de Luz y Fuerza de Córdoba, 1969–1974*, Amsterdam, 1978

Rotundaro, Ruben, *Realidad y cambio en el sindicalismo*, Buenos Aires, 1972

Roxborough, Ian, 'Unity and diversity in Latin American history', *Journal of Latin American History*, vol. 16, part 1 (1984), pp. 1–26

Sartre, Jean-Paul, *Critique of Dialectical Reason*, vol. 1, London, 1976

The Communists and Peace, London, 1969

Senén González, Santiago, and Torre, Juan Carlos, *Ejército y sindicatos*, Buenos Aires, 1969

Stedman Jones, Gareth, *Languages of Class: studies in English working class history*, Cambridge, 1984

Tamarin, David, *The Argentine Labor Movement, 1930–1945: a study in the origins of Peronism*, Albuquerque, 1985

Torre, Juan Carlos, *El proceso político interno de los sindicatos argentinos*, Instituto Torcuato di Tella, Documento de Trabajo, no. 89, Buenos Aires, 1974

Los sindicatos en el gobierno, 1973–1976, Buenos Aires, 1983

Vigo, Juan M., *La vida por Perón: crónicas de la Resistencia*, Buenos Aires, 1973

Viñas, Ismael, *Orden y progreso: Análisis del frondicismo*, Buenos Aires, 1960

Walsh, Rodolfo, *Quién mató a Rosendo?*, Buenos Aires, 1969

Williams, Raymond, *Marxism and Literature*, Oxford, 1977

Wright, Mills, C., *The New Men of Power*, New York, 1948

Zuvekas Jr, Clarence, 'Economic growth and income distribution in post-war Argentina', *Inter-American Economic Affairs*, vol. 20, no. 3 (1966), pp. 19–39

'Argentine economic policy, 1958–1962: the Frondizi government's development plan', *Inter-American Economic Affairs*, vol. 22, no. 1, pp. 45–75

Index

CAMBRIDGE LATIN AMERICAN STUDIES